Survival Governance

Survival Governance

Energy and Climate in the Chinese Century

PETER DRAHOS

OXFORD
UNIVERSITY PRESS

Oxford University Press is a department of the University of Oxford. It furthers
the University's objective of excellence in research, scholarship, and education
by publishing worldwide. Oxford is a registered trade mark of Oxford University
Press in the UK and certain other countries.

Published in the United States of America by Oxford University Press
198 Madison Avenue, New York, NY 10016, United States of America.

Library of Congress Cataloging-in-Publication Data
Names: Drahos, Peter, 1955– author.
Title: Survival governance : energy and climate in the Chinese century /
Peter Drahos.
Description: New York : Oxford University Press, 2021. |
Includes bibliographical references and index. |
Identifiers: LCCN 2020041608 (print) | LCCN 2020041609 (ebook) |
ISBN 9780197534755 (hardback) | ISBN 9780197534779 (epub) |
ISBN 9780197534786
Subjects: LCSH: Energy policy—China. | Sustainable development—Government
policy—China. | Energy policy. | Sustainable development—Government policy.
Classification: LCC HD9502.C62 D73 2021 (print) |
LCC HD9502.C62 (ebook) | DDC 333.790951—dc23
LC record available at https://lccn.loc.gov/2020041608
LC ebook record available at https://lccn.loc.gov/2020041609

DOI: 10.1093/oso/9780197534755.001.0001

1 3 5 7 9 8 6 4 2

Printed by Sheridan Books, Inc., United States of America

To my brother, Paul, and my son, Nikolai

Contents

Preface

Five of the world's largest 10 companies in 2020 were oil companies. They lead innovation of the wrong kind. They matter to the war machines of war-making states. They need to disappear from the Fortune Global 500. Can China lead world capitalism into low-carbon cycles aimed at ecological rejuvenation? A world of cheap and clean bio-digital energy might also be a more peaceful world.

China has two of those oil companies—the conglomerate Sinopec and China National Petroleum Corporation. China is the world's biggest emitter (27%) of greenhouse gases. It is deeply dependent upon coal for its energy. It continues in its planning to refer to the importance of Marxist thought; it aims for tight planning control over its economy. But China's economy is also a mix of market mechanisms, private investment, entrepreneurs, and state-owned enterprises. This complex hybridity means that it is not a classical Marxist state of the kind Lenin or Mao would have recognized. What they would recognize, however, is a state in which party cadres play a key role in decision-making. The hierarchical and organized ferocity of this system would be familiar to Lenin and Mao. China's present leader Xi Jinping continues to emphasize the need for the Communist Party of China to revitalize its Marxist roots, so as not to lose its radical edge. The idea that such a state will plan and diffuse the necessary innovations to create a new kind of low-carbon economy for global capitalism seems, at best, odd.

When I began trying this China-led scenario of transformation on colleagues, the reactions ranged from disbelief to shocked disbelief. China, went the usual response, is incapable of fixing its own environmental problems, let alone the world's energy and climate problems. Those Chinese scholars on whom I tried the hypothesis listened politely and would, after a pause, relate some story of government incompetence, oppression, or corruption. Many believe that the next global financial crisis will have Chinese characteristics.

My reason for ignoring these perfectly sensible reactions is that we do not have enough exploration of how, in a world that has shifted to governing through networks composed of state and non-state actors, a strong state might provide the impetus for such a transition. At this point in the history of world capitalism, its commanding networks of investment and innovation have to move, quickly, in the direction of carbon reduction and adaptation to deepening ecological crises. As monster firestorms reaching temperatures of over 1,000 degrees Celsius moved across Australia's landscape in the summer of 2019–20, consuming forests, burning animals in the billions, and destroying human lives, Australians watched the arrival of a future wild-fire world that the climate science had been predicting for some time. The United States could lead us to a better future, and perhaps still may, but in my scenario it does not. Instead China ends up catalyzing a network reorganization that avoids some of the worst of our possible climate futures. The Intergovernmental Panel on Climate Change has put together more than 900 mitigation scenarios. We have plenty of analysis of important policy options such as carbon taxes, emissions trading schemes, energy efficiency measures, technology transfer options, and possible financing flows. We do not lack for mitigation scenarios and policy prescriptions. We have less analysis of the geo-political "how" of a low-carbon world. My focus in these pages is on the geo-political "how" of a strong state organizing an exogenous shock that sets world capitalism on a different commodification path, one more consistent with the system's long-term survival. Of course, much more than strong leadership from a state is needed to accomplish this, but it cannot be done, I argue, without such strong leadership.

This book comes out of a larger project on the global governance of energy on which I worked with my then colleagues Julie Ayling, Christian Downie, and Neil Gunningham while based at the Regulatory Institutions Network (RegNet) at the Australian National University (ANU). My conversations with Julie, Christian and Neil triggered many of the ideas and arguments contained in this book. Together we collected interview data over a period of nine years in 17 countries, data I describe in more detail at the end of chapter 1. Dr. Wenting Cheng, a former PhD student at RegNet, quietly drew my attention to aspects of Chinese governance that I would otherwise have missed. Gary Lea, also a PhD student at RegNet, helped me to understand the digitalization of energy. Arpitha Kodiveri from the European University Institute provided comments on the chapter on India. I am fortunate to have worked with such wonderful researchers. I finished the writing of the book at my new academic home in the Law Department of the European University Institute (EUI), Fiesole. Both the ANU and the EUI are places that help individuals develop and push on with ideas. I am lucky to have been surrounded in both these places by colleagues who, after having listened to me, have responded with the kind of encouragement an author needs on a long trail.

Julie Ayling, John Braithwaite, and Nikolai Drahos read the entire manuscript and provided many detailed suggestions. They helped me to cross the finish line. There are no words to thank them. Will Steffen's work on climate science has been profoundly important, and he more than anyone else alerted me to the depth of the climate crisis. He read parts of the manuscript and encouraged me to push on with the argument. Neil Gunningham, a long-time friend, did what a friend should do by providing an incisive critique of my argument that helped me to formulate a better one. I also thank two anonymous reviewers who both engaged so constructively with the whole manuscript.

This book is dedicated to my brother, Paul, and my son, Nikolai. Niko, who is trained in international relations and economics, made many of the suggestions that set me on the path leading out of the thickets to a view of the forest. His knowledge of energy markets was an invaluable resource. Paul has had a long interest in renewable energy, perhaps triggered by my father, who many decades ago was an early embracer of rooftop solar. Renewable and cheap energy turned out to be a recurring topic of conversation around the family dinner table. My brother, unlike me, is gifted with practical skills, and over the years, often with my father, has spent many hours in his garage working on energy alternatives to petrol engines. Today the scale of organized firm innovation dwarfs the garage innovator, but I still like to think that the can-do spirit to be found among those who tinker and invent in their garages will help us arrive at the climate solutions we so desperately need.

Peter Drahos
European University Institute, Fiesole

Abbreviations

AASE	Association for Applied Solar Energy
BR	Belt and Road Initiative
CCS	carbon capture and storage
CIAB	Coal Industry Advisory Board
CoCom	Coordinating Committee for Multilateral Export Controls
EIA	Energy Information Association (US)
EIB	European Investment Bank
FDI	foreign direct investment
GATT	General Agreement on Tariffs and Trade
HVDC	high-voltage direct current
ICGCC	integrated coal gasification combined cycle
ICSU	International Council of Scientific Unions
IEA	International Energy Agency
IEC	International Electrotechnical Commission
IPCC	Intergovernmental Panel on Climate Change
IRENA	International Renewable Energy Agency
ISA	International Solar Alliance
ISO	International Organization for Standardization
LG	Limits to Growth
OECD	Organisation of Economic Co-operation and Development
OPEC	Organization of the Petroleum Exporting Countries
SAC	Standardization Administration of China
TRIPS	Trade-Related Aspects of Intellectual Property Rights
UNCTAD	United Nations Conference on Trade and Development
UNDP	United Nations Development Programme
UNEP	United Nations Environment Programme
UNFCCC	United Nations Framework Convention on Climate Change
WEO	World Energy Outlook
WMO	World Meteorological Organization
WTO	World Trade Organization

1

The Argument in Summary

A Chess Problem

Imagine a variation of Bergman's movie *The Seventh Seal* in which the central character is playing chess with Death in order to save the human species from a combination of climate-related ecological crises. Our player has lost his queen, and one of his castles is trapped. Everything now depends on what he can do with his remaining castle. The position looks hopeless. Even the kibitzers gathered around the board have become silent.

In this book the queen is time. The trapped castle represents the United States. China is represented by the other castle. The position seems unwinnable. China is responsible for more than half of the world's coal demand.[1] On some accounts, it is systemically corrupt and in the final stages of decay.[2] Some say it is not a state capable of leading the kind of innovation needed to shift the earth system from the worst of the coming intense climate fluctuations.

Many mitigation scenarios exist showing possible paths to limiting global temperature increases to 2°C. The International Energy Agency (IEA) for many years has been refining scenarios, including most recently a "Faster Transition Scenario."[3] This scenario requires, among other things, all countries to introduce carbon pricing in their power and industry sectors by 2020, the elimination of fuel subsidies by 2025, about a quarter of the world's truck fleet to be electric by 2020, and the retrofitting of the world's entire building stock. How can we possibly achieve this? The sands of the hourglass are rapidly taking us past these years.

---

[1] International Energy Agency, *World Energy Outlook 2017*, OECD/IEA, Paris, 2017 (hereinafter WEO 2017), 474.
[2] Minxin Pei, *China's Crony Capitalism: The Dynamics of Regime Decay*, Harvard University Press, Cambridge, MA, 2016.
[3] WEO 2017, 149.

A Staccato Answer

States compete under conditions of world capitalism. Rapid innovation has become the principal means of competition. States have been and remain war makers. Fossil fuel innovation has fed the war machines upon which they base their national security. For example, napalm, a petrochemical invention, was widely used to burn cities and citizens in World War II firebombing strategies. Price didn't entrench coal and oil as fuels. States entrenched these fuels because they increased their military capabilities.

The United States, much more than other states, has been responsible for continuous innovation in fossil fuel extraction. This innovation success has helped make its economy more competitive and increased the energy security of its military. The price of these geo-political gains has been a slowing of world capitalism's response to the climate crisis. Capitalism produces its own gravedigger; however, this turns out not to be an angry proletarian force but rather an earth system shifting to new equilibria at an exponential speed that overwhelms capitalist states.

A strong state has to organize an exogenous shock to change the direction, speed, and scale of innovation in world capitalism. Trillions of dollars of financing will have to be directed away from the fossil fuel industry and into circular and green economy projects. Big climate treaty meetings, filled with calculated bargaining and conditionality, deliver too little, too late. This exogenous shock has to target the energy system in the first instance. Oil and gas companies have to stop dominating the list of the world's largest companies.[4] They need to be extinguished. CO_2 emissions from fossil fuel burning represent around 75% of the world's greenhouse gas emissions.[5] Coal (27%), oil (32%), and gas (22%) dominate the world's total primary energy supply.[6]

Energy systems go through long transformations rather than revolutions. Beginning with the first Industrial Revolution, coal took well over a century to work itself fully into processes of energy generation and industrial manufacturing.[7] Renewables account for less than 2% of the world's primary

---

[4] Sinopec Group (2), China National Petroleum Corporation (4), Royal Dutch Shell (5), Saudi Aramco (6), BP (8), Exxon Mobil (11). See Fortune Global 500, http://fortune.com/global500/.

[5] International Energy Agency, *CO_2 Emissions from Fuel Combustion (2018 Edition)*, OECD/IEA, Paris, 2018, xix.

[6] Figures taken from International Energy Agency, *Key World Energy Statistics 2018*, OECD/IEA, Paris, 2018, 6.

[7] Astrid Kander, Paolo Malanima, and Paul Warde, *Power to the People: Energy in Europe over the Last Five Centuries*, Princeton University Press, Princeton, NJ, 2013, 14.

energy supply.[8] There is not the time for bottom-up processes of market aggregation or social movements to accomplish this initial shock. A state is needed to accelerate the global project of survival governance.

Lying at the heart of this project is the building of a bio-digital energy paradigm. Decarbonizing electricity and heating systems is the first task. They account for over 40% of global CO_2 emissions.[9] From a decarbonized electricity system, flows of electrons can be directed to the transformation of transport systems and the use of heat in industrial processes. There are many more prototype solutions to explore than we realize, and they have been around for much longer than we realize. For example, hydrogen-powered jet flight was the subject of US Air Force research programs in the 1950s.[10] Hydrogen fuel powered the Saturn rocket that put US astronauts on the moon in 1969. Our capacity to innovate technologically is not the problem.

Lying at the heart of the bio-digital energy paradigm is a global city-based network of endogenous innovation. Exogenous shock is needed to start networked endogenous innovation. A state has to organize a sufficiently large number of cities into such a network. The basic logic is of city markets drawing in low carbon technologies and then funding their scaling and diffusion. Something on the scale of China's Belt and Road (BR) Initiative is needed.

No capitalist state is in a strong position to deflect world capitalism from its current trajectory. China probably represents the best of a set of poor chances. The critical issues are whether China can, in a matter of decades, retire carbon capital, reorganize global finance sufficiently to open up the right combination of technology frontiers, and price the results so as to maximize their global diffusion rather than its own global rents. Through this great transformation, the Communist Party of China will have to persuade citizens to place survival governance ahead of the continuous rise in material improvements in living standards. Ecological wealth will need to be seen as glorious.

The objections as to why China cannot or will not do these things form something of an endless procession. They generally begin with China's authoritarianism and corruption and its poor track record of environmental

---

[8] This excludes hydro, which accounts for 2.5%. International Energy Agency, *Key World Energy Statistics 2018*, 6.

[9] International Energy Agency, *CO_2 Emissions from Fuel Combustion*, xiv.

[10] See John L. Sloop, *Liquid Hydrogen as a Propulsion Fuel, 1945–1959*, NASA, Washington, DC, 1978.

protection, and then shift to China's lack of innovation capabilities and "rampant theft of intellectual property," to borrow Donald Trump's description.[11] Chapter 2 explores these objections in more detail.

Worried about the technology monopolies that underpin its hegemony, the United States may engineer a truly serious confrontation with China. Climate change, however, will turn all coming hegemonic contests into Pyrrhic victories.

Why States?

State leadership, my staccato answer asserts, is necessary for a rapid transition out of the era of fossil fuel energy. As we will see in chapter 7, states were fundamental to the emergence of the coal-electricity paradigm. Among the lessons emerging from this earlier transition are that changing an energy paradigm takes longer than you think and that one should be wary of networks of incremental innovation as they can kill you. If you want to delay life-saving disruptive innovation, give it to the market as soon as possible. A rapid transition requires a network-building and standards-setting exercise in which ever-expanding circles of decision-makers act to decarbonize the world's economies and standard-setting bodies collectively move to publish standards for a low-carbon world in many different crucial areas, such as digitization, energy efficiency, and energy production.

Anchoring such a network and standard-setting exercise requires the lure of a large domestic market. In such a market, renewable energy innovation along with regulatory models for the bio-digital energy paradigm can be created, scaled, and then diffused globally. Such a market can require others to have emissions trading schemes as part of the entry price to trade. To be a contender in leading such a rapid transformation, a state has to possess a networked influence in international organizations that provide the regulatory infrastructure for markets on core matters such as property rights, contracts, technical standards, rules of trading, and the rules of financial intermediation. It has to be capable of organizing a banking system that embraces the risk and return of a global economy based on survival governance.

---

[11] At a speech given at the Detroit Economic Club in 2016. See https://www.npr.org/2016/08/08/488816816/donald-trump-looks-to-turn-the-page-on-bad-week-with-economic-speech?t=1537452311543.

Using network leadership and a large domestic market as criteria, four states emerge as possible agents to trigger rapid paradigm change: China, India, the European Union, and the United States. (The European Union can be treated as a unitary actor in key areas such as climate change and trade.) These states are also the world's four largest emitters. I say more about their respective capacities and incentives in this chapter and the next.

As a side note, Japan does not feature in my scenario. Japan is one of the 20th-century's great, perhaps greatest, development success stories, but as John Braithwaite and I concluded in our study of global business regulation, Japan's economic success has not spilled over into the successful globalization of its regulatory agendas.[12] When it has tried to push such an agenda, as with a proposal for an Asian Development Bank during the time of the Asian financial crisis, Japan has not been successful. The resurgence of right-wing politics in Japan is unlikely to change this particular historical track record.

What of Non-State Actors?

Over the last two decades or so, a large literature has grown around the role of non-state actors in regulatory change within world capitalism. Non-state actors, whether from business or civil society, have played vital roles in coalitions that have led to progress on issues such as the regulation of the ozone hole, whaling, access to medicines by poor people, and improving the incomes of farmers in developing countries.[13] Weak actors, when networked, can become potent agents of change, as my former colleagues John Braithwaite, Hilary Charlesworth, and Adérito Soares have shown in their account of the networks of resistance that freed Timor-Leste from Indonesian rule.[14] Business leadership is also helping to demonstrate how the potential of low-carbon technologies can be fulfilled. For example, in 2017 Elon Musk gambled tens of millions of dollars that his company Tesla could build in South Australia a 100-megawatt lithium iron battery storage

---

[12] John Braithwaite and Peter Drahos, *Global Business Regulation*, Cambridge University Press, Cambridge, 2000.

[13] See Braithwaite and Drahos, *Global Business Regulation*; John S. Odell and Susan K. Sell, "Reframing the Issue: The WTO Coalition on Intellectual Property and Public Health, 2001," in John S. Odell (ed.), *Negotiating Trade: Developing Countries in the WTO and NAFTA*, Cambridge University Press, Cambridge, 2006, 85; and Anna Hutchens, *Changing Big Business: The Globalisation of the Fair Trade Movement*, Edward Elgar, Cheltenham, UK, 2009.

[14] John Braithwaite, Hilary Charlesworth, and Adérito Soares, *Networked Governance of Freedom and Tyranny: Peace in Timor-Leste*, ANU E Press, Canberra, 2012.

facility within 100 days or deliver it for free. It was done in 60 days. In a preliminary report on the facility, the Australian Energy Market Operator concluded that it was providing a rapid and precise service compared to large conventional turbine services.[15]

But climate change presents a challenge of a completely different order. It is not a question of powerful states agreeing to reform a single sector or of weak actors escaping the domination of a single power. In the case of climate change, the most powerful states have to change established structures in key sectors such as energy, transport, building, and agriculture.

At a deeper level, world capitalism has to change its current circuits of commodity and capital circulation. Fossil fuel, I argue in chapter 3, is an established institution of capital accumulation. This gives it huge advantages in being able to meet threats to its survival. Its resources extend to political networks of support, innovation networks within research institutions, and the legitimacy that comes with being an employer and provider of energy security. Fossil fuel as an institution will not suddenly collapse. Too many giant banks like JPMorgan Chase and Bank of America continue to provide it with the finance it needs to extract, emit and accumulate profit. It believes that it has time on its side. My argument is not that states can do without the agency of non-state networks but that only a state can organize the exogenous shock needed to change the current trajectory of world capitalism. Non-state networks are deeply important to fulfilling the potential of that new trajectory.

Perhaps, it might be argued, there are other sources of exogenous shock. One source might be mass tort litigation based on a breach of a duty of climate care owed by defendants to the world at large or some smaller class of plaintiffs. Another could be civil disobedience.

Climate change litigation is increasing, with one database reporting more than 1,000 cases in the United States and almost 300 outside of the United States.[16] Based on the experience of tobacco litigation, courts collectively around the world will likely take many decades to sort out issues of liability. We do not have decades. In any case, it is not as if litigation has put the tobacco industry out of business. We need to extinguish the fossil fuel industry, rather than obtaining a settlement from its rich members.

---

[15] See Australian Energy Market Operator, *Initial Operation of the Hornsdale Power Reserve Energy Storage System*, Melbourne, April 2018, https://www.aemo.com.au/-/media/Files/Media_Centre/2018/Initial-operation-of-the-Hornsdale-Power-Reserve.pdf.

[16] See US Climate Change Litigation Database at http://climatecasechart.com/about/.

Carefully planned campaigns of civil resistance could be used to disrupt people's everyday routines in order to bring the climate emergency to the forefront of their attention. A lot of crises do, after all, compete for people's attention. Perhaps civil resistance could help found a global social movement of the kind that organized against slavery in the eighteenth and nineteenth centuries. The campaign conducted by Extinction Rebellion in London in 2019—in which people took actions like climbing on top of trains, barricading roads, and gluing themselves to bridges—provides one potential model of exogenous shock. Here I would argue that the threats of climate change can only be contained through changes to the trajectory of world capitalist accumulation. Civil disobedience on its own may change the ruling politics of a single capitalist state. The Marcos regime did come to an end in 1986 when hundreds of thousands of Filipinos walked the streets in peaceful protest. But civil disobedience cannot on its own change circuits of capital accumulation in which large capitalist states remain invested for reasons of military and economic security. Is it plausible to think that Extinction Rebellion–style campaigns could be scaled, sustained, and co-ordinated across China, India, the European Union, and the United States? The proposal of Boris Johnson's government to classify Extinction Rebellion as an organized crime group is one telling example of how political elites may use police powers to defend the law and order behind which fossil fuel interests hide.

I do not dismiss the power of civil disobedience or of social movements. Perhaps a global carbon abolitionist movement will prove to be the long lever of profound change. At some point mass publics in many countries connected by the sharing of images and evidence will, more or less simultaneously, conclude that there is nothing left to lose. At that point paper law will do little to protect elites. In the context of climate change we are in scenarios of improbability. A large state capable of creating new circuits of capital accumulation is a less improbable source of the required scale of exogenous shock than globally orchestrated civil disobedience.

Innovation and the Geo-Energy Trilemma

My staccato answer claims that innovation is central to both the problem of climate change and its solution. States have been simultaneously too directive and too agnostic about the sources of energy innovation. The direction of innovation in energy has been heavily influenced by a militarized version of the geo-energy trilemma (see chapter 4). This trilemma emerges when states dependent on fossil fuel strive to improve their competitiveness in the global economy, to increase their climate mitigation efforts, and to maintain energy security for their military and industries. The United States has supported innovation in the fossil fuel sector while remaining relatively agnostic about the disruptive potential of renewables. Disruptive innovation in retail therapy (Amazon) or in social feedback loops (Facebook) matter much less than organizing the extinction of the fossil fuel industry and fast-tracking innovation in renewables. The US fracking revolution has created a powerful network of resistance capable of slowing down a rapid transition to a low-carbon world. The fracking of oil and gas offers the United States the holy grail of energy security, employment growth, and more influence in trade negotiations (countries signing free-trade agreements with the United States receive better access to US oil and gas exports). President Barack Obama, an opponent of coal, became something of a missionary for fracking, overcoming the resistance of US environmental groups domestically and traveling to Europe to encourage major states there to embrace the use of new fracking technologies.[17] Today the United States is the world's biggest producer of gas, with two-thirds of its output being shale gas.[18]

China has vast reserves of shale gas and, as the world's largest importer of gas, also has incentives to embrace the fracking revolution. But fracking in China will almost certainly take longer and be more costly for China. Its shale gas is trapped within complex fault lines, often at depths of more than three kilometers and in areas of seismic activity.[19] The environmental costs of fracking include huge amounts of water consumption, a significant cost for a water-stressed China. Through innovation, the United States has locked itself into being a fossil fuel export superpower. China can still choose not to go down this path. China, as I argue here, has more incentives to finance and build the bio-digital energy paradigm that I discuss in the next section.

<hr>

[17] John Graham, *Obama on the Home Front: Domestic Policy Triumphs and Setbacks*, Indiana University Press, Bloomington, 2016, 244–45.

[18] International Energy Agency, *Gas 2018: Analysis and Forecasts to 2023*, IEA/OECD, Paris, 2018, 5.

[19] United States Energy Information Administration, *Technically Recoverable Shale Oil and Shale Gas Resources: China*, Washington, DC, 2015, https://www.eia.gov/analysis/studies/worldshalegas/pdf/China_2013.pdf.

Bio-Digital Energy Paradigm

I use the term "bio-digital energy paradigm" to refer to a paradigm based on the use of biology and software languages to regulate the generation, storage, and distribution of energy from sources that are renewable and consistent with ecosystem preservation. (The constraint of ecosystem preservation may rule out some renewable energy, such as large-scale hydro projects.) Software languages are flexible, cheap, and extraordinarily powerful tools for writing and implementing a renewable energy future. Through software we can intervene in the flow of electrons for the purpose of storing them, releasing them, redirecting them, or joining together different sources. Energy-efficient appliances, smart grids, smart meters, apps for comparing energy prices, algorithmic trading of electricity, and solar-wind hybrid systems of generation are just some of the examples of the digitization of energy. There is a long way to go in understanding the language of DNA, but we have also come a long way. The costs of decoding and recoding DNA have fallen. We have an endless supply of bacteria that can be converted into clean factories for the production of many useful things, such as vitamins and antibiotics, as well as clean energy. Bacteria have been used to build solar cells.[20] Biological processes have reduced energy use in the manufacture of electrodes for batteries. Parts for lithium batteries, it has been demonstrated, can be extracted from microbial-based production.[21] The language of biology is heading in the same direction as software language, offering flexible cheap and powerful tools with which to write a renewable energy future for ourselves.

The shift from wood to coal as a fuel opened up new innovation horizons as industries changed furnaces and discovered new chemical worlds. The shift from fossil fuel to bio-digital energy will do the same.

The future of energy lies in its bio-digitization. Less clear is which actors will win the contests over how the future of digitization will be written. The oil and gas industries continue to invest in digitization of technologies for the drilling of oil. Their vision is one of fleets of smart drilling automatons advancing across fields and landscapes in the search for hydrocarbons, fleets that can be rapidly sent into slumber or switched on in response to price

---

[20] Sarvesh Kumar Srivastava, Przemyslaw Piwek, Sonal R. Ayakar, Arman Bonakdarpour, David P. Wilkinson, and Vikramaditya G. Yadav, "A Biogenic Photovoltaic Material," *Small*, 14 (2018), https://doi.org/10.1002/smll.201800729.

[21] Oluwakemi Adesina, Isao A. Anzai, Jose L. Avalos, and Buz Barstow, "Embracing Biological Solutions to the Sustainable Energy Challenge," *Chem*, 2 (2017), 20–51.

signals. Perhaps China will embrace this techno-hydrocarbonic apparition. But, as the next section shows, world capitalism is moving into the era of survival governance. China can also choose a very different innovation future for itself and world capitalism, one of governance for humanity's and other species' survival.

Survival Governance

Survival governance refers to an actor, whether state or non-state, intervening in systems for the purpose of maintaining the ecological systems upon which it is dependent. The aim of survival governance is to avoid a descent into an ecological maelstrom. In the way that I have formulated it, survival governance has a specific ecological context. It should not be confused with a much broader claim that states seek to survive in a world of competing sovereigns by seeking to maximize their power. The usefulness of this broader claim in explaining state behavior continues to be a source of debate within international relations theorizing.

The evidence for the existence of a deep and global ecological crisis is clear. In 2005 a global study found that 15 of 24 major ecosystem services were being degraded or used unsustainably.[22] A little less than 15 years later, another large-scale multicountry assessment revealed a picture of even faster decline.[23] Regulation is not managing to reverse the rapid extinction of biodiversity. States have moved into a world where the ecosystems related to the supply of the essentials of life—such as water, clean air, fertile soil, and fish stocks—could change abruptly and irreversibly. Climate change is not the only driver of ecological crisis, but depending on levels of carbon emissions, it may become so.

My assumption is that, in the face of rapidly tipping climate dominoes, states will increasingly focus on survival governance. States will have to approach ecological issues with a survival governance mentality if, for example, the 1.6 billion people currently living in countries where there is physical water scarcity grows to a possible 3.2 billion in the next 20 years.[24]

---

[22] Millennium Ecosystem Assessment, *Ecosystems and Human Well-Being: Synthesis*, Island Press, Washington, DC, 2005, 1.

[23] See Intergovernmental Science-Policy Platform on Biodiversity and Ecosystem Services, *Summary for Policymakers of the Global Assessment Report on Biodiversity and Ecosystem Services*, Bonn, 2019, https://www.ipbes.net/event/ipbes-7-plenary.

[24] World Bank, *High and Dry: Climate Change, Water, and the Economy*, World Bank, Washington, DC, 2016, 1.

In this book I explore one instrumentally rational path of survival governance in which China leads. However, the rationality of state survival dictates no single path. The motive of survival amid fast-moving ecological collapse makes the world less predictable. In a situation where the earth's ecosystems are moving in rapid and dangerous ways for the life of most of its current species, differently resourced actors will calculate how best to survive in different ways. Some states, confronting scared and angry populations, may gamble on high-risk geo-engineering technologies. Biological threats to survival can lessen, not increase, cooperation. In 2004–2005, for example, when states were confronted by the increased threat of a pandemic avian influenza, a scramble took place to stockpile antivirals, with rich countries, which faced less of a threat, doing much better.[25] There was little sharing of stockpiles, and the sharing that took place was symbolic. Countries like the United States were able to get the attention of pharmaceutical companies in ways that developing countries simply could not. More generally, the case of continuing limited access by poor people to life-saving medicines shows just how difficult it is for states to cooperate in the equitable distribution of technologies of survival.

States may look inward, focusing on the development within their borders of techno-bubbles of adaptation to climate extremes, giving little priority to global cooperation. Treaties governing water resources shared between upstream and downstream countries, such as those in the Mekong River basin, may end up counting for precious little. The current US indifference to the world's multilateral trading rules as embodied in the World Trade Organization (WTO) may be a glimpse of what is to come.

Survival Governance in China

China is an authoritarian state but not a scientifically incompetent state. Various authorities in China, such as the China Meteorological Administration, have pointed to the different kinds of high-level risks that climate change is creating for China in the form of rising sea levels, drought, and net losses in food production.[26] China's scientists are increasingly being

---

[25] B. Lokuge, P. Drahos, and W. Neville, "Pandemics, Antiviral Stockpiles and Biosecurity in Australia: What about the Generic Option?," *Medical Journal of Australia*, 184 (2006), 16–20.

[26] National Climate Center, China Meteorological Administration, *Non-Party Stakeholder Submission to the Talanoa Dialogue of the UNFCCC*, Beijing, March 2018, https://unfccc.int/sites/default/files/resource/162_Talanoa_Dialogue_Submission_NCC_China_2018.pdf.

called upon to devise ecological zoning policies aimed at the preservation and restoration of ecosystems.[27] The major flooding of the Yangtze River basin in 1998 was a warning signal to which China's policymakers began to respond. China's rulers know better than to dismiss climate science as fake science. My assumption here is that political elites in China more or less understand the deep threat of climate change to China and their authority. China's famine of 1959–1961 killed, by some estimates, 30 million people. If climate change impacts food systems in ways that bring deaths on this incomprehensible scale, China's present rulers might not survive an ancient test of their legitimacy. Heaven's mandate would be seen to have been withdrawn.

Experimental Cities of Survival Governance

China is urbanizing. By 2030 China is predicted to add another 310 million people to its cities.[28] But China is not just urbanizing. It is urbanizing innovation. One way of seeing its urbanization process is to say that China has the chance to add 50 or more innovative Singaporean city-states to its economy. From around 2007, Singapore's government networks began to think more systematically about being a "living laboratory for companies to develop and test green solutions" (interview). Some four years later Singapore announced the opening of the Experimental Power Grid Centre, as well as collaborations between the Centre and US and Japanese companies on smart grid projects. Singapore's goal then and now is to be a magnet for research and development excellence in clean energy technologies. Singapore saw, probably sooner than others, the waves of city innovation starting to roll across China. In 2007 Singapore caught that wave by agreeing to develop the Sino-Singapore Tianjin Eco-City.[29] By definition these city-scale experiments are risky, but for Singapore it is much better to be part of the city-innovation paradigm than not.

Cities, as chapter 8 shows, form the experimental backbone of China's strategy of survival governance. China is building experimental cities of many kinds—such as forest cities, sponge cities, hydrogen cities, and eco-cities—to test whether these technologies can in fact be rolled out across

---

[27] Jixi Gao, "How China Will Protect One-Quarter of Its Land," *Nature*, 569 (May 23, 2019), 475.

[28] United Nations Development Programme, *China Human Development Report. 2013: Sustainable and Liveable Cities: Toward Ecological Urbanisation*, Beijing, 2013, 3.

[29] See https://www.tianjinecocity.gov.sg/bg_intro.htm.

China's urban areas, as well as the cities outside of China that form part of its Belt and Road city network initiative.

Designing experimental cities to link people more closely with the countryside is not a novel idea. For example, British planner Ebenezer Howard's 1898 book gave rise to a garden city movement in the United Kingdom and had an influence on urban planning in many Western states.[30] What is different about China are the scale and variety of experimentation with cities. No other country in the world is seeking to test so many technologies of eco-survival and management using so many types of cities.

For China there is a strong case for taking on the risks of city experimentation. For instance, large port cities around the world are at risk from sea-level rise at only small temperature increases.[31] China has 10 of the world's top 20 container ports, including four of the world's five largest (Shanghai, Shenzhen, Ningbo-Zoushan, Guangzhou Harbour).[32]

Cities and Innovation

In taking this city-based approach to innovation, China is scaling up an approach that occurred earlier in Europe and the United States, but that, as Peter Taylor's wonderful book *Extraordinary Cities* argues, we are only now coming to understand. The interlinked processes of industrialization and population growth in Europe in the second half of the 19th century and the beginning of the 20th saw the growth of large cities in European states. While no city rivaled the growth of London, large cities spread across France, Germany, Italy, and all the way to Russia. These cities became centers of endogenous innovation, as well as places of both intellectual experimentation and dissent. City density made collective action against established orders much easier to organize. It was in Paris that Marx met Engels. London offered Marx and his wife, Eleanor, the intellectual resources of the British Library, as well as contacts with other political activists and organizations such as the International Workingmen's Association, whose political program Marx helped to define.

---

[30] The original title was E. Howard, *Tomorrow: A Peaceful Path to Real Reform*, Swan Sonnenschein & Co., Ltd., London, 1898.

[31] Intergovernmental Panel on Climate Change, *Global Warming of 1.5°C: An IPCC Special Report*, World Meteorological Organization, Geneva, 2018, 231.

[32] See http://www.worldshipping.org/about-the-industry/global-trade/top-50-world-container-ports.

In the hands of urban planners, geographers, and regional economists, the connections between cities, creativity, and innovation, which began to be explored in the 1980s, have become a new project of interdisciplinary synthesis leading to richer spatial concepts, such as the creative city.[33] As Richard Florida, one of the most influential writers on cities, observes, in a world of hyper-cyber connectivity, "place and community are more critical factors than ever before."[34] Climate change will reshape relations between citizens and their cities because cities will be the places where survival governance is seen, felt, and lived. City networks of innovation form our best chance for the bio-digital energy revolution.

Cities also offer opportunities for residents to do something practical about climate change. Not many of us receive invitations to Davos in the Swiss Alps to chew the cud behind closed doors with oil companies and energy ministers. But there are thousands of opportunities for action on climate in cities. Cities are where most of us can make manifest the local action of a broader change on energy and climate. The chances to do so come through networks made up of a diversity of actors such as local councils, resident action groups, religious communities, community groups, clubs, and local businesses. Cities are places where we can overcome our feelings of helplessness about climate change.

Universities also have an opportunity to play a much greater role in those city networks. Managers of universities have for decades greatly harmed the independence of universities, pushing them into the service of military establishments and petro-chemical corporate interests. Universities guided by civic purpose rather than corporate or military research agendas could produce more of the research needed to find appropriate technologies of climate mitigation and adaptation for local communities.

One can safely speak of there being a world capitalist system by the end of the 19th century.[35] This world system coincided with the launch in the 19th century of great technical projects of infrastructure for the carbon economy, such as the creation of railway networks, the state-led expansion of road systems, the electrification of state economies in the West, the linking of states

---

[33] David Emanuel Andersson, Ake E. Andersson, and Charlotte Mellander, *Handbook of Creative Cities*, Edward Elgar, Cheltenham, UK, 2011.

[34] Richard Florida, "Cities and the Creative Class," *City & Community*, 2 (2003), 3–19, 4. See also Richard Florida, *Cities and the Creative Class*, Routledge, New York, 2005.

[35] Immanuel Wallerstein, *Historical Capitalism with Capitalist Civilization*, Verso, London, 2011, 19; Immanuel Wallerstein, *World-Systems Analysis: An Introduction*, Duke University Press, Durham, NC, 2004, 23–24.

through transatlantic telegraph cables, and the beginnings of wireless telegraphy networks (radio). In the current century, world capitalism's survival depends on great infrastructure projects of decarbonizing, such as forest cities, hydrogen cities, and smart grids.

As they fill Asia's newly built cities, hundreds of millions of people create the opportunity for those cities to be centers of endogenous innovation and ideas experimentation, but on a much larger scale than their 19th- and early-20th-century European city counterparts. For both China and India, the possibility of building a new, low-carbon developmental model lies in each seeing their cities as centers of poly-plural innovation, places where innovation of different types takes place guided by principles of sustainability.

Cities and Multinational Capital

Cities represent huge focal points of technological convergence, infrastructure projects, and systems solutions. They are opportunities to set standards for a long list of technologies, such as low-carbon building materials, water efficiency, lighting systems, glazing systems, insulation, sensor systems, meter technologies, and many other areas. No multinational that cares about the development of its technology or the impact of standard-setting on the future of its technology can stay out of China's cities. Many multinationals have arrived at this conclusion. Multinationals in China are participating in the world's largest technology experiments and pilots, experiments being run in hundreds of cities involving hundreds of millions of inhabitants (see chapter 8).

For multinationals it is not just about access to China's cities. As more and more people end up in cities in China, those cities will evolve into a vast network of agglomeration economies stretching into neighboring countries such as Vietnam, where urbanization is also taking off.[36] Technologies tested in one part of the network can be rolled out to other parts.

In dealing with multinational capital China has to land gently on a surface tension on which it must float, not break. It must project an image of China as a place where the knowledge monopolies of foreign capitalists are safe and

---

[36] World Bank and Ministry of Planning and Investment of Vietnam, *Vietnam 2035: Toward Prosperity, Creativity, Equity, and Democracy,* World Bank, Washington, DC, 2016, 207, doi:10.1596/978-1-4648-0824-1.

secure. At the same time it must ensure that exclusive knowledge is eventually freed from the clasp of the monopolist so that market competition can make the technologies of the bio-digital energy paradigm affordable for billions of people. Survival governance has to be a project that includes billions of poor people, not one that simply saves elites. A glimpse of what China can do in this paradigm can be seen with solar. In a five-year period beginning in 2008, Chinese solar manufacturers caused an 80% drop in world prices.[37]

China's cities represent giant levers in standard-setting exercises of decarbonization. The building sector brings with it the potential of investment partnerships with global capital and significant local employment. All this can only be done, as Jeroen van der Heijden argues, by a brave government prepared to use fine-grained powers of regulation to turn cities, old and new, into engines of carbon reduction, sustainability, and resilience.[38]

China's City Belt and Road Initiative

In 2013 in Kazakhstan, President Xi Jinping put forward a big idea—the old Silk route could be transformed into an economic belt, bringing benefits to almost three billion people.[39] The timing of this idea can be seen as fortunate, for in the years following its announcement, cooperation through the multilateral trade regime has become more and more difficult. The Trump administration triggered in 2018 a tit-for-tat tariff war in which China has become the main target.

BR is made up of two great global circuits of transport infrastructure, trade and finance, in the form of the Silk Road Economic Belt and the Maritime Silk Road. The Silk Road heads toward Europe via Central Asia. The Maritime Road takes in the South China Sea, the Strait of Malacca, the Indian Ocean, and ultimately ends up in the Mediterranean. BR is a vision of cooperation based not on fragile trade agreements but on the concreteness of infrastructure projects. High-speed trains and digital communication technologies will replace the camels and carts of the old Silk Road to link city economies

---

[37] John Fialka, "Why China Is Dominating the Solar Industry," *Scientific American E & E News*, December 19, 2016, https://www.scientificamerican.com/article/why-china-is-dominating-the-solar-industry/.

[38] Jeroen van der Heijden, *Governance for Urban Sustainability: Responding to Climate Change and the Relevance of the Built Environment*, Edward Elgar, Cheltenham, UK, 2014.

[39] Xi Jinping, "Work Together to Build the Silk Road Economic Belt," September 7, 2013, in Xi Jinping, *The Governance of China*, Vol. 1, Foreign Language Press, Beijing, 2014, 315–319.

in China to city economies in Central Asia, Russia, and Europe. For China such links would bring greater economic growth to some of its poorer provinces and regions, such as Xinjiang, a northwestern province whose shared borders include Kazakhstan, Mongolia, Russia, and Tajikstan.

There are many indeterminacies about the BR initiative and a number of ways in which it might fail to deliver. The economics of large infrastructure investment are not straightforward. Large infrastructure projects such as the 50-kilometer Channel Tunnel between the United Kingdom and France can fail to deliver net economic benefits, ending up as very expensive white elephants. China has gained a reputation for being an infrastructure building machine, but one study of some 95 road and rail projects in China concluded that less than one-third of these had been really economically productive.[40] A scattershot investment approach to infrastructure carries with it the twin risks of ever-mounting debt and poor returns.

China's opportunities to make gains from the export of its infrastructure building skills may also run into trouble, especially if partner countries come to see China's motives through a "rising power" lens. Infrastructure projects can be easily slowed down. For example, worried about a breach of procurement rules, the EU Commission in 2016 opened an investigation into China's successful bid to build a high-speed railway line between Budapest and Belgrade.[41] Europe does need investment in its railway and port infrastructure. Railway transport can be more climate friendly than air transport. The danger for China lies in a protectionist reframing of its investment initiatives in which the giant transport corridors of the BR are portrayed as transmission belts for cheap Chinese exports to Europe. The experience of importing cheap photovoltaics from China into Europe has created a nagging worry among European policy-makers about who will really benefit in manufacturing and employment terms from renewables.

The BR plan is also the basis for energy cooperation with the countries encompassed by it.[42] More oil and gas exploration is one of its very real possibilities. If the BR initiative sends three billion people down a carbon-intensive

---

[40] Atif Ansar, Bent Flyvbjerg, Alexander Budzier, and Daniel Lunn, "Does Infrastructure Investment Lead to Economic Growth or Economic Fragility? Evidence from China," *Oxford Review of Economic Policy*, 32 (2016), 360–390.

[41] James Kynge, Arthur Beesley, and Andrew Byrne, "EU Sets Collision Course with China over 'Silk Road' Rail Project," *Financial Times*, February 20, 2017, https://www.ft.com/content/003bad14-f52f-11e6-95ee-f14e55513608.

[42] See the speech by Xi Jinping, "Revolutionize Energy Production and Consumption," June 13, 2014, in Xi Jinping, *The Governance of China*. Vol. 1, Foreign Language Press, Beijing, 2014, 143–145.

development path, some of the worst-case climate scenarios identified by the Intergovernmental Panel on Climate Change (IPCC) are likely to come to pass. China and India would together be responsible for the culmination of a historical project of resource ruinous growth started and legitimized by Western powers. East and West together will have been partners in ending history.

The future of the BR is, I would argue, still a matter of choice. It may wind its way toward some of the negative outcomes I have mentioned. But it may also help to create a global city network of innovation and technology diffusion that will help billions of city residents to survive in new climate equilibria. Identifying the high-quality infrastructure needed to support the rapid creation of the bio-digital energy paradigm is the great challenge. Wall Street's financial capitalism, I argue in chapter 2, will not deliver this. China's experimental cities and the BR drive may be the means to this infrastructure and paradigm. More than 120 countries are participating in BR projects. There has never been a better opportunity for the global greening of the world's infrastructure. There has never been a better opportunity to require bankers and financiers to go green as part of the price of entry into this global network of projects, and to finally exit, once and for all, the institution of fossil fuel.

Belt and Road: The Transport of Ideas

China may build an extraordinary infrastructure of networks and connectivity in the coming decades, but Xinru Liu's world history of the old Silk Road suggests that cultural flows and their impacts along the network are likely to be multidirectional, full of the rustle of changing ideas about the world system.[43] Under the Han dynasty (206 BCE–220 CE), agricultural knowledge spread along the route, turning remote oases into caravan cities. Trade was not one way. Products coming from the lands to China's west were hugely valued by Han elites. For 200 or so years from the first century CE, a large part of the Silk Road running through Central and South Asia fell under the control of the Kushan kings who were Buddhists. Under their influence the Silk Road became a route for pilgrims and preachers to spread an intangible into China: the ideas of Buddhism. The old Silk Road evolved into

---

[43] Xinru Liu, *The Silk Road in World History*, Oxford University Press, New York, 2010.

a complex network stretching across China, Central Asia, Europe, and parts of Africa that rose above a simple trade in goods to include flows of technological knowledge, religious ideas, and cultural practices among the many nomadic societies, empires, and dynasties that at different times exercised patronage over some of its routes. Ancient and medieval China did not control the old Silk networks. Modern China will not likely control the new Silk networks it is building. Silk networks of commerce and culture will evolve, often in surprising ways.

Perhaps some of the strands of this eventual surprise already exist. It is almost impossible for outsiders to tell, but one of our Chinese interviewees, who was close to city design projects, spoke of more "scientific and democratic" alternatives to the Shenzen model of governance.[44]

The Opportunity of Belt and Road

The Belt and Road Initiative offers countries a chance to negotiate another approach to infrastructure investment. Whether a country has enough institutional agency to set a course toward the bio-digital energy paradigm is another question, but China, by putting on the table the largest global infrastructure networking exercise in history, has created that chance. Africa provides an example. Historically much of the investment in Africa from the West was linked to resource extraction. For example, 73% of US investment in Africa was directed toward petroleum resources and the import of crude oil into the United States.[45] The United States became the biggest customer of oil from Equatorial Guinea following Mobil's major discovery in the Zafiro field in 1995. By the early 2000s three US oil (and gas) companies dominated the petroleum industry in Equatorial Guinea: ExxonMobil, Amerada Hess, and Marathon Oil.[46]

Equatorial Guinea had been a small Spanish colony in which Spain had taken little interest other than to organize forced labor to work the cocoa plantations. It entered independence in 1968 with electricity in only three towns. Its newly elected leader, Francisco Macias Nguema, through a program of

[44] For a description of the sources of interview data see the final section of this chapter, "A Note on Data".

[45] Richard Knight, "Expanding Petroleum Products in Africa," *Review of African Political Economy*, 30 (2003), 335–339, 336.

[46] Jędrzej George Frynas, "The Oil Boom in Equatorial Guinea," *African Affairs*, 103 (2004), 527–546, 530.

torture and murder, eliminated the opposition, including two-thirds of the members of Parliament. Nguema was himself executed in 1979 after his nephew Teodoro Obiang Nguema Mbasogo led a military coup.[47] By then about one-third of the population had been killed or had fled the country. Obiang has held onto power for four decades, turning the apparatus of government into a network to entrench his power, enrich his clan, and carry out purges of political opposition.[48] US oil companies remain the main producers of oil. Access to electricity by the general population remains low.[49]

Will China's BR money make a difference in Equatorial Guinea? Perhaps not. History has made it a tough case for change. Even if Equatorial Guinea does nothing about a transport and electricity network for its population, other African leaders may see China's BR investment differently. Some of them will understand the imperatives of survival governance.

A Note on Data

The writing on energy is full of statistics, along with models and scenarios. One is confronted by a sea of tables and graphs showing patterns of demand and supply, current costs, likely levelized costs of electricity, generation capabilities of technologies, the impact of learning effects on market penetration, and many other things. My most frequently used sources of statistics on energy are the various reports authored by the International Energy Agency (IEA). The IEA has, I was told in interviews more than once, the best databases on energy in the world. Now, there might be some or many complaints about my reliance on the IEA because, as I also heard in interviews, it is hardly an objective actor in the energy space. It was born a fossil fuel organization, one of the reasons some countries pushed for the creation of the International Renewable Energy Agency (IRENA).

As chapter 4 shows, the IEA has tilted the analytical field on energy in ways that have slowed our response to the global climate emergency. The IEA member states probably do not share the blame for this equally. More of it can be laid at the feet of the United States and Australia. In the case of the United

---

[47] Randall Fegley, "The Human Rights Commission: The Equatorial Guinea Case," *Human Rights Quarterly*, 3 (1981), 34–47.

[48] Geoffrey Wood, "Business and Politics in a Criminal State: The Case of Equatorial Guinea," *African Affairs*, 103 (2004), 547–567.

[49] See "Equatorial Guinea," https://www.eia.gov/beta/international/analysis.php?iso=GNQ.

States, the Eisenhower administration passed up the opportunity to support solar research in the 1950s, and then in the 1970s the US government found itself having to scramble to ensure supplies of oil from the Middle East. The IEA, a Henry Kissinger initiative, was designed to be an instrument of fossil fuel security, not climate security. Australia squandered the opportunity its scientists provided for solar leadership, effectively confining solar research in an academic tower and, among other things, using the IEA to defend its coal export interests. That said, the IEA is now signaling in much stronger terms to states about the need to take strong action on carbon emission reduction. It has tempered its club approach with more of an open-door policy, resulting in Brazil, China, India, Indonesia, Morocco, Singapore, and Thailand joining as association countries.[50] Despite the IEA's recent analytical openness on renewable energy issues and climate change, one of its core missions is to underpin a regime of cooperation over oil security. This regime needs to be phased out as soon as possible and replaced by a regime in which the central actor is IRENA. If we are to avoid a world beyond the 2°C boundary, most of our remaining oil, coal, and gas will have to stay in the ground and the IEA will need to be rendered irrelevant.

My other source of data for this book is the more than 250 interviews I undertook as part of a project on global energy governance. Funded by the Australian Research Council, the project began in 2009 and ran for nine years. My colleagues on the project were Julie Ayling, Christian Downie, and Neil Gunningham. With Neil and Christian I conducted interviews in a number of countries, as well as interviews at the European Commission, the Organisation for Economic Co-operation and Development (OECD), and the IEA. We interviewed actors from government, business, and the non-government sector in the following countries: Australia, Belgium, Brunei, China, France, Germany, India, Indonesia, Italy, the Netherlands, Norway, Poland, Singapore, South Korea, Sweden, the United Kingdom, and the United States. Ten of these countries are G20 members (the European Union also counts as a member of the G20). This group also captures the EU's internal diversity when it comes to matters of energy security and renewables. Brunei is a low-cost venue for obtaining insights into the oil industry. Singapore is a city-state model that offers interesting lessons for China's own urbanization. Indonesia is a populous and developing country dependent upon fossil fuel even though it has the world's largest geo-thermal resources.

---

[50] WEO 2017, 67.

Obviously, China, the United States, the European Union (using a mix of member state leaders and laggards on energy and climate change), and India, the world's four largest emitters, had to be part of the data-gathering strategy.

In the end, however, this book is not about what we found in the interviews but rather the possibility of humanity keeping temperature increases below 2°C because of what China could do. The idea for this possibility emerged from the interviews, especially those in the United States and China. Korea, a country that watches China closely, was also important. In the words of one Korean official, China's "speed and scale is unbelievable. Changes in China should be carefully observed." We were fortunate in being able to gain access to highly placed individuals. When senior people from US manufacturing multinationals say things like, "Everyone realizes that CCS is not viable," one begins to read IEA scenarios, which assume carbon capture and storage (CCS), in a different way.

The collective reflections of our interviewees also suggested the likely failure of a strategy for a 2°C limit based on incremental innovation by the fossil fuel sector in which a combination of CCS and the replacement of coal with gas in the power sector is used to lower carbon emissions. Incremental innovation is one way in which industries hang on in global markets. We have seen this with the tobacco industry and its new generation of products based on vaping. But incremental innovation in the fossil fuel industry is, I argue in chapter 7, dangerous because it prolongs the industry's existence in the marketplace. The use of gas technology as a long bridge to the wider use of renewables is, in reality, a bridge to hotter worlds. The interviews in the United States with utility companies on the question of commercial-scale CCS were especially revealing. Experienced industry insiders suggested it made no sense as an option because of its cost. Claims that commercial CCS already existed or was in reach were being made by people who "do not run power stations."

If incremental innovation does not get us there fast enough, this leaves the rapid and radical scaling of a renewable energy system as the only option. China, our interviews made clear, no longer thinks of climate change as a capitalist plot designed to bring it asunder, if it ever thought that at all. The technical or scientific background of many of China's political elites probably helps them to engage with the evidence of climate change.[51] Scientific literacy among political leaders matters. Margaret Thatcher, one of the first influential politicians to raise climate change as an issue, understood the science because

---

[51] Cheng Li, *China's Leaders: The New Generation*, Rowman & Littlefield, Lanham, MD, 2001, 224.

she had worked as a research chemist.[52] Compared to the interviews in India, there also seemed to be more reflection going on in China about positive ways forward. In particular, some interviewees talked about the possibility of China using its urbanization processes to drive low-carbon innovation.

The genesis of this book lies in these interviews in the United States and China, as well as India. But I also draw on the many interviews outside of these countries. Over the course of nine years we interviewed people in 17 different nations and everywhere found people who had been reflecting on why, as one interviewee observed, governments had not been "more honest" with their populations about the nature of the climate crisis.

We had begun the interview process before the Copenhagen Climate Conference of 2009 when expectations of a breakthrough deal on climate change were high. In the United States, more businesses were joining broad-based coalitions such as the Apollo Alliance. Businesses, environmental groups and unions were joining forces to work for a clean energy innovation future for the United States. In July 2009, five months before the Copenhagen summit, the Obama administration signed a deal with China outlining a plan for more cooperation on energy, climate change, and the environment.[53] Obama also announced a provisional emissions target for the United States. Even though modest, it was at least a signal of more serious intent for a climate deal than had come from previous US administrations. The dialogue at the highest levels seemed to be moving in the right direction. Everyone had been waiting for some US leadership on climate. A treaty to inspire hope on climate seemed possible. It did not turn out that way.

We continued interviewing in the years after Copenhagen when a darker realism had set in about the possibilities of reforming the world's energy system in time. In the words of one activist:

Working in the environmental sector is about losing and trying to lose a little less the next time. The comfort is in the history.

Drawing on the collective reflections of our interviewees, I also provide some account of why, in the end, the story of renewable energy and climate has been a history of lost opportunities.

---

[52] Brendan Montague, "How Margaret Thatcher Came to Sound the Climate Alarm," *Ecologist,* August 21, 2018, https://theecologist.org/2018/aug/21/how-margaret-thatcher-came-sound-climate-alarm.

[53] U.S. Department of State, *U.S.-China Memorandum of Understanding to Enhance Cooperation on Climate Change, Energy and the Environment,* July 28, 2009, https://2009-2017.state.gov/r/pa/prs/ps/2009/july/126592.htm.

2

Choosing among Implausible Leaders

The Case against China

One objection to the possibility of China leading on climate change is to say that governmental decision-making in China is nontransparent, often corrupt, and lacks the public participation upon which any progressive environmental regulation must ultimately depend. Widespread bribery, for example, can ruin the independent verification procedures needed to check the reporting of company emissions data on which carbon markets and governments depend.

On this line of thinking China will struggle to save itself from environmental collapse, let alone be able to help world capitalism veer away from the worst-case scenarios. To this one might add that China's great urbanization is part of the problem and not the solution. More people in cities means more demand for cars, cement, steel, heat, and cooling—in short, more emissions. The climate risks of the building sector are well understood. China's and India's urbanization, it could be argued, are a guaranteed entry into hotter worlds, not an exit.

Some security analysts might argue that the most likely scenario is one of military conflict between the United States and China. Global governance scholars might argue that the United States and the European Union still remain better exponents of the craft of soft-power governance than China. The work I carried out with my colleague John Braithwaite on the globalization of regulation does reveal the remarkable post–World War II influence of the United States and US multinationals in many fields of regulation ranging from nuclear power to technical areas of private law such as contract and intellectual property. What is the evidence of China's global regulatory influence?

One can go on multiplying objections. Surely US financial capitalism is a more likely source of funding for the kind of paradigm-changing innovation that we need. Has China produced a Silicon Valley? US innovation will certainly have to underpin the emergence of the bio-digital energy paradigm.

Does China have the unitary existence that my scenario supposes? Is it not more a case of a fragmented authoritarian state in which the center must constantly invest in webs of coercion in order to remain the center? The power of China's central government is overplayed. If that is right, how can China organize itself to lead a global transition?

Corruption Problems

On Transparency International's Corruption Perception Index, China ranks 79th out of 176 countries. Researchers employing empirical methods to study corruption in China have found evidence consistent with China's rank on this index.[1] Inadequate levels of funding for local courts create incentives for Chinese judges to use their powers of office to raise money.[2] Despite the hundreds of anticorruption decrees issued by the central government, a large-scale perception survey in China pointed to the belief that the corrupt took little risk and gained much benefit in practicing corruption.[3] The origin of this corruption is a matter of debate, but on one line of analysis it is linked to the opportunities and privileges given to officials and party members during China's transition to a market economy.[4] On some accounts the presence of foreign multinationals does not bring improvements to the rule of law but more investment money for Party officials to divert.[5] Big growth has led to big corruption. To complete a bleak picture, corruption, according to some, is rife among the Chinese leadership.[6] As criminologists sometimes say, a fish rots from the head down.

What of the anticorruption drive led by Xi Jinping? He has emphasized the importance of the fight against corruption. Critics see in this fight a purge of political opponents. For others the target really is corruption because of the

---

[1] Yong Guo, "Corruption in Transitional China: An Empirical Analysis," *China Quarterly*, 194 (2008), 349–364.

[2] Yuhua Wang, "Court Funding and Judicial Corruption in China," *China Journal*, 69 (2013), 43–63.

[3] Xuguang Song and Wenhao Cheng, "Perception of Corruption in 36 Major Chinese Cities: Based on Survey of 1,642 Experts," *Social Indicators Research*, 109 (2012), 211–221.

[4] Yan Sun, *Corruption and Market in Contemporary China*, Cornell University Press, Ithaca, NY, 2004.

[5] Boliang Zhu, "MNCs, Rents, and Corruption: Evidence from China," *American Journal of Political Science*, 61 (2017), 84–99.

[6] He Zengke, "Building a Modern National Integrity System: Anticorruption and Checks and Balance of Power in China," in Kenneth Lieberthal, Cheng Li, and Yu Keping (eds.), *China's Political Development: Chinese and American Perspectives*, Brookings Institution Press, Washington, D.C., 2014, 366–395.

dangers that the scale of China's corruption poses for governance.[7] Xi Jinping has made clear that the successful governance of China depends on its Marxist Party being run with strict discipline in which every local member and official understands fully the importance of working with the Central Committee's plans and guidelines. Since 2012, various Party discipline enforcement mechanisms, such as the Central Commission for Discipline Inspection of the Party and the various commissions under the Ministry of Supervision and Party Discipline, have been at work catching "tigers" and "flies" in breach of Party rules.[8] A five-year work plan for combating corruption was issued by the Central Committee in 2013 and made a priority. To date one and a half million officials have been disciplined, including 35 members of the Central Committee.[9] Before this is over, millions more will probably face proceedings of some kind. In 2018 the anticorruption campaign saw the establishment of the National Supervision Commission, with wide powers to investigate allegations of corruption outside of the Party.

This widespread corruption has to have been a factor in China's poor environmental record. During Hu Jintao's time, the goal of "scientific development" toward a "harmonious society" looked to slip further away as rich people's networks enabled them to increase their incomes by a factor of 60 or more compared to the incomes of the bottom 10% in China.[10] At the same time, poor people bore the brunt of China's deteriorating ecosystems. Rivers provide a good example. China has more than 50,000 rivers and a large overall supply of water, but data show China being closer to a water stress situation than its overall supply would suggest.[11] During the past few decades, various studies have highlighted China's water shortage and water pollution problems. In 2002, of China's then 668 cities, 400 had some degree of water shortage, of which 108 were classified as serious.[12] By 2002, Yellow

---

[7] Andrew Wedeman, "Xi Jinping's Tiger Hunt: Anti-Corruption Campaign or Factional Purge?," *Modern China Studies*, 24(2) (2017), 35–94.

[8] See the speech by Xi Jinping, "Power Must Be 'Caged' by the system," January 22, 2013, in Xi Jingping, *The Governance of China*, Vol. 1, Foreign Language Press, Beijing, 2014, 425–431.

[9] D. Gueorguiev and J. Stromseth, "New China Agency Could Undercut Other Anti-Corruption Efforts," *Brookings Blog*, March 6, 2018, https://www.brookings.edu/blog/order-from-chaos/2018/03/06/new-chinese-agency-could-undercut-other-anti-corruption-efforts/.

[10] Guoguang Wu, "China in 2010 Dilemmas of 'Scientific Development.'" *Asian Survey*, 51 (2011), 18–32.

[11] Xiaoliu Yang and Jinwu Pang, "Implementing China's 'Water Agenda 21,'" *Frontiers in Ecology and the Environment*, 4 (2006), 362–368, 363.

[12] Yang and Pang, "Implementing China's 'Water Agenda 21,'" 365.

River carp had gone from being a staple to something only high officials or rich businessmen could afford.[13] In 2007, 300 million rural Chinese were reported not to have access to safe drinking water.[14] There is a seemingly endless supply of statistics about the scale of pollution of China's air, soil, and water.

Rational actor–style arguments posit that powerful authoritarian governments will do little to address negative environmental externalities because environmental regulation will reduce the personal opportunities of authoritarian elites to grasp wealth.[15] Of course, context affects these abstract arguments. China's elites have a grip on long terms of power. They may calculate that they should satisfy the demands of present and future generations for a better environment because not to do so may turn out to be a rapidly escalating source of destabilization of their power. This is especially true if they understand that climate change will deliver rapid and exponentially scaling shocks. Fires, as the case of Australian bushfires of 2019–2020 demonstrated, arrive to burn the land on a vast scale.

Even if an authoritarian government is prepared to do something about domestic pollution levels in order to reduce domestic unrest, it faces no such constraint in exporting pollution. In 2017, one report identified the major role of Chinese companies like the Shanghai Electric Group and the China Energy Engineering Corporation in building coal power plants in a number of countries, including Egypt, Iran, Malawi, Pakistan, and Vietnam.[16] Allowing Chinese companies to add tens of thousands of coal-based megawatts to national grids around the world is consistent with a prioritization of profit-seeking above all else. An ecological future for China depends on decarbonizing the world system, not just China's economy.

---

[13] Corliss Karasov, "Water Pollution. Reviving China's Ruined Rivers," *Environmental Health Perspectives*, 110 (2002), A510–A511, A511.

[14] Jian Xie with Andres Liebenthal, Jeremy J. Warford, John A. Dixon, Manchuan Wang, Shiji Gao, Shuilin Wang, Yong Jiang, and Zhong Ma, *Addressing China's Water Scarcity: Recommendations for Selected Water Resource Management Issues*, The International Bank for Reconstruction and Development / The World Bank, Washington, DC, 2009, xxi.

[15] Thomas Bernauer and Vally Koubi, 'Are Bigger Governments Better Providers of Public Goods? Evidence from Air Pollution," *Public Choice*, 156 (2013), 593–609.

[16] See   https://www.banktrack.org/news/new_database_reveals_world_s_biggest_coal_plant_developers.

Cadres of Collapse

China collapse scenarios are rooted in the idea of a Chinese Communist Party more interested in governing to entrench its monopoly power than in adapting state structures and policies for the benefit of Chinese citizens irrespective of the effects of this adaptation on its own power.[17]

In order to maintain power, the Chinese Communist Party adopted a version of the former Soviet Union's nomenklatura system in which the Communist Party controls power by controlling appointments to public office.[18] As a system it has been and continues to be reformed.[19] As a principle of party power it remains inviolable. Nomenklatura systems lead to an insularity of governance in which the primary focus is control of loyalty through party control of appointments to crucial positions. Through its appointees a party controls a state's economy, police, army, education system, cultural organizations, media, and so on. Everyone who succeeds in being appointed becomes beholden to someone. The incentive to chase privilege through the system is great. Soviet historian Michael Voslensky, writing of the Soviet nomenklatura system, described a world of elite treatment based on access to superior homes, hospitals, shops, and schools, along with many other rewards.[20] Its beneficiaries bypassed the drudgeries of daily life. Nomenklatura systems turn revolutionary cadres into a stable caste and then an aristocratic class as their children come to be born into positions of privilege. The supposedly linear dialectic working its way toward the classless society circles back to its starting point of deep inequality, ready to restart the dialectic of oligarchy.

Nomenklatura systems do not align with good governance. Mounting governance deficits in crucial areas such as financial, health, environmental, and welfare regulation might unexpectedly combine into a powerful current that drags China back to its recent past of crumbling state competence, internal dissension, and conflict. Whether the currents of collapse mix to produce some bright-line event such as the revolution of October 1911 that

---

[17] Minxin Pei, "China's Governance Crisis," *Foreign Affairs*, 81 (2002), 96–109.

[18] For the history of the Chinese system, see Melanie Manion, "The Cadre Management System, Post-Mao: The Appointment, Promotion, Transfer and Removal of Party and State Leaders," *China Quarterly*, 102 (1985), 203–233.

[19] See, for example, Hon S. Chan, "Cadre Personnel Management in China: The Nomenklatura System, 1990–1998," *China Quarterly*, 179 (2004), 703–734.

[20] Michael Voslensky, *Nomenklatura: The Soviet Ruling Class: An Insider's Report* (tr. Eric Mosbacher), Doubleday, Garden City, NY, 1984.

swept away the Qing imperial state, or instead feed a slow, state-destroying repeated sequence of crisis and leadership failure, is anyone's guess.

My response to the objections for why China cannot lead on climate and energy is to acknowledge their weight. I make no attempt in this book to read the tea leaves of the Communist Party's future in China. This is a job for China specialists. There are those who are more optimistic about the possibility of the Communist Party creating a viable and new political model in which access to and maintenance of political power leadership is determined through a knowledge meritocracy designed to select for superior skills in the craft of ruling and regulating.[21]

This book is not an exercise in political theory in which different political systems are analytically or normatively compared for strengths and weaknesses. Rather, I am exploring a possible future in which an unlikely agent, the Chinese Communist Party, has an opportunity to do the improbable: shift us from a terrible global public bad to one less bad. My reading of the scientific evidence is that this is probably the best we can hope for in the time we have left.

I see this as a possible rather than probable scenario, given what many experts would say about the variable of Chinese Communist Party leadership and the problems of corruption in China. But if I am estimating a low probability for the success of a China scenario, why am I even less optimistic about the other three possible actors I identified in chapter 1 as possible sources of exogenous shock? I deal with India in detail in chapter 9 because by virtue of its population and coal resources it represents a huge climate risk. Here I want to say more about the United States and the European Union.

Why Not the United States?

The United States remains a hegemonic power. It has a demonstrated track record of globalizing regulatory regimes in a variety of areas of business regulation, such as trade, intellectual property, and nuclear power. I do not in this book focus on the role of the Trump presidency. US presidents come and go but what has remained in the United States is its military power and security state network, its capacity to influence business regulation globally, its innovation system, and its pluralism of factional elites. On the last point, by way of example, James A. Baker III (former Secretary of the Treasury under

---

[21] Daniel Bell, *The China Model*, Princeton University Press, Princeton, NJ, 2015.

Reagan), Henry M. Paulson (former secretary of the treasury under George W. Bush) and George P. Shultz (secretary of state under Reagan) are part of a coalition pushing for a gradually increasing carbon tax in the United States.[22] This group of conservatives sees a carbon tax as central to stimulating US economic growth and innovation. It has also managed to obtain the support of Exxon and some other oil companies for the tax.[23] Probably this is just symbolic politics on Exxon's part, but the broader coalitional work of figures like Baker, Paulson, and Shultz contribute to the possibility of significant changes in direction by the United States. The door to another future remains ajar.

Another example of how US climate and energy politics remains a game of shifting factions and networks, generating the potential for abrupt changes in direction, can be seen in one response to the Trump administration's announcement on June 1, 2017, that it intended to withdraw the United States from the Paris Agreement. On June 5, 2017, leaders from many city, business, education, and faith organizations in the United States, drawing on the deep wellspring of American civic life and business entrepreneurialism, signed the "We Are Still In" declaration.[24] To date it has 2,700 signatures. "We Are Still In" is a large and expanding network helping to coordinate existing climate actions and find resources for new ones. Climate mitigation action from this network along with others in the United States—such as America's Pledge, an initiative led by Jerry Brown and Michael Bloomberg—may, according to one study, deliver as much as half of the US commitment pledged by the Obama administration under the Paris Agreement.[25]

The progress on emissions reductions from bottom-up networks in the United States depends significantly on California, Colorado, and New York. California is the world's fifth-biggest economy and New York would sit around the 17th spot in the world as a separate state. Sub-state actors, no matter how powerful, realize the importance of leadership by a state at the global level. In 2013 Jerry Brown, the governor of California, signed a memorandum of understanding for cooperation on clean energy with China's most important agency, the National Development and Reform Commission.

---

[22] See Americans for Carbon Dividends, https://www.afcd.org/publications.

[23] John Schwartz, "Exxon Mobil Lends Its Support to a Carbon Tax Proposal," *New York Times*, June 20, 2017, https://www.nytimes.com/2017/06/20/science/exxon-carbon-tax.html.

[24] See https://www.wearestillin.com/about.

[25] Takeshi Kuramochi, Niklas Höhne, Sebastian Sterl, Katharina Lütkehermöller, and Jean-Charles Seghers, *States, Cities and Businesses Leading the Way: A First Look at Decentralized Climate Commitments in the US*, New Climate Institute, Cologne, 2017, https://newclimate.org/wp-content/uploads/2017/09/states-cities-and-regions-leading-the-way.pdf.

Building multilayered networks with centers of energy innovation such as California is how a sovereign state might harness the bottom-up activism of non-state and sub-state actors for a clean energy world.

The United States, more than any other country in the world, sends shock waves of innovation around the globe to disrupt the most settled business practices. After Uber, there is another alternative to hailing a cab. After Airbnb, people have less to worry about when all the hotels in a city are booked. After Amazon, retail therapy is more or less perpetually available. After Netflix, there is no need ever again to stream one's own consciousness. Companies like Alphabet, Apple, Amazon, and Facebook have sped into the list of the world's top corporations (in seven years in the case of Facebook).

Of the four national players, the United States has the greatest capability to catalyze change. However, it does not provide this catalytic leadership in my scenario. To begin with, its constitutional system of checks and balances is now enveloped by a sophisticated legal adversarialism, which in turn is delivering interruptions and blocks to its green economy leadership. Lawyers, litigation, and lobbying make for legislative gridlock, not innovation leadership. From the moment the Obama administration moved to regulate emissions from coal power plants, the industry began to "build a record for litigation in the courts" (industry interview).

The rule of law in the United States has become dominated by a tit-for-tat executive power struggle. Obama's Clean Power Plan of 2015, aimed at reducing emissions from coal power plants in particular, saw the US Supreme Court in 2016 issue a stay on the Environmental Protection Agency's implementing rules. In 2017 President Trump signed an executive order revoking important Obama executive decisions on climate and energy. In 2019 the Clean Power Plan was repealed and replaced by the Affordable Clean Energy rule, a rule much more favorable to prolonging the life of coal-fired power stations. The Affordable Clean Energy rule, like the Clean Power Plan before it, is providing a feast for lawyers as it winds its way through a long legal maze that will likely end at the US Supreme Court building.

It is not that good things on climate and energy regulation do not happen in the United States. They do. Twenty-nine states in the United States impose a renewable energy portfolio standard of some kind on their electricity suppliers.[26] This requires those suppliers to incorporate a specified degree of

---

[26] Galen L. Barbose, *U.S. Renewable Portfolio Standards: 2018 Annual Status Report*, Lawrence Berkeley National Laboratory, November 2018, http://eta-publications.lbl.gov/sites/default/files/2018_annual_rps_summary_report.pdf.

renewable energy into their systems. Under the Obama administration, the Department of Energy lifted the tempo of its standard-setting for the energy efficiency of appliances and equipment. Savings for consumers in terms of utility bills are estimated to amount to $1 trillion by 2020. Cumulative savings from emissions up to 2030 will be around three billion metric tons. [27] The problem does not lie in an absence of the good, but rather the growing bad of fossil fuel innovation and its networks of influence in the United States.

It is difficult to overstate the speed and scale of the US fossil fuel energy transformation. In 2009 it overtook Russia to become the world's biggest producer of natural gas and it remains so.[28] By the end of 2019 the United States will be the third-biggest exporter of liquefied natural gas (after Australia and Qatar).[29] Similarly, after the ban on oil exports from the United States was lifted, the United States has become a major exporter of crude light oil to Latin America, Europe, and Asia.[30] Aside from the domestic employment benefits, energy export on this scale adds to US hard power. For example, it is in a position to contest Russia's gas export markets in Europe.[31]

The success of fracking in the United States has created an interest-group network that stretches well beyond the gas and oil industry. For General Electric, the more gas used to generate electricity, the more gas turbines it sells. Chemical manufacturers see in fracking a "manufacturing renaissance." As long as sufficient quantities of both coal and gas are kept in the US market, companies like Dow will be guaranteed low costs of energy and natural gas feedstock with which to make plastics. Their line to government is that US global leadership of manufacturing is at stake. "Does Dow bring on four [ethanol] crackers or one?" (interview).

Insiders understand the long-term military importance to the United States of this manufacturing leadership. Its origins lie in the birth of the

---

[27] United States Department of Energy, *Saving Energy and Money with Appliance and Equipment Standards in the United States,* Washington, DC, 2016, https://www.energy.gov/sites/prod/files/2016/02/f29/Appliance%20Standards%20Fact%20Sheet%20-%202-17-2016.pdf.

[28] See "United States Remains the World's Largest Producer of Petroleum and Natural Gas Hydrocarbons," https://www.eia.gov/todayinenergy/detail.php?id=36292.

[29] See "U.S. Liquefied Natural Gas Export Capacity to More Than Double by the End of 2019," https://www.eia.gov/todayinenergy/detail.php?id=37732.

[30] International Energy Agency, *World Energy Outlook 2017,* OECD/IEA, Paris, 2017, 474, 193.

[31] See "U.S. Liquefied Natural Gas Exports up by 272% as EU and U.S. Host High-Level Business-to-Business Energy Forum," European Commission press release, May 2, 2019, http://europa.eu/rapid/press-release_IP-19-2313_en.htm.

national security state in the years immediately after World War II, a period when the US government opened the dams of federal money to its corporations through research and development contracts, as well as defense procurement contracts.[32] For example, companies like Du Pont and Dow developed different versions of the petrochemical napalm for use in bombs and flamethrowers. For these giant companies, the United States can and should continue to capture the highest-value elements—both military and economic—of the hydrocarbon economy.

Shale gas has made some poor people much better off. One of our interviewees spoke of the "generational wealth" that had been created for people in the counties of South Texas that are part of the Eagle Ford shale play. Before the shale industry, most of these counties had small rural communities in which families only remembered hardship. Education, workforce development, tens of thousands of jobs (50,000 in 2011), and many billions of dollars in investment have come to the counties of South Texas because of shale gas.[33] Shale has made tangible for thousands of struggling rural people the wealth promised by the amorphous American Dream.

Could a Green New Deal rally enough American voters and lead the United States into a rapid change in direction? There is support from some Democrats for a Green New Deal.[34] The global financial crisis of 2007–2008 drew many parallels with the Great Depression of the 1930s, leading to, among other things, a call for a global Green New Deal.[35] In the United States, Green New Deal thinking links back to the 1930s, when, following Franklin Roosevelt's election to the presidency in 1933, the United States entered what was in essence a period of intense regulatory institutional experimentation with its banking, farming, welfare, and labor systems. There was little choice but to experiment. Banks by the thousands failed. Millions had fallen into a jobless oblivion. In the previous year, tens of thousands of war veterans and their families had marched into Washington, DC, demanding bonuses they had been promised for their war service. They were driven by

---

[32] Daniel Yergin, *Shattered Peace: The Origins of the Cold War and the National Security State*, Andre Deutsch, London, 1978.

[33] Railway Commission of Texas, *Eagle Ford Shale Task Force Report*, March 2013, https://www.rrc.state.tx.us/media/8051/eagle_ford_task_force_report-0313.pdf.

[34] For details, see https://www.gp.org/green_new_deal.

[35] E. B. Barbier, *Rethinking the Economic Recovery: A Global Green New Deal*, report prepared for the Economics and Trade Branch, Division of Technology, Industry and Economics, United Nations Environment Programme, April 2009.

desperation and destitution. Evidence of a collapsing capitalism was everywhere. Roosevelt won both the 1932 and 1936 elections in landslides, among the biggest in American history. The success of his election promise of a "new deal" reflected a widespread acceptance and desire for deep and rapid reform.

The effects of the climate crisis are not yet perceived by a sufficient number of Americans in the way that Americans in the 1930s saw the effects of the Great Depression. Here the United States faces its own systemic corruption problem, one in which the integrity of its information and knowledge systems have been compromised by close-knit networks of the very rich. Through often anonymous donations, billionaire families such as the Koch brothers have built a network of many tentacles that draws in political appointees, think tanks, advocacy groups, and university-based programs to thwart action on climate change.[36] Corporate wealth has been used to purchase and spread falsehoods about climate. No organism, social or biological, can survive for long if it receives false information about a rapidly changing and hostile external environment. News mouthpieces such as *Fox & Friends* are part of a deeply dangerous informational feedback loop.

The famous checks and balances of the American system have been reduced to instruments of political warfare. They were intended to be mechanisms to share power among those holding common basic values. They were meant to preserve the potential and efficacy of democratic politics, not destroy it. For the moment the stage is not yet set in the United States for a cooperative New Deal–style politics around climate.

And in the short term at least, no US president is likely to be able to do what is required: send the oil and gas industry into extinction. A president would have to manage the politics of a confrontation with JPMorgan Chase, Wells Fargo, Citi, and Bank of America, the four biggest bankers to fossil fuel in the world.[37] The bankers and miners would speak to the public of the destruction of an American success story of roustabouts—risking everything, making a fortune, and along the way creating jobs and delivering energy security to the nation.

[36] See Jane Mayer, *Dark Money: The Hidden History of the Rise of the Billionaires behind the Radical Right*, Doubleday, New York, 2016.

[37] See Rainforest Action Network, BankTrack, Indigenous Environmental Network, Oil Change International, Reclaim Finance, and the Sierra Club, *Banking on Climate Change: Fossil Fuel Finance Report 2020*, 8, https://www.banktrack.org/article/banking_on_climate_change_fossil_fuel_finance_report_card_2020.

Why Not the European Union?

The European Union has, if policy and regulatory proposals are a guide, the best understanding of the role of innovation in resolving the geo-energy trilemma. In 2015 the European Commission, with its Energy Union package, turned to the serious orchestration of a unified energy-climate policy.[38] The European Union was importing some 53% of its energy needs. In the case of gas imports, six members were largely dependent on Russia, a dependency allowing for the possibility of divide-and-conquer strategies.

The Energy Union is about much more than energy security. It represents an aspiration to a different kind of economy, one in which EU citizens gain more control over their lives through the control of energy and the European Union cements itself as the innovation leader in energy-related technologies. Central to the Energy Union plan is innovation. Through it comes renewable energy to guard the European Union against energy shocks and provide new industries and jobs in Europe, reductions in greenhouse gas emissions, and cheaper energy prices for consumers. There are other important complementary initiatives, such as the 54 actions outlined in the Circular Economy Action Plan that the commission adopted in 2015.[39]

The European Union is also some way down the road to a green deal. In December 2019 the European Commission set out an action plan for the "European Green Deal."[40] The aspiration is to create, on the basis of fairness for all, a path to a climate-neutral Europe by 2050. This was followed by an announcement of an investment of €1 trillion in the European Green Deal.[41] The sources of money include the EU budget, the national budgets of EU member states, and the hope of private-sector investment.

Through thousands of hard and soft rules the European Union is binding itself to goals of ecological and climate sustainability. Many of these rules

[38] European Commission, *A Framework Strategy for a Resilient Energy Union with a Forward-Looking Climate Change Policy*, Brussels, 25.2.2015 COM (2015) 80 final.

[39] European Commission, *Closing the Loop—An EU Action Plan for the Circular Economy*, Brussels, COM (2015) 614 final.

[40] Communication from the Commission to the European Parliament, the European Council, the Council, the European Economic and Social Committee, and the Committee of the Regions, The European Green Deal, COM (2019) 640 final.

[41] See "Financing the Green Transition: The European Green Deal Investment Plan and Just Transition Mechanism," European Commission press release, January 14, 2020, https://ec.europa.eu/commission/presscorner/detail/en/ip_20_17.

may have an effect outside of the European Union. Regulatory standards set in the European Union have a modeling effect well beyond its borders.[42]

Beyond this profusion of rules there is also evidence of steps toward a low-carbon economy. So, by way of example, coal regions such as Trenčín in Slovakia are being helped to shift away from coal production; more EU money is being channeled into areas likely to be decisive for innovation leadership, such as battery storage; there are bottom-up energy efficiency initiatives, such as the Covenant of Mayors, which began in Europe in 2008; and step-by-step improvements to electricity interconnection capacities (for example, Spain-Portugal) are in place so that EU members can reach their 10% interconnection target.

Complementing the commission's policy orchestration of energy and climate policy is the European Investment Bank's financial orchestration of Europe's transition to a cleaner energy economy. Whether it is creating public-private partnerships to fund small-scale renewable energy projects in southeastern Europe, participating in funding aimed at helping member states meet renewable energy targets, financing circular economy initiatives, developing framework loans for cities to pursue sustainable development projects, issuing the Climate Awareness Bond, promoting best practice around green financing products, or working with other major multilateral development banks to channel more money globally into climate finance, the European Investment Bank is finding evermore ways to fund the building of a green and innovative Europe.

The European Union does have a financing plan for a green deal. It rests on the shoulders of the European Investment Bank and ultimately the European Central Bank. Presumably the Central Bank will end up buying many of the green bonds that will be issued in the next decade. Work is being done on an EU Green Bond Standard.[43] Put starkly, the European Union has a path to quantitatively easing its way into financing the European Green Deal.

The European Union's single market of some 500 million consumers provides it with leverage. To achieve its climate strategy Brussels has the option of turning to its cannons of trade power. Trump's trade wars have probably helped to encourage tariff-for-tariff thinking in trade relations. The European Green Deal contains a message shorn of niceties. The commission

---

[42] Joanne Scott, "From Brussels with Love: The Transatlantic Travels of European Law and the Chemistry of Regulatory Attraction," *American Journal of Comparative Law*, 57 (2009), 897–942.

[43] EU Technical Expert Group on Sustainable Finance, *Report on EU Green Bond Standard*, June 2019.

is prepared to design a carbon border adjustment mechanism to minimize the risks of carbon leakage.

The European Union can point to climate mitigation successes, as well as successes in renewable energy production. EU emissions were in 2016 almost 18% less than in 2005, and the European Union's global share of emissions at 9.6% has been constant since 2015.[44] Germany is a world leader in solar photovoltaics and Denmark in wind technology. As I show later, Germany played a crucial role in the establishment of the International Renewable Energy Agency (IRENA). There have also been hard-won regulatory milestones such as the EU Emissions Trading Scheme, even if the success of this scheme lies in the eyes of the modeler.

The Answer to "Why Not the European Union?"

When one looks at all the integrated activity going on in Europe around energy, climate, and innovation, why, one might reasonably ask, does the European Union not feature more prominently in my scenario? As with any scenario, I make assumptions. In the case of the European Union, I assume that a constraining factor on its capacity to move quickly is the effect of perpetual negotiation among its members. Behind every grand EU package there lies a many-stranded helix of negotiation. This helix connects, for example, the finance and environmental ministries within a member state; the finance ministries of member states, ministries, and the EU Commission; member states and the commission; and so on and so forth. Everyone comes to the table armed with a perspective, a partial truth and an interest. Finance people want to know what they will get for their money before they put it on the table. Environmental people want to put money on the table in order to get something going. If some member states do less on climate targets, then other states have to do more. EU members are always in wrangling mode. If a position finally emerges from all this, mutating to another position is not likely to be quick.

Behind the wrangling lie hard judgments about the innovation and industrial strength of members and which members will really benefit from

---

[44] See G. Janssens-Maenhout, M. Crippa, D. Guizzardi, M. Muntean, E. Schaaf, J. G. J. Olivier, J. A. H. W. Peters, and K. M. Schure, *Fossil CO$_2$ and GHG Emissions of All World Countries*, EUR 28766 EN, Publications Office of the European Union, Luxembourg, 2017, doi:10.2760/709792, JRC107877, 6.

tough emission reduction measures. Interviewees in Germany saw economic opportunities. It was different in Poland.

> We don't have the [technological] sophistication of Germans. Poland doesn't have the university, private sector R&D, and German banking system to match Germany. (interview)

A less than 2°C world requires a revolutionary and rapid energy system change. Do the intensive internal negotiating dynamics that underpin the European Union's soft federalism project allow it to take the radical action required? Unified radical action is tough to deliver where one member has lurched to an exit from the union. No matter how brave the faces in Brussels look, some must wonder if the European Union has entered a Habsburg tunnel. Making this possibility seem far-fetched will consume vast amounts of the European Union's nonrenewable political negotiating time.

There is also a more specific constraint on the European Union's Energy Union strategy. It is more a union of energy sovereigns than a sovereign energy union. For example, the reforms of the European Union's electricity sector have been deep, but it is still a market in which there are 28 national energy regulators, with quite different regulatory capacities and powers.[45] A recognition of the need for collective action when it comes to energy security is not lacking. The launch in 2011 of the Agency for the Cooperation of Energy Regulators is a good example. It helps to push action on issues such as gas interconnector capacity, doing its best to promote the Europeanization of gas.

However, the European Union is a net energy importer, especially of crude oil and gas.[46] Every member assesses the national link between energy costs and competitiveness. Every member has its own version of the geo-energy trilemma. There are complex linkages to consider, such as those between the type of oil it imports, its oil refinery capacity, and the industries for which its refineries produce. Every member forms a view about the role of renewables in its economy and what it is fair for it to do when it comes to contributing to the "burden-sharing operation being run in Brussels," as one interviewee put

---

[45] See Vincent Rious and Nicolo Rossetto, "Continental Incentive Regulation," in Leonardo Meeus and Jean-Michel Glachant (eds.), *Electricity Network Regulation in the EU: The Challenges Ahead for Transmission and Distribution*, Edward Elgar, Cheltenham, 2018, 28–54.

[46] See EU Imports of Energy Products—Recent Developments, Eurostat, May 29, 2019, https://ec.europa.eu/eurostat/statistics-explained/pdfscache/46126.pdf.

it. National energy sovereignty has to be guarded by member states because, in their eyes, national industrial policy is still crucial. The cost and security of energy supply are never too far away from issues of firm capability and competitiveness in any country.

The exercise of energy sovereignty matters to EU member states in other ways. As pictures of explosions at the Fukushima plant flashed around the world, German chancellor Angela Merkel announced on March 14, 2011, the temporary shutdown of seven reactors that had been constructed prior to 1980. One guesses she did not spend much time coordinating with Brussels on what this might do to Germany's use of coal-fired power. Germany's plans for extending the life of its nuclear power reactors ended up in tatters. In June 2011 the Bundestag voted to phase out nuclear power by 2022.

At the EU country level, our interviews revealed policy networks concerned less with reducing carbon emissions and renewables and much more about the oversubsidization of renewables, the manufacturing rents being captured by China, and the likely underdelivery of the green revolution in employment terms. For Italy, escaping its dependence on gas is not easy. Engineering a German-style energy revolution is not in the cards. Denmark has a much better chance than Italy of being a renewable energy economy. For France, allowing members a diversity of energy choices remains fundamental. Poland sees sense in using its coal because it does not want to depend on gas from Putin's Russia more than is absolutely needed. Not everyone sees Russia in the same way: "Negotiating with Russia is hard. Negotiating with Algeria is impossible" (Italian interview). Tough emissions targets, in the words of one Polish official, "allow some countries to impose their technologies on the world." For smaller, formerly communist European countries, the main game is to attract investment and jobs from industries using the lure of cheaper energy prices. Winning an innovation and manufacturing race in green technologies is not a game for them.

Of course, the European level of law-making can push the national regulatory levels into processes of convergence and harmonization. In November 2016, the commission published 1,000 or so pages of new rules in the form of regulations and directives relating to the redesign of the electricity market, the setting of renewable energy and energy efficiency goals, and the improvement of consumer capacity to act as informed forces of demand, as well as producers in their own right. But harmonization, no matter how many draft directives and regulations are proposed, takes time to emerge and only after long-running phases of negotiation and implementation.

The member cogs of the European Union make choices about the harmonization speed at which they want to run. From time to time they choose to throw some sand into the machinery of implementation. Even if, for example, Poland has the benefit of electricity interconnectors with other EU members like Germany, the way it sets up its bidding processes for the supply of electricity to its market may end up favoring its coal-fired power producers. In theory, sending a flow of electrons across a transmission line that spans a border should be as easy as sending a flow down a line that does not. In reality, as Rumpf and Bjørnebye show in their detailed analysis of the European Union's interconnector market, the electrons have to jump a lot of regulatory hurdles before they can flow across a border.[47] Within the European Union, the various transmission system operators responsible for the interconnectors have superior information about the complexity of network supply and security. They can game the rules around the use of interconnector capacity. The upshot is that the interconnection lines crossing borders remain severely underutilized, with electrons circulating in regional markets rather than one integrated market.

When it comes to member states transposing and implementing EU law, the commission's annual monitoring reports reveal significant compliance gaps in many areas. In 2016, a year in which the commission launched 986 new infringement actions, it also kept on with infringement procedures it had previously commenced across more than a dozen directives relating to the Energy Union, as well as opening 31 new procedures on energy efficiency and nuclear power.[48]

The European Union has been and remains an indispensable part of a trajectory to a less than 2°C world. It is a model in many ways for what is possible in terms of climate financing and leadership on renewable energy targets. But it is also a real-world model for why, absent more radical leadership of some kind, there is a strong risk of too slow a transition to a clean energy world. So, for example, the price consequence for emitting a tonne of carbon under the EU Emissions Trading Scheme (introduced in 2005) could be likened to the effect of a slowly increasing dripping tap—eventually there is an effect. The price has fallen below €5 and at the time of writing was around

<hr>

[47] Julius Rumpf and Henrik Bjørnebye, "Just How Much Is Enough? EU Regulation of Capacity and Reliability Margins on Electricity Interconnectors," *Journal of Energy & Natural Resources Law*, 37 (2019), 67–91.

[48] European Commission, *Monitoring the Application of European Union Law, 2016 Annual Report*, Brussels, 6.7.2017 COM (2017) 370 final, 7.

€25. A defense of this low price band might be that it has minimized the unexpected consequences for industries of the scheme and is slowly having an effect. A climate scientist might reply, "Wait till you see the unexpected consequences and rapid effects of the rise in global temperatures."

Similarly, Europe will likely move too slowly on eliminating gas from its energy mix. Bulgaria, Germany, Hungary, and Italy have sought through infrastructure projects to improve their access to gas from Russia.[49] The construction of the Nord Stream Gas Pipeline between Russia and Germany, completed in 2012, is being followed up with the laying of two additional pipelines (Nord Stream 2). More pipelines into Europe meet Gazprom's market access goals and will tie Europe and Russia into a relationship of mutual dependency. Using these pipelines, Russia will be able to manage delivery and prices to maximize its revenues from its huge gas fields, leaving less to be stranded by the inevitable growth of renewable energy sources. Nord Stream 2 is an example of how investment is keeping fossil fuels competitive against renewable energy sources, helping to keep a major fossil fuel supplier in the game. By supporting the growth of this web of pipelines, European states are likely lessening the chances of not exceeding a 2°C limit, an issue taken up in chapter 4.

The commission signaled in its European Green Deal that it was considering carbon tariffs, but whether it could ever obtain a consensus on the design, let alone the use, of such a mechanism is far less clear. The French, with an electricity system predominantly based on nuclear power, could possibly live in a world of retaliatory carbon tariffs, but could Germany or Italy? Italy's reliance on gas, along with the importance to it of the US export market, would see it much more vulnerable to carbon tariffs. Every member state's support for carbon tariffs would rest on a calculation about its use of carbon in the production of goods and its export markets.

The European Union does have an imposing edifice of rules for a low-carbon world. But it is an edifice resting on the fluidity of national energy sovereignty—a sovereignty, as Merkel's decision on nuclear energy revealed, that will set limits on energy coordination among its members. As we will see, China has implementation capacities that the European Union does not; it can scale the production of clean energy technologies in ways that the European Union cannot, and ultimately, through its BR initiative, it can build

---

[49] Robert L. Larsson, *Tackling Dependency: The EU and Its Energy Challenges*, Swedish Defence Research Agency, 2007, 11.

a market to dwarf that of the European Union. For these reasons, China, rather than the European Union, takes center stage in my scenario.

That said, even if the European Union cannot provide the needed scale of exogenous shock on its own, it is a potential partner for a fast-moving China in both global and regional projects of survival governance. Whether Europe looks south to Africa or east along the largest continent of Eurasia, how China shapes its Belt and Road investment planning matters to the European Union's green deal aspirations. Some of the more obvious partnership possibilities, such as joining the European Union's emissions trading scheme to China's scheme, have already been signaled.[50]

Why Not Wall Street?

Capitalism becomes finance capitalism when agents in the financial sector shift into the invention and trade of instruments of finance as profit ends in themselves. The entire sector becomes a distinct and autonomous force with directional power over the real-world economy. The reengineering of the world's energy systems depends heavily, one might think, on financial engineers. As we will see in a moment, to date not much engineering appears to have been done.

Solar photovoltaic and solar thermal along with wind power have in recent years dominated the financing of renewable energy projects, together capturing 93% of all investment in renewables in 2016. The maturing of solar and wind technologies along with their cost reductions have seen renewable energy installations from 2012 contribute more to global generating capacity than nonrenewable energy installations.[51] The rise of renewable energy capacity looks impressive, but it is off a pitifully low base. In 1973, renewables (excluding hydro) represented 0.1% of the world's overall primary energy supply. In 2016 they accounted for 1.7% of supply.[52]

The supply dominance of fossil fuels shows why the probability of ever-more dangerous climate scenarios keeps increasing. Renewable energy is

---

[50] See "Emissions Trading: European Commission and China Hold First Policy Dialogue," April 26, 2018, https://ec.europa.eu/clima/news/emissions-trading-european-commission-and-china-hold-first-policy-dialogue_en.

[51] International Renewable Energy Agency and Climate Policy Initiative, *Global Landscape of Renewable Energy Finance 2018*, International Renewable Energy Agency, Abu Dhabi, 2018, 11.

[52] Figures taken from International Energy Agency, *Key World Energy Statistics 2018*, OECD/IEA, Paris, 6.

a significant source of investment ($263 billion in 2016 and $330 billion in 2015), but this has to be seen in the context of overall investment in the global energy sector. Despite the fall in oil prices, oil and gas remained the single largest category of investment in 2015, capturing some 45% of the $1.8 trillion invested globally in energy.[53] Fossil fuel remains a large investment target. In 2017, $790 billion was invested in fossil fuel supply, with investment in renewable power attracting almost $300 billion.[54] Some investors continue to see in fossil fuel multi-decadal opportunities of profit. As chapter 5 shows, this has everything to do with the oil and gas industry's innovation capacity.

In any scenario of rapid transition to a low-carbon world, finance is central. IRENA, for example, estimates that $25 trillion of investment in renewable energy will be needed by 2050 if the upper limit of 2°C of warming is to remain realistic.[55]

The interests of US financial engineers during the first decade of the 21st century did not lie in renewables. In the two years before the financial crisis of 2007–2008, they issued $2 trillion in nonconventional mortgage-backed securities.[56] Their incentive lay in the fees they made from inventing and selling cryptic financial products to investors who made little effort to decrypt them. Perhaps in the next few decades Wall Street financial engineers will play a larger role in the renewable energy transition. Power purchase agreements in the energy sector do constitute regular income streams over a long period of time and so have the potential of being aggregated into an asset that underpins a financial product. Some new variants of existing approaches to the financing of renewable energy investment have emerged, such as the "yieldco" company structure in which a utility creates a public subsidiary through which it channels the income flows from its power purchase agreements to shareholders in the subsidiary. Those income flows gain the tax depreciation advantages available to developers of power generation plants. The capital that the utility raises in this way can be used to fund further power generation projects.

While some of those we interviewed in the United States thought that this kind of vehicle might be a "game changer," a phrase one hears a lot in

---

[53] International Energy Agency, *World Energy Investment 2016*, OECD/IEA, Paris, 2016, 13.

[54] International Energy Agency, *World Energy Investment 2018*, OECD/IEA, Paris, 2018, 14.

[55] IRENA and CPI, *Global Landscape of Renewable Energy Finance, 2018*, 14.

[56] Neal Fligstein and Adam Goldstein, "The Transformation of Mortgage Finance and the Industrial Roots of the Mortgage Meltdown," Institute for Research on Labor and Employment, Working Paper #133-12, Berkeley, CA, October 2012, http://sociology.berkeley.edu/sites/default/files/faculty/fligstein/The%20Transformation%20of%20Mortgage%20Finance2.pdf, 22.

the renewable energy sector, progress with this kind of vehicle has slowed. Yieldcos did raise almost $8 billion of finance in 2014–2015, but the bankruptcy of one of the largest renewable energy companies—SunEdison in 2016, which held two of the biggest yieldcos—has seen a dramatic decline in the use of this financing mechanism.[57]

Wall Street financial engineers do not feature in my scenario. Perhaps firms like Goldman Sachs will make some contribution to renewable energy generation when they structure deals for firms like SolarCity based on the leasing of solar rooftops to consumers and the packaging of individual tax credits as an income stream. Firms that understand complex systems can create various income streams for investors from all the government subsidies and incentives for renewables.

But for the moment this is more of a sideline of portfolio diversification. In 2018, solar photovoltaics made up 1.5% of US electricity generation.[58] If renewables have a revolutionary future, Wall Street is not writing it. Of course, if governments miscalculate and over-incentivize renewables, "The locusts come in from everywhere" (interview).

Financial engineering will not usher in the bio-digital energy paradigm. Research and innovation in renewable energy have to continue apace if emissions are to fall. Back in 1962 Kenneth Arrow pointed out that, because of uncertainty, appropriation, and indivisibility problems, markets would tend to underinvest in research, with the risk of underinvestment being greater for basic research.[59] This particular economic insight holds true today. Not much, it follows, can be expected from venture capitalists. For obvious reasons they favor technology projects that are likely to return some sort of revenue stream within five years or so. They tend to favor software over hardware.

Financial engineers are not in the business of covering the risk of providing public goods, especially global public goods. They are in the businesses of covering up the risks of the private commodities they engineer and sell—and engineering products for tax benefits. They gain, as the mortgage securities

---

[57] Brian Eckhouse, "Wall Street Sours on $9 Billion Mechanism for Green Projects," *Bloomberg News*, July 10, 2017, https://www.bloomberg.com/news/articles/2017-07-10/wall-street-sours-on-9-billion-mechanism-for-green-projects.

[58] See https://www.eia.gov/tools/faqs/faq.php?id=427&t=3.

[59] Kenneth J. Arrow, "Economic Welfare and the Allocation of Resources for Invention," in National Bureau of Economic Research, *The Rate and Direction of Inventive Activity: Economic and Social Factors*, Princeton University Press, Princeton, NJ, 1962, 609–626.

market showed prior to the global financial crisis, from the massive scaling of financial products while dissembling about the true risks of those products.

Climate change is a real-world problem requiring responses from the real economy, necessitating hardware and software investment. Strong leadership and investment from states in research and innovation are needed in order for the real economy to respond in terms of the manufacture and deployment of low-carbon technologies. Stable financial intermediation on a large scale is needed. Not needed is a financial engineering sector that hides the excessive risk it generates for its own profit aggrandizement.

For similar reasons I do not spend time investigating the exotic possibilities of the "fintech" world, such as those offered by blockchain technology for the building of cryptocurrencies and the automation of financial contracting and trading. States in the course of the 20th century, through institutions such as central banks, acquired massive regulatory power over the financial system. Central banks in turn have developed many technical tools, like quantitative easing, to help them in their pursuit of monetary and financial stability. States, especially those with hegemonic interests, have strong incentives to defend core central bank powers like those relating to the issue of money, monetary policy, banking supervision, and exchange rates. Hegemonic states will develop techniques of surveillance over fintech innovation because it is in their interests to do so. Fintech, I have little doubt, will create many contracting and trading possibilities within the bio-digital energy paradigm I describe in chapter 7, but it will not usher that paradigm into existence. At this moment in world capitalism's history, much more depends on the directed use of state powers of financing than on fintech innovation.

States have many creative options at their disposal. For example, they could agree to give banks relief from the global standards for capital requirements in cases where banks were financing renewable energy projects. Long-term state-based strategies of finance are needed if, for example, Indonesia is ever to unlock its geothermal potential for electricity generation. States agreed to reform capital adequacy standards in response to the global financial crisis.[60] They can equally change them to respond to the global climate crisis. There is little point in a "resilient" banking system if it fails to respond to a global existential threat—or perhaps that is the logic of financial capitalism: to have a system calculating trillions of transactions long after humans have departed.

---

[60] Basel Committee on Banking Supervision, *Basel III: Finalising Post-Crisis Reforms*, Basel, December 2017, https://www.bis.org/bcbs/publ/d424.pdf.

In my scenario, China makes the commitment to fund the research needed to drive the evolution of low-carbon technologies because of the scale of its existing environmental problems, its population size, and the potentially huge range of threats it faces from rapid climate change. It invests because it wants to avoid the bleakest forms of survival governance.

China also has another advantage. The BR initiative is a potential market of three billion people, a large market in which to rapidly deploy low-carbon technologies. If we think of this as a market made internal through webs of relationships, investment agreements, and other interdependencies, then the players in this market have learning and scaling opportunities unlike that of any other player. Multinational capital, I argue in chapter 8, cannot afford to stay out of this market.

The potential of the giant BR network to create a safer world for global capital has been seen by some financial players. Beginning in 2017, green finance committees from China and the City of London drafted a set of voluntary principles for investment in BR initiatives. Known as 'Green Investment Principles for the Belt and Road' they were released in 2018. By mid-2019 some 27 significant financial institutions had signed on to these principles, including all of China's major banks involved in BR, as well as other large banks such as Deutsche Bank, Mizuho Bank (one of Japan's megabanks), and Standard Chartered Bank.[61]

China's Global Regulatory Influence

World capitalism depends on multilayered regulatory systems that involve global, regional, and national regulatory authorities and standard-setting bodies. The United States, along with its various networks of global corporate influence, has been the consummate architect of global regulatory change in domains such as antitrust, intellectual property, investment, and corporate regulation. There are many experienced practitioners in the United States, both in the public and private sectors, of the craft of global governance. Obviously they do not have a monopoly on the craft, but by virtue of their size and skills they allow the United States to be a consistent and powerful

[61] For details and text of the principles see Belt and Road, "Twenty-seven global institutions sign up to green investment principles for Belt & Road", 3 May 2019, https://beltandroad.hktdc.com/en/insights/twenty-seven-global-institutions-sign-green-investment-principles-belt-road.

presence in the inner and informal circles of global governance. Through them, the United States influences the outcomes of many technical areas of negotiation, such as the international rules for corporate insolvency.[62]

Until now a very wide gap has existed between the United States and the successive number-two economic powers—Japan, then China—in shaping global architectures of regulation. There is some evidence that China has embarked on a strategy aimed at narrowing this gap. China's establishment of the Asian Infrastructure Development Bank, and its participation with Brazil, Russia, India, and South Africa in establishing the New Development Bank in 2014, are examples of global regulatory initiatives in a field that the United States and the European Union have dominated. Many of the technical skills and knowledge needed to influence standard-setting processes are embodied in the private sector, with US multinationals in particular possessing a real depth of expertise. As more and more Chinese companies enter the lists of the world's top companies, they will become a collective force in standard-setting. There are both qualitative and quantitative dimensions to standard-setting games. It is not just about numbers. But in terms of numbers, China in 2019 had 129 companies (including 10 from Taiwan) in the Fortune Global 500.[63] The United States had 121.

The transition to a bio-digital energy paradigm will require the redefinition of tens of thousands of technical standards that regulate food production, agriculture, mobile phones, computer communication, the production and use of chemicals, aircraft transport, standards for building materials, and more—the list is very, very long. Just how long can be seen from the work of the International Organization for Standardization (ISO) with its 161 national standards bodies as members, its 780 technical committees and subcommittees, and its more than 20,000 published standards. The ISO itself is part of a much larger global web of standard-setting for products, services, and systems that citizens come into contact with on a daily basis. This web includes sector-specific bodies such as the International Telecommunications Union or broader-based technology organizations such as the Institute of Electrical and Electronic Engineers Standards Association.

The speed at which states will achieve a transformation of their respective energy systems depends hugely on the work of thousands of obscure technical committees working in highly climate- and energy-sensitive sectors such

---

[62] For a rich account, see Susan Block-Lieb and Terence C. Halliday, *Global Lawmakers: International Organizations in the Crafting of World Markets*, Cambridge University Press, Cambridge, 2017.

[63] See https://fortune.com/2019/07/22/china-takes-lead-in-fortune-global-500-ceo-daily/.

as the aircraft, car, cement, steel, fertilizer, and aluminum industries. ISO, for example, has a technical committee working on standards for the management of greenhouse gases (ISO/207), which in turn has subcommittees working on specific issues such as organizations' reporting of greenhouse gas inventories.

Participation in the key nodes of global governance, such as the G20 or the International Monetary Fund (IMF), is clearly important in terms of big-picture agenda setting. Equally as important is the ability to play in the thousands of standard-setting contests that collectively shape the success or failure of the big-picture agenda. One can, for example, release a G20 statement extolling the virtues of knowledge diffusion and open science. But this big picture may simply end up gathering dust if the many technical standard-setting games in intellectual property in trade negotiations, among patent offices, and in international organizations like the World Intellectual Property Organization (WIPO) end up favoring exclusivity and secrecy.[64] The visions and principles of high summits, if they are to have a life beyond speech-making, have to be turned into the rules and standards of systems. For a state to be a real force in the craft of global governance, the skills of summit negotiation have to be matched by skills in the persistent grind of technical rule negotiation.

In a speech in 2016 Xi Jinping recognized the importance for China of both continuing "to pursue the transformation of the global governance system" through nodes of governance such as the G20 and, at the same time, creating a large enough "talent pool" of professionals with the skills to negotiate international rules.[65] It was the latter where he identified a need to improve.

China's engagement with ISO has, as in so many areas, grown. China is represented at ISO by the Standardization Administration of China (SAC). SAC was set up by the State Council to coordinate China's involvement with international standard-setting bodies, while within China the General Administration on Quality Supervision, Inspection, and Quarantine is the lead player on standards.

SAC participates in some 730 of ISO's 780 technical committees. In 2008 it became the sixth permanent member of ISO's core governance body, the ISO Council (the other five being France, Germany, Japan, the United Kingdom,

---

[64] See the G20 statement "G20 Innovation Action Plan," released in 2016, https://www.mofa.go.jp/files/000185872.pdf.

[65] Xi Jinping, "Improve Our Ability to Participate in Global Governance," September 27, 2016, in Xi Jinping, *The Governance of China*, Vol. 2, Foreign Language Press, Beijing, 2017, 487–490.

and the United States).[66] Obviously, detailing China's work on these many committees would take us into a zone beyond tedium. But what we see from China is active participation in many areas of strategic importance to it, such as energy management and energy savings, internal combustion engines, and reactor technology. Sometimes SAC will be the sole secretariat for the relevant committee, as it is for the committee working on standards for water reuse in urban areas. At other times it will share secretarial responsibility, as it does with the German standards authority, Deutsches Institut für Normung e.V., on the committee for building construction machinery and equipment.

The lofty goals Xi Jinping has articulated—a beautiful China, an ecological China, an innovative China—in significant part depend for their fulfillment on many thousands of Chinese officials and experts regularly attending standards meetings, getting involved in the tiny details of the drafting process, not dropping the ball on issues, staying awake after lunch, and politely but firmly steering the process to an outcome convergent with those big goals. In global capitalism, power does not so much grow out of the barrel of a gun as it does out of holding the drafting pen on a standards committee.

Of course, China does not have to lead in some fine-grained way the work of each and every one of the thousands of committees working on standards around the world, but it does have to impel the standard-setting system in the direction of decarbonization and a postcircular economy.

How China Gets Things Done—The Pressure-Driving Mechanism

Since its independence in 1949 China has had to manage the parallelism of ongoing technology and knowledge revolutions within its borders. For today's developed economies, these revolutions occurred in a more temporally linear and therefore manageable way. In the case of Western states, a rough sequence begins with the Industrial Revolution in Europe (from the mid-eighteenth century), continues with the industrial organization of science in the 19th century (and its many subsequent networked reorganizations), the Fordist revolution of mass manufacture of the early 20th century, and the waves of information and knowledge economy changes after World

---

[66] See http://www.loc.gov/law/foreign-news/article/china-permanent-membership-in-iso-council/.

War II. The story of China's industrial revolution begins in the 1940s as it started to reform a vastly populated rural economy with a very low rate of electrification. In the following decades, the other waves of change I mentioned also reached its shores.

Over the years China has appeared to have remarkable success in terms of meeting its various economic growth targets. From time to time there have been suggestions of some cooking of the books, particularly at the provincial level of data collection, but there are also signs of improvement in China's economic data-gathering and reporting capabilities.[67]

An example of where China has moved swiftly to reach a target comes from its patent system. In 2011 its patent office received more patent applications than any other patent office in the world, a notable achievement for a developing country in which a modern patent office only began operating in 1985. The electrification of China's economy is another remarkable story. Here one has to keep in mind that the electrification of the US economy, which mainly took place in the 1910–1930 period, occurred when its population had risen from about 92 million to a little over 123 million. China's predominantly rural population in 1980 was something over 981 million, with a substantial part of that population not having access to electricity and struggling to find fuel to meet basic heating and cooking needs.[68] Twenty-five years later China's electrification rate was 99%.[69] Its population had grown to something over 1.3 billion. In comparison, India's electrification rate in 2005 was estimated at 62%.

In this section, my interest is in sketching an answer to the question of how China manages to achieve these feats of rapid scaling. An important part of the answer lies in something called the *pressure-driving mechanism*, a mechanism for obtaining compliance with the state's economic planning and target-setting. I credit the term to my coauthor Wenting Cheng, who translated the concept and brought the Chinese governance literature on the pressure-driving mechanism to my attention. Together, using reams of Chinese patent data, we were able to show how the mechanism functions.

---

[67] M. T. Owyang and H. G. Shell, "China's Economic Data: An Accurate Reflection or Just Smoke and Mirrors?" *The Regional Economist*, Second Quarter, 2017, https://www.stlouisfed.org/~/media/publications/regional-economist/2017/second_quarter_2017/china.pdf. See also Dmitriy Plekhanov, "Quality of China's Official Statistics: A Brief Review of Academic Perspectives," *Copenhagen Journal of Asian Studies*, 35 (2017), 76–101.

[68] International Energy Agency, *World Energy Outlook 2007*, OECD/IEA, Paris, 2007, 281 (hereinafter WEO 2007).

[69] WEO 2007, 281.

Readers with a thirst for the thrill of patent data are welcome to read what we have written elsewhere.[70] Here I simply provide a brief outline because it helps to show how China could organize the scale of exogenous shock required to send world capitalism on a different course.

The geo-energy trilemma has a sharp temporal dimension. Every year in which the world delays peaking greenhouse gas emissions and then reducing them is a year in which the probability of limiting temperature rise to 2°C is lowered. Treaties, as an instrument of exogenous shock, do too little and arrive way too late. Prolonged muddling through using treaties is simply not an option in a climate emergency. We cannot repeat the history of trade negotiations. In 1947 the major trading powers began negotiating tariff reductions, a process that in the following decades was expanded to include more states and nontariff trade barriers. This ultimately led to the creation of the World Trade Organization (WTO) in 1994. But then the gains of this multilateralism have been compromised by the rapid rise of preferential trade deals.

The wheels of multilateralism turn too slowly and can slip backward. So how could China acting unilaterally start the necessary process of exogenous shock?

In his collection of essays on the governance of China, Xi Jinping, after suggesting it is not easy to govern a country with 56 ethnic groups and 1.3 billion people, draws on a metaphor from Chinese literature: "Governing a big country is as delicate as frying a small fish."[71] How to apply heat to something to get exactly the right result is one way in which to think about governance. The pressure-driving mechanism can be thought of as a process for adjusting the heat so that the fish ends up perfectly fried.

In broad outline, China's levels of government consist of the center, the provincial level, sometimes a prefectural level, and then a county and town level. These different levels are populated by government agencies and departments all standing in complex vertical and horizontal relationships with each other. It is a world of official hierarchy, status, and competition for resources. Most bureaucracies can be described in this way. However, China's, it is fair to say, is larger than most and has the Communist Party as its watchful master. A system as large as China's could fragment into conflicting

<hr>

[70] Wenting Cheng and Peter Drahos, "How China Built the World's Biggest Patent Office: The Pressure-Driving Mechanism," *International Review of Intellectual Property and Competition Law*, 49 (2018), 5–40.

[71] Xi Jinping, "Governing a Big Country Is as Delicate as Frying a Small Fish," March 19, 2013, in Xi Jinping, *The Governance of China*, Vol. 1, Foreign Language Press, Beijing, 2014, 457–459.

parts that fail to meet the targets of central planning. China is sometimes described as a system of fragmented authoritarianism. But, as the examples mentioned earlier show, the Chinese Communist Party does find ways to overcome the dangers of fragmentation and loss of control.

The pressure-driving mechanism plays a crucial role in uniting the different fragments of China's bureaucracy. There are three components of the mechanism: quantified task disaggregation and assignment, problem solving, and performance evaluation. Quantified task disaggregation sees the bigger goals of central planning turned into numerical targets that are sent down the many pipelines of bureaucracy to the appropriate level of implementation. In this process officials end up signing letters of accountability, formally obliging themselves to deliver the targets to those higher up and in turn receiving such letters from those below them. The problem-solving phase refers to the chase for resources, especially by those carrying letters of obligation. Those letters of obligation represent career-making or -failing opportunities. In the performance-evaluation phase, officials are assessed against the targets they have promised to deliver, with rewards flowing to those who have delivered and promotion vetoes to those who have missed their targets.

These three components of the pressure-driving mechanism work together as a highly focused and structured system of carrots and sticks. Since performance is generally evaluated on an annual basis, local governments have incentives to be responsive in adjusting their implementing strategy when a target is changed. Everyone is caught up in loops of continuous driving pressure. Ministries from the central level of government cannot simply rest on their laurels once they have sent targets down to lower levels. These ministries have to push their priority goals so that lower-level governments in the provinces and prefectures assign enough budget resources to lower-level officials so that they in turn can implement those numerical targets. Everyone has their sights on measurable outcomes and is competing for resources to meet those outcomes. No one wants a promotion veto next to their name at the end of the year. Whether it is patent applications, electrification rates, solar installations, roads built, water pollution measures, or some other target, pressure travels up and down the governmental network responsible for delivering the target. Perhaps employees in a large multinational like Amazon would see something familiar in the pressure-driving mechanism, a system in which people are turned into cogs in the service of system outputs.

The pressure-driving mechanism is a means to unite China's many layers of local government and its complex network of central ministries into a system of target implementation. Once the mechanism swings into operation, China's bureaucracy enters a phase of cybernetic operation in which the focus is on constant communication about the delivery of measurable targets.

At the planning stage, Party leaders remain open to input, often floating cryptically worded goals in order to see whether players at the technocratic level of governance come back with data-based blueprints worth backing. At this technocratic level, a huge pool of talented individuals all want to catch the attention of the Party's elites. This is not a world of elevator pitches, the dazzling TED Talk, or the slick visual presentation. Rather it is a world in which those with ideas have to persuade circles of impassive but alert audiences, using blueprints and data to demonstrate a measurable and verifiable pathway to the goal being discussed. The big-picture thinking of China's leaders is transformed, layer by governmental layer, into specific action plans, strategy papers, laws, regulations, opinions, and so on.

When the interpretation, critique, discussion, and probing have come to an end and the goals have been set, the system enters its cybernetic phase. Measurable outputs are defined and individuals are checked for their delivery of agreed-upon targets; feedback is given; and refinement of the targets takes place. The system remains closed until the targets are hit or something triggers a major change of direction.

This is a bare-bones description of the pressure-driving mechanism, but nevertheless one can see how China can deploy it to hit various targets that matter to the constitution of a bio-digital energy paradigm. Using the mechanism to drive China's emerging national carbon emissions trading scheme is one obvious area of application. It could be used to set targets for low-carbon technologies—as well as transport, communication, and energy infrastructure—for the many hundreds of cities that are or will become linked through its BR initiative.

Another obvious target for the pressure-driving mechanism is green finance, particularly as it relates to BR. The People's Bank of China (China's central bank) has, since 2014, been leading detailed work on action plans for a green financial system for China.[72] The focus of these plans is on system

<hr>

[72] See Green Finance Task Force, *Establishing China's Green Financial System (Final Report)*, People's Bank of China and United Nations Environment Programme, Beijing and Geneva, 2015.

elements such as local green banks, green bonds, green ratings, and green equity indices. As I mentioned earlier in this chapter, voluntary Green Investment Principles were released for BR in London in 2018. They have been signed by the Chinese banks funding BR. These principles, which one suspects were never all that optional for Chinese banks, could be turned into a rigorous system of targets and measures for those banks. Global financial capitalism will only exit the carbon economy if there is a safer and profitable alternative in which to invest. The pressure-driving mechanism could see China deliver that alternative in the form of a green BR at a speed the world needs to avoid the worst climate catastrophes. BR was publicly born as an idea in Kazakhstan in 2013. The frameworks needed to underpin a larger systems shift in the entrenched flows of global finance have been put in place quite quickly.

Finally, the pressure-driving mechanism should not be thought of as a magic wand of governance that China's leaders simply need to wave in order to obtain results. The mechanism helps to explain how some targets have been met with surprising speed. But China does not always hit the targets that it sets, especially in the environmental field. The governance of China takes place in many rooms, many networks, and in many places. There is, beyond the world of formal command and control, a much larger informal world, one in which Party members, bureaucrats, and those in business are constantly circling back to each other to negotiate, to test their freedom to operate, and to read the political winds. *Fragmented authoritarianism* is, at times, the right label for China's governance. At other times, the system unites into the pressure-driving mode, and woe betide those who do not deliver what has been commanded.

3

Technology Choices

Various climate scenarios point to the need to organize some comparatively rapid-acting colossal force of intervention if warming is not to move past 2°C. The International Energy Agency (IEA) scenario in which renewables play the greatest role is the new sustainable development scenario. It has renewables in 2040 accounting for 29% of total primary energy demand and 60% of electricity generation.[1] The International Renewable Energy Agency (IRENA) has developed a road map in which renewables by 2050 provide 65% of final energy consumption and have an 85% share of the power sector. The agglomeration economies of China's cities could provide the colossal force needed for these kinds of scenarios to come into being.

I do not attempt to build the case for a particular renewable energy technology, principally because these days each renewable technology has its ardent supporters and knowledgeable advocates. In the case of the most developed renewables, such as solar and wind, there are national associations and an international association working to make the case to governments for more support and investment. Structures of representation and networks of influence are fundamental to the growth and success of any industry. These do not emerge overnight. WindEurope (formerly the European Wind Association) has some 450 members, and the World Wind Energy Association some 600 members. In the geothermal sector there is emerging representation at national levels, such as the Australian Geothermal Energy Association, the Canadian Geothermal Energy Association, and the US Geothermal Energy Association. Ocean energy has nothing like the representational structures of wind and solar, but there is the EU Ocean Energy Association.

Over time, as various claims about these technologies are evaluated and the technologies themselves advance, states will have much better information about the basket of technology options from which they can choose.

---

[1] International Energy Agency, *World Energy Outlook 2017*, OECD/IEA, Paris, 2017, (hereinafter WEO 2017), 299.

Australia's central deserts and Indonesia's archipelago of more than 17,000 islands each offer very different possibilities and challenges for the extraction and delivery of renewable energy. No one energy technology will fit all the ocean and land terrains of the world.

State funding of research remains a vital component of creating a large set of technology choices. The OPEC oil crisis of 1973–1974 saw the beginnings of something like the right kind of government approach to energy research. It was a time when all sorts of portals to new energy futures were being opened. Creative minds in science had their best chance to obtain funding to turn their big ideas about new sources of energy into flourishing research paradigms. By way of example, the US Department of Energy dramatically increased research funding into ocean energy systems, as did a number of other states, including France, Japan, the Netherlands, and the United Kingdom.[2] With the inauguration of Ronald Reagan in 1981, funding for exploring these alternative energy worlds dropped dramatically, and a policy-as-usual mentality saw government funding go to oil and nuclear options. These same fuels were fundamental to military security.

The United States was not the only country to pull back on developing a broader research and development agenda around renewable energy. The French, who in 1966 had built what remains one of the biggest tidal power plants in existence in the Rance River, withdrew from tidal power, preferring to focus on nuclear power development. Building a nuclear arsenal would ensure that France's voice and position would always figure in the strategic calculations of other nuclear states.

Only a few small tidal power plants were built around the world over the next half century. Ocean energy research did not stop, but nor was it a funding priority for governments. Now some 40 years later, the ways in which one might harness the energy of the oceans (tidal, wave, current, temperature differences between surface and deep currents) are once again being explored with a little investment going into small tidal lagoon projects.[3]

The scope for variety in the design of national renewable energy systems is great. Geography itself functions as a selection mechanism for particular renewable energy technologies. Self-evidently, tidal power will not be a high priority for landlocked countries. Countries rich in geo-thermal

---

[2] For a succinct statement of the history, see http://www.oceanenergycouncil.com/about-oec/history-oec/.

[3] International Renewable Energy Agency and Climate Policy Initiative, *Global Landscape of Renewable Energy Finance 2018*, International Renewable Energy Agency, Abu Dhabi, 2018, 21.

energy have the opportunity, especially in an investment environment where investors are looking for renewable energy projects, to exploit its potential. Hydropower is presently the world's single biggest source of renewable energy, but it has risk dimensions. Giant dams often push local people off their lands. The Sardar Sarovar Dam in India saw more than a quarter of a million indigenous people moved out, a small number compared to the 1.2 million people that the construction of the Three Gorges Dam in China displaced.

Hydropower is also a potentially fragile source of power at large scale in a climate system where rainfall patterns and inflows are changing. In the Australian state of Tasmania, drought brought dam levels to such lows in 2016 that the hydro power generator had to bring in diesel generators. Water levels in the Snowy Mountains hydro scheme in southeastern Australia fell to about 10% in 2007, requiring the use of gas-fired plants in order to conserve water in the scheme.

Countries do not have to go big in the case of hydropower. Smaller and lower-cost pumped hydro projects can be used as a means of storing energy obtained from other renewable energy sources, such as wind and solar. Water from one reservoir is pumped uphill to another using renewable energy and then released through turbines when other sources of renewable energy are not available. In a world where drought events become more frequent, recycling water for energy storage purposes makes more sense than large-scale hydro projects. As more and more creative engineering solutions emerge for the generation and storage of renewable energy, countries will have more technology options in order to shift to a zero-emissions energy grid. Renewable energy technologies are perhaps best thought of as forming a portfolio in which the risks of one system are covered by another (the use of wind generation and pumped hydro to cover problems of solar generation).

As the preceding paragraphs imply, my arguments rest on technological indeterminacy. By this I mean that the establishment of a technology will not of itself specify a known end for the technology. Science and technology form a loop in which the discovery of new knowledge takes place and then in some cases widens into a spiral of innovation and diffusion. When investigating the history of a technology, historians reveal, at least on a nonphilosophical level, the contingency of technological development. In other words, the outcomes of technological contests could have been different. Tesla with the backing of George Westinghouse defeated the formidable combination of Thomas Edison and General Electric over whether the transmission of electricity was to be an alternating or direct current. There was nothing inevitable about the outcome. If anything, prior to the contest one might have bet on direct current becoming the standard because of Edison's relentless entrepreneurial drive and capacity for winning over investors. Once alternating current became the standard, debates over the advantages of direct current were largely confined to electrical engineering journals. Over the last few decades direct current has made something of a comeback, especially in the long-distance transmission of electricity using renewable sources. The history of electricity transmission standards shows how many different variables are at play in the technology products and standards that eventually gain national market ascendancy: entrepreneurial talent, investor perceptions, firm alliances, and market structure are all on the list in the case of electricity.

We live in a time when many discoveries relevant to managing the risks of climate change are being made and have the potential to enter the innovation system. The hunt is on for the next big thing in the green economy. The hunters include risk-taking entrepreneurs, entrepreneurial scientists in universities, venture capitalists willing to fund start-ups, multinational companies capable of scaling innovation into giant energy infrastructure projects, nonfirm networks of innovators drawn together by the value of openness, investment banks and international banking institutions, governments with subsidies to hand out, government departments with research and development grants to allocate, independent government agencies empowered to invest in renewable energy innovation, the mayors of cities wanting jobs and a cleaner urban environment, and large foundations with energy poverty alleviation agendas. No one theory of innovation captures all that is happening. Most capture a part.

Climate science has endogenized innovation in technologies of climate mitigation and adaptation. Within the present context of world capitalism, the potential for new circuits of capital and commodity has been created. The lure of future profits in a global economy on the edges of a monumental transformation into a low-carbon business cycle is drawing more capital into renewable energy innovation. Whether enough capital will flow quickly enough to a large enough range of technologies is very much an open question. Commodity accumulation through innovation continues on all technology fronts, including fossil fuel.

The flow of finance also carries risks. Financial markets may place too huge a bet on too small a range of technologies. Still, the endogenous effects of climate science on discovery and innovation processes will see an increasing number of interesting discoveries with which to contest the dominance of the fossil fuel paradigm. So, for example, the energy from processes of natural evaporation from lakes could be harnessed by evaporation engines to produce enough electricity to generate something like 70% of US electricity.[4] Many other interesting possibilities like this one will emerge. The more that do and begin to make the "valley of death" crossing to successful commercialization, the better. Few start-ups survive this valley crossing in which they have to remain a team, find strong financial backers, continue research development, avoid legal minefields, and find the right marketing strategies. We need many of them to make the attempt. States have a crucially important role in the funding of discovery research. Without such funding there is little chance of novel ideas like evaporation engines eventually becoming part of the technology basket of options for states when it comes to decarbonizing their economies.

Research networks need to become even bigger hatcheries of ideas about energy futures in order for some of those ideas to come to maturity as technologies. The rapid global diffusion of knowledge should be our categorical imperative of survival. Here there is a great struggle of paradigms going on in our universities and research institutions on which much of our innovation future rests. Many of our public institutions of knowledge have, through systems of intellectual property rights, been drawn into a paradigm of commodification and exchange value for knowledge. Secrecy and exclusivity of knowledge are the hallmarks of a capitalism that sees in knowledge new horizons of appropriation. Intellectual property monopoly privileges are a destructive influence upon the global diffusion of knowledge. On a positive note, there is also an embrace of the value of openness in capitalism: open science, open data, open source, open standards, open innovation. There is also some defiance in complying with the terms that knowledge monopolists dictate. A consortium of German universities, for example, has refused to meet Elsevier's terms for access to its paywalled journals, demanding a deal based on a much stronger commitment to open-access principles. We cannot in the context of world capitalism escape the commodification of knowledge, but states have to harden their regulation of knowledge monopolies in favor of openness if the project of survival governance is to have any chance of success.

---

[4] Ahmet-Hamdi Cavusoglu, Xi Chen, Pierre Gentine, and Ozgur Sahin, "Potential for Natural Evaporation as a Reliable Renewable Energy Resource," *Nature Communications*, 8 (no. 617) (2017), doi:10.1038/s41467-017-00581-w.

This is not a philosophy book, so I do not defend my premise of technological indeterminacy. My position can be contrasted with the arguments of the lawyer-sociologist of *la technique*, Jacques Ellul.[5] Ellul's view of technology stretches beyond machines into a systems view of it as a set of methods for driving the expansion of standards and technical solutions. On this expanded view, technology begins as a servant of our means and grows to dictate our ends. Political relations become absorbed into relations of technology in which human agents play bit roles in maintaining systems of technical operation beyond their individual capacity to change.

I mention Ellul's position because those who argue that it will be difficult to shift societies away from reliance on fossil fuel in anything like the time required are, whether they know it or not, drawing on Ellul's idea of the powerlessness of humans to change the path on which *la technique* has set them. Rex Tillerson, the former CEO of Exxon Mobil, more than implies that societies are locked into a long-term dependence on fossil fuel energy systems:[6]

> The reality is there is no alternative energy source known on the planet or available to us today to replace the pervasiveness of fossil fuels in our global economy, in our very quality of life, and I would go beyond that and say our very survival.

As the next chapter shows, the IEA, in its early years, played a role in projecting a technological future in which fossil fuel technologies would inevitably dominate the 21st century.

In the end, I think Ellul would say that there is a high probability that systems of techniques will drive us toward a dehumanized end, but that this probability might change if enough people take the first step of thinking about how to change it. To meet the existential threat of climate change we will have to embrace the freedom to choose that lies at the heart of existential philosophy. Technological determinism is, for the existentialist, apparent, not real. We can choose otherwise.

How people could bring change after their transformation of consciousness about technology was not a question Ellul sought to answer. His

---

[5] Jacques Ellul, *The Technological Society* (tr. John Wilkinson), Vintage Books, New York, 1964.
[6] Matt McGrath, "Oil Change? Fossil Fuel Advocate to Run State Department," *BBC News*, December 13, 2016, http://www.bbc.com/news/science-environment-38303209.

arguments were aimed at the need to create an active consciousness, one that was socially sentient about the channels of *la technique*.

The Nuclear Power Option

"Nuclear power generation will never be like another industry." With these words a member of the French National Assembly whom we interviewed summed up the many difficulties facing the nuclear power industry, not least of which is the burden of safety it faces. "Nuclear safety is every second of your life," this member went on to say. Or at least it ought to be. The former Soviet Union, this member suggested, cared more about production targets than safety.

Our interviews about the role of nuclear power in reducing the risks of climate change did not reveal other than what is clear from the public debates in many nations: namely, that its role remains deeply controversial. The nuclear power industry continues to present evidence about the objective risk of nuclear power. So, for example, the World Nuclear Association points out that in *17,000 years* of cumulative reactor years of commercial operation across 33 countries, only three major accidents have occurred: Three Mile Island (1979), Chernobyl (1986), and Fukushima (2011).[7] Climate-change scenarios involving drought, fire, or flooding all lead to much greater projections for loss of life than were directly caused by these three accidents (fewer than 40, according to the World Nuclear Association).

But judgments of risk are not settled by objective or actuarial risk, even if—as is often not the case—there is agreement on how to calculate that objective risk. Political risk and sociocultural risk (the risks to a group's identity and social endeavors) are in play in any country's systems of decision-making.[8] The brute fact of nuclear power's permanently controversial status sets limits on its capacity to help us meet the climate targets in the short time we have to meet those targets. Because nuclear power generation is too often seen as too risky, it is too risky a bet.

The IEA has warned about the dangers of a fading contribution from nuclear power to low-carbon electricity generation.[9] In 2018 nuclear power

---

[7] https://www.world-nuclear.org/Information-Library/Safety-and-Security/Safety-of-plants/Safety-of-Nuclear-Power-Reactors.aspx.

[8] For a discussion of these risks, see Fiona Haines, *The Paradox of Regulation: What Regulation Can Achieve and What It Cannot*, Edward Elgar, Cheltenham, UK, 2011, chap. 3.

[9] International Energy Agency, *Nuclear Power in a Clean Energy System*, IEA, Paris, 2019.

was responsible for 10% of global electricity supply. But the industry faces problems, especially in advanced economies where aging nuclear power plants require substantial capital investment if they are to be replaced or renovated. The IEA estimates a range from $500 million to $1 billion to extend one gigawatt of nuclear capacity for 10 years. This capital investment has to be found in environments where the costs of both solar and wind power and wholesale electricity prices have declined. In the IEA's analysis, the looming danger is of a loss of some two-thirds of nuclear power generating capacity in advanced economies by 2040 that would probably have to be replaced by gas and possibly coal. But, as is generally the case with IEA analysis, this claim rests on contestable assumptions about the price of renewable sources of energy.[10] Money not going into nuclear power may be much better spent on scaling and diffusing renewable energy solutions.

What is also clear is that China is not likely to be a source of renaissance for the nuclear power industry. China's nuclear reactor fleet is not growing to the extent that was projected a few years ago. Its 47 reactors is the third largest number after the United States and France. But there has also been a decline in the build of new reactors because of price competition from renewable energy sources. In 2019 there were 10 reactors under construction in China, compared to 20, two years earlier.[11] Unlike in China's other industry sectors, the Chinese nuclear program has seen long delays in construction times. For example, back in 2007 Westinghouse was given permission to build four AP1000 pressurized water reactors in China. The construction times for these reactors averaged between eight and nine years, roughly double of what had been expected.[12] As a result, the Chinese market for AP1000 reactors has "all but evaporated."[13]

One final point adds to nuclear power's problems as a source of rapid scaling of low-carbon electricity, a point that came up in our interviews with those in the French nuclear industry. A firm like Westinghouse, which historically has been the single most important firm in providing commercial nuclear power plants to other countries, will, as part of the technology transfer process, hold back some knowledge from the transfer. This knowledge—often described as proprietary knowledge, know-how, or trade

---

[10] M. Schneider, and A. Froggatt, *The World Nuclear Industry Status Report*, Mycle Schneider Consulting Project, Paris, Budapest, 2019, 233.

[11] Schneider and Froggatt, *The World Nuclear Industry Status Report*, 60.

[12] Schneider and Froggatt, *The World Nuclear Industry Status Report*, 41.

[13] Schneider and Froggatt, *The World Nuclear Industry Status Report*, 61.

secrets—forms the basis of its competitive advantage against existing or potential competitors. The logic of withholding knowledge that makes a firm a global design leader in nuclear reactors is commercially straightforward. A country might—if it acquires, say, Westinghouse reactor products—aim to develop its own trade secrets and know-how. The French nuclear industry did so after it acquired Westinghouse technology under patent licenses. But this process of building up know-how takes many years and is only possible if one has the engineering scale that comes with building a domestic commercial nuclear power industry. Since the small number of vendors of reactor technology are all playing the same game, customers of their reactors become locked in over the long term because other vendors do not have the trade secrets and know-how relevant to the reactor in question. These are ideal conditions under which to charge customers higher prices over the reactor's life. Reactor technology is expensive to start with and operates in a highly regulated market in which a few vendors can find ways to continue to extract profits from their customers. This is completely at odds with the global climate emergency in which states have to very quickly diffuse low-cost technologies for producing low-carbon electricity.

Self-Fulfilling Prophecies

One assumption does not feature in my analysis: the inevitability of war between the United States and China. A conventional way to think about China's future is through the lens of international relations theory and in particular a realist-inspired security framework in which the rise of China threatens US hegemony. The hegemon and would-be hegemon are drawn into an escalating power struggle in which only one winner can emerge. People of a pessimistic disposition see in this struggle the inevitability of war. Who will wear the crown of hegemony will likely be decided through military confrontations and trade contests. The United States will not quietly shuffle off to occupy its pedestal in history's hall of past hegemons. China will have to send it there.

Perhaps the possibility of military conflict between China and the United States is much higher than is generally realized.[14] War might arise in other

---

[14] Hugh White, "Without America: Australia in the New Asia," *Quarterly Essay*, 68, (November 2017), 1-81.

ways, such as a nuclear exchange between India and Pakistan. But if this were to occur, it would set back enormously the possibility of decarbonizing the world. War would rob the world of the time it needs to organize a different kind of global economy. War also consumes vast amounts of oil, reinforcing in the mind of the military the dependency the oil industry so loves and on which it relies. The US Department of Defense, for example, is the largest single consumer of petroleum on the planet.[15]

Those who argue for the United States to do all it can to slow China's economic growth and influence may well be increasing the risk of war.[16] Defining war between two nations as inevitable creates the perceptual filters of suspicion and fear needed to lay the path to that "inevitable" war. Self-fulfilling prophecies, Robert Merton pointed out many years ago, are initially false definitions of situations, the repeated incantation of which changes behavior, thereby making it seem as if a true prediction has been made.[17]

A US politics of China containment could bring even more fear and uncertainty into climate survival governance. A United States moving aggressively to manage high-tech flows into China would be likely to elevate the power of hawks in China. It would allow them to make the "Century of Humiliation" an even more potent narrative of China's need to defend itself against injustice and repeated humiliation. (This century begins after the First Opium War of 1839, when China progressively lost command over much of its territory and trade to foreign powers.) The opportunities for warmongering will multiply. The United States, by frustrating at every turn China's desire for greater mastery over technologies of development, may slow China's development, but it will also root China's future relations with the United States and its allies in a past of aggression, colonization, and subordination. The vastness of history allows us to choose and construct lessons. In the case of future US-China relations the lessons chosen will be those extracted from wars of the 20th century. If this is how things play out, world capitalism will be propelled into a much greater ecological crisis.

[15] Moshe Schwartz, Katherine Blakeley, and Ronald O'Rourke, *Department of Defense Energy Initiatives: Background and Issues for Congress*, Congressional Research Service Report for Congress, Washington, DC, 2012.

[16] John Mearsheimer, *The Tragedy of Great Power Politics*, W. W. Norton & Company, New York, 2001, 402.

[17] Robert K. Merton, "The Self-Fulfilling Prophecy," *The Antioch Review*, 8 (1948), 193–210.

4

The Geo-Energy Trilemma and
Its Mismanagement

The Shackles of the Trilemma

The geo-energy trilemma refers to three goals: climate mitigation, energy security, and competitiveness/development. Labeling it a trilemma implies the necessity of making trade-offs among these three goals—of having to compromise by underachieving on one goal in exchange for achieving better outcomes on the other two. India, for example, can achieve a higher level of energy security by exploiting its domestic reserves of coal and probably lower its costs of energy, but at the expense of achieving climate goals.

In Korea some see renewables as offering both climate and energy security because renewables give some refuge from oil and gas market volatility. Renewables seem to make sense for one of the world's biggest importers of fossil fuel. But, of course, policies on renewables have to run the gauntlet of approval of the dominant business groups in the economy. In those richly paneled meeting rooms belonging to those who run Korea's chaebols, green growth policies face their real audience. Persuading high-carbon-industry success stories like steel and shipping to embrace green growth is tough. The message from companies like Posco to government has been, "Please do carbon regulation step by step." For Korea there is also the close reality of competing with Japan and China for shares of various technology markets.

But Korea, a close watcher of China, also knows that China can quickly change the way in which it approaches the trilemma. So Korea has been preparing for the possibility of a China switch in which green technology exports to China and other markets become much more important to Korea's competitiveness. Korea's expertise in semiconductors can be leveraged in smart grids and other green technologies. Its engineering capabilities in shipbuilding can be deployed to develop renewable energy projects. And step by step it has moved its firms into a new regulatory environment for carbon. It knows that China's emissions trading scheme will dwarf that of any other country. In 2003 the Korean Energy Management Corporation did some emission trade simulations with major companies in that nation. The Voluntary Emission Reduction Program was established in 2005. A target management system for controlling greenhouse gas emission and energy consumption in large companies came into operation in 2010. Other initiatives, such as a domestic emissions trading pilot project, followed. Korea launched a mandatory emissions trading scheme in 2015.

One might decide, as Germany has done, that one can potentially escape from the trilemma by engineering a renewable energy revolution. Feed-in tariffs have been at the core of Germany's road to an energy revolution (Energiewende). First introduced in Germany in an experimental way in 1990, a national scheme came into operation a decade later. It gave investors the security of tariff rates over a 20-year period and gave electricity from renewables priority of access to the grid. An important principle behind the scheme was to build in preset discounts to the various tariff rates in order to take into account declining costs of installing renewable energy, as well as to keep up the pressure on suppliers to look for further cost-reducing innovations. There have been reports of Germany's electricity demand on given days being almost completely met through renewable energy generation.[1]

The trilemma, however, is far from resolved in Germany. The extra cost of the tariff is borne by electricity consumers in the form of a surcharge calculated on the basis of the difference between wholesale electricity prices and the tariff price. For domestic energy-intensive industries the temptation is to locate existing or new production in European states such as the Czech Republic or Poland where energy is cheaper (the competitiveness prong of the trilemma). In order to keep industries in Germany, the German government grants exemptions. Naturally, more and more companies push to be exempted. As a result, German consumers have had to foot much of the bill for Germany's transition to renewables. As more exemptions are granted and more renewable energy enters the market, the bill for consumers grows. Energy security concerns in Germany have also kept fossil fuels in the energy mix. Germany's Energy Concept paper of 2010 made clear that Germany would continue to rely on a flexible fleet of coal- and gas-fired power stations.[2]

---

[1] For a report that 100% of Germany's power came from renewables on January 1, 2018, see https://www.cleanenergywire.org/news/renewables-cover-about-100-german-power-use-first-time-ever.

[2] See Federal Ministry of Economics and Technology and Federal Ministry of Environment, Nature Conservation, and Nuclear Safety, *Energy Concept for an Environmentally Sound, Reliable, and Affordable Energy Supply*, Berlin, 2010, 16.

Reliance on fossil fuel may also have been increased by the Bundestag's decision in June 2011 to phase out nuclear power by 2022. Prior to 2011, nuclear power had supplied about 25% of Germany's electricity needs.

German consumers continue to bear the costs of feed-in tariffs, fossil fuel plants continue to operate as buffers on the German grid, and electricity prices remain high. Germany's Energiewende shows just how difficult it is for a state to escape the trilemma, even one as rich as Germany in regulatory capability and technology innovation. Financing an energy revolution faces the twin hazards of decreasing the competitiveness of national firms and having regressive effects, depending on who pays and how much.

In this chapter I want to do two main things. The first is to set out the emergence of the geo-energy trilemma. As the discussion shows, knowledge of the trilemma arrived among various public and private networks in the 1970s and 1980s. My second purpose is to show how the International Energy Agency (IEA) fundamentally mismanaged the response to the trilemma, thereby leading us into a much deeper climate emergency than would otherwise have been the case. Moreover, one has to ask whether an IEA-centered regime is at all useful. If the scenario I am suggesting is likely to have any chance of coming to pass, fossil fuel industries will have to be managed out of existence, requiring new nodes and networks of influence, not old ones in which the losers find ways to hang on and frustrate the pace of a global Energiewende. The IEA represents one means for fossil fuel interests to slow the ebb of their historically embedded influence.

The Military Version of the Geo-Energy Trilemma

The trilemma is a geo-energy trilemma because energy systems underpin states' economic and military power. In the military version of the trilemma, military power replaces competitiveness. States continue to invest in the fossil fuel paradigm, as well as nuclear energy, despite a deepening climate crisis because they prioritize their military capabilities above all else. Right from the beginnings of their industrialization, states have provided deep support for carbon-heavy industries such as iron, steel, and chemicals because those industries form the core of their military prowess[3] Without those

---

[3] Gautam Sen, *The Military Origins of Industrialisation and International Trade Rivalry*, Frances Pinters Publishers Limited, London, 1934.

industries a state has had to look outside of its borders to fill its orders for aircraft, battleships, and tanks.

War-making states focused on fossil fuels in the 19th and 20th centuries because of the security those fuels offered to their militaries. Without energy security there is no military power. Armies need fuel to be mobile. Air forces need aviation fuel to fly. Navies needed large supplies of coal and then oil to stay at sea for long periods. Toward the end of World War II, much of the Luftwaffe was grounded because of chronic fuel shortages, leading to a scramble to develop jet engines that could use unrefined fuels.[4] Serious oil shortages affected the German military as early as 1941, leading Hitler to embark on a campaign, which ultimately failed, to capture the giant Caucasus oil fields. Around 90% of Soviet production came from these fields.[5] In the 19th and early 20th centuries, the strategic use of navy fleets in Great Power calculations and contests rested on reliable access to coal. The US Navy, for example, needed around 300,000 tons of coal to mobilize its fleet in the Caribbean and 150,000 tons a month to keep it operational.[6]

Today the US military is interested in renewable energy because of its promise to increase the endurance of its war machines. Hydrogen fuel cells and solar could keep vehicles and drones in action for much longer[7]—"more fight for less fuel" (interview). Water and sunlight are readily available in most places. Oil fields lose some of their strategic significance if armies find ways to harness renewable energy. Low-emission war machines are, one supposes, a collateral benefit.

We have very imperfect information about the emissions for which militaries around the world are responsible. As the IEA points out, states treat this information as sensitive and so merge it with other categories or simply do not report it.[8]

Control by one state of another state's energy supply gives the supplier state a potential lever of threat. For example, during the Soviet Union era, Estonia, Latvia, and Lithuania became highly dependent on Russian oil and

---

[4] Hermione Giffard, "Engines of Desperation: Jet Engines, Production, and New Weapons in the Third Reich," *Journal of Contemporary History*, 48 (2013), 821–844.

[5] Joel Hayward, "Too Little, Too Late: An Analysis of Hitler's Failure in August 1942 to Damage Soviet Oil Production," *Journal of Military History*, 64 (2000), 769–794.

[6] John H. Maurer, "Fuel and the Battle Fleet: Coal, Oil, and American Naval Strategy, 1898–1925," *Naval War College Review*, 34 (1981), 60–77, 61.

[7] See "Hydrogen as a Military Fuel," https://www.hydrogen.energy.gov/pdfs/review18/ia001_darling_2018_o.pdf.

[8] International Energy Agency, CO_2 *Emissions from Fuel Combustion (2018 edition)*, OECD/IEA, Paris, 2018, 1.5.

gas imports, a dependence that continued after their independence in the 1990s. It was not just an import dependence, but an infrastructure dependence in the form of pipelines. These Baltic states, along with other European states, experienced the evolution of an integrated Russian geo-energy policy in which, by 2006, Russia had suspended its exports of energy on 40 or so occasions.[9] Small to medium-size states are especially vulnerable to these kinds of geo-energy plays.

The Arrival of the Trilemma

The geo-energy world of the 20th century was always a world of complex management, well before the arrival of the trilemma. Britain and then the United States were key players in putting together, in the second decade of the 20th century, the first oil regime. The regime took the form of a state-supported private oligopoly. The oil majors (known as the "Seven Sisters") extracted oil from producing states and exported it to consuming states on economic terms that largely favored the oil companies and their Western customer states.[10] Under the first oil regime, the energy security and competitiveness needs of Western states were largely met by cheap and plentiful oil. After World War II, this oil regime came under increasing pressure as producer states such as Venezuela began to push for better profit-sharing deals. A crucial step in the reshaping of relations within the regime was the formation of the Organization of the Petroleum Exporting Countries (OPEC) in 1960. The OPEC oil crisis of 1973–1974 is generally taken as the endpoint of the first oil regime. Around this time scientists were also beginning to see evidence of another growing crisis involving oil.

Article 2 of the United Nations Framework Convention on Climate Change (UNFCCC) 1992 contains a goal, or perhaps what will increasingly be come to be seen as a duty, "to prevent dangerous anthropogenic interference with the climate system." The risks of CO_2 emission were known before 1992. The science leading up to this conclusion had begun in the 19th century.

In 1827 physicist Joseph Fourier suggested that the atmosphere acted like glass in a greenhouse, letting in the sun's rays but trapping the heat. By the end

---

[9] Agnia Grigas, *The Politics of Energy and Memory between the Baltic States and Russia*, Ashgate, Aldershot, UK, 2013, 44.

[10] Lawrence P. Frank, "The First Oil Regime," *World Politics*, 37 (1985), 586–598.

of the century, the research was suggesting a more detailed hypothesis. The absorption by the atmosphere of heat radiated from the earth depended on small concentrations of two gases: aqueous vapor (water vapor) and carbonic acid (the term then used for carbon dioxide). Svante Arrhenius, a Swedish chemist generally regarded as laying the foundations for the modern scientific explanation of the greenhouse effect, suggested in 1896 that the "influence of this absorption must be of great importance."[11] The next century was to reveal just how important.

Science in the United States made a huge difference to our understanding of the climate system.[12] During the 1970s the Geophysical Fluid Dynamics Laboratory at Princeton and the National Academy of Sciences were at the forefront of developing the first climate models. Various individual scientists pushed the results and issues into the work agendas of the World Meteorological Organization (WMO), the International Council of Scientific Unions (ICSU), and the United Nations Environment Programme (UNEP). The 1980s saw more reports and warnings from scientists, as well as more international action. A conference in 1985 at Villach, Austria, saw experts publicly agree on the likely rise of global mean temperatures in the next century. Acting on a recommendation of the conference, the ICSU, UNEP, and WMO established an Advisory Group on Greenhouse Gases in July 1986. Two years later the Intergovernmental Panel on Climate Change (IPCC) was formed. Also in 1988 James Hansen suggested it was "time to stop waffling so much and say that the evidence is pretty strong that the greenhouse effect is here."[13] In 1990 the IPCC expressed confidence in the calculation that carbon dioxide had been responsible for more than half of the enhanced greenhouse effect.[14]

Hansen was not being alarmist. By 1988 there had been almost 100 years of science around the mechanism since Arrhenius had put forward some estimations of its effects. During the course of the 20th century more data became available with which to explore and test the effects of the mechanism.

<hr>

[11] Svante Arrhenius, "On the Influence of Carbonic Acid in the Air upon the Temperature of the Ground," *Philosophical Magazine and Journal of Science*, 41 (1896), 237–276, 239.

[12] Shardul Agrawala, "Early Science—Policy Interactions in Climate Change: Lessons from the Advisory Group on Greenhouse Gases," *Global Environmental Change*, 9 (1999), 157–169.

[13] Philip Shabecoff, "Global Warming Has Begun, Expert Tells Senate," *New York Times*, June 24, 1988, Section A, 1.

[14] J. T. Houghton, G. J. Jenkins, and J. J. Ephraums (eds.), *Climate Change: The IPCC Scientific Assessment*, Cambridge University Press, Cambridge, 1990, xi.

The most important of this data came from Hawaii. On the northern flank of the Mauna Loa volcano, a US weather observatory started recording in 1958 the concentration of CO_2 in the atmosphere. The idea for the measuring program had come from a young chemist, Dr. Charles Keeling. Keeling had developed high-precision techniques for measuring the amount of CO_2 in the air, reducing the uncertainty and error of earlier approaches. Keeling's program was the beginning of the world's longest-running data gathering exercise for CO_2 levels in the atmosphere. It also inspired the creation of a more rigorous global monitoring network for the collection of data on greenhouse gases.

By 1988 Keeling's data clearly showed concentrations of CO_2 in the form of a steeply rising curve, known today as the Keeling curve. Hansen was right to say it was time to stop waffling. On the face of it, the global response times of many nation-states to an emerging climate crisis look pretty good. Two years after the first IPCC report, the Rio Earth Summit of 1992 delivered, among other things, the UNFCCC. But the UNFCCC did not turn out to be the path to a rapid and integrated risk management strategy for the geo-energy trilemma. Instead it became a doorway into delay, or what Christian Downie has termed "prolonged international negotiations" over climate.[15] Managing the energy regime was largely left in the hands of the IEA, a fossil fuel agency with a narrow membership of states. There was no coordinated response to the trilemma.

The IEA: Born Fossil

During the 1973–1974 oil crisis, Arab oil-producing states imposed an embargo on the United States and some European countries because of their support for Israel in the Arab-Israeli War that had begun in October 1973. In that same month, Arab oil ministers agreed to a policy of systematically reducing exports to countries based on where those countries stood on the Arab-Israeli conflict. An embargo was imposed on the United States because it was providing arms to Israel, as well as the Netherlands for its pro-Israeli support. Saudi leadership in the person of King Faisal drove the boycott policy. Faisal was responding to pressures from within Saudi Arabia and

---

[15] Christian Downie, *The Politics of Climate Change Negotiations: Strategies and Variables in Prolonged International Negotiations*, Edward Elgar, Cheltenham, UK, 2014.

from more militant Arab states for Saudi Arabia to play a greater role in helping the Palestinians.

The creation of the IEA was the fruit of an intense period of cooperation among a group of Organisation of Economic Co-operation and Development (OECD) countries, a group led by the United States. Prior to the crisis, the members of the OECD had not collaborated much on energy policy. There was an energy committee and an oil committee in the OECD, but these were essentially talking shops. The European members of the OECD weathered the crisis because they had, acting on an OECD recommendation, been developing stockpiles of oil. During the time of crisis they had reserves amounting to an average of 70 days. Oil-importing states were also helped by the relatively short period of the crisis. By December 1973, Arab states were not acting on planned cutbacks in production. July 1974 saw an end to the embargo for all countries.

The 1973–1974 crisis was a reminder, if a reminder was needed, that economies depend on the reliable supply of energy. Henry Kissinger in December 1973 likened the crisis to a "Sputnik challenge" and proposed the formation of an Energy Action Group.[16] From there states moved with lightning speed. February 1974 saw the United States bring together key oil-importing countries at the Washington Energy Conference. This led to the formation of an Energy Coordinating Group. Meeting in Brussels, this group produced the documentation that set OECD countries on a path of cooperation on energy policy, especially on the issue of security of oil supplies.

An OECD Council decision of November 15, 1974, established the IEA as an autonomous body within the OECD. Three days later, the Agreement on an International Energy Program, which required its members to commit initially to holding 60 days of emergency oil reserves, was signed on behalf of 16 founding members.[17] The Governing Board of the IEA met later on the same day.

The IEA had energy in its title, but as might be expected of a creature born of an oil crisis, it was administering a treaty that was all about oil. Aside from the provisions establishing the oil emergency mechanism, the treaty

---

[16] Richard Scott, *The History of the International Energy Agency: The First Twenty Years*, Vol. 1, OECD/IEA, Paris, 1994, 44.

[17] The founding members were Austria, Belgium, Canada, Denmark, Germany, Ireland, Italy, Japan, Luxembourg, the Netherlands, Spain, Sweden, Switzerland, Turkey, the United Kingdom and the United States. See the copy of the 1974 Agreement available at *International Legal Materials*, 14 (1975), 1.

required the establishment of an information system about the international oil market and a framework for consulting with oil companies. One of the lessons of the crisis was just how little information states had about the oil industry and sources of supply. The IEA was to turn itself into a super-analyst of the oil market on behalf of its OECD members. A standing group on long-term cooperation was given the task of reporting on the development of alternative energy sources such as coal, natural gas, nuclear energy, and hydroelectric power.

The IEA's fossil-centric view of energy security saw it recommend to its members strategies based on the greater use of coal to reduce the demand for oil. In 1979 its governing board adopted Principles for Action on Coal. The same year saw the formation of a Coal Industry Advisory Board (CIAB), a vehicle for feeding the coal industry's expertise into the IEA. In 1980 a report from the CIAB Coal Action Programme recommended a doubling of coal use by 1990 and tripling it by 2000.[18] In 1982 there were more positive suggestions about the use of coal in industry and the establishment of a Coal Information System. A review in 1984 recommended that IEA members increase their reliance on coal.[19]

States entered the negotiations over climate with a schizophrenic regime structure for addressing the geo-energy trilemma. The IEA pushed on with its fossil fuel–centric views, while the climate change negotiations became bogged down because of the domestic politics of denial in some states, the growth agendas of large developing countries, and blocking behavior by fossil fuel exporters such as Saudi Arabia.

The IEA's strategy of increasing oil security by recommending the substitution of coal drew states more deeply into the trilemma. One of the IEA's mandates was to improve information about oil supplies and markets. This it did. It also created databases concerning coal supplies and markets. Its statistical data and depth of expertise were all tilted in the direction of a policy of energy security based on fossil fuel. It had much less expertise when it came to projecting the future of renewables. The clear danger of this tilt was the statistically self-fulfilling prophecy. Its depth of data and knowledge about fossil fuels backed its views about coal's key role in states' energy security. Coal use would help oil security, and oil security was at the core of the IEA's mission.

---

[18] Scott, The History of the International Energy Agency, 417.
[19] Scott, The History of the International Energy Agency, 419.

The commitment to coal was very much in evidence in our interviews at the IEA in 2009: Coal, it was pointed out, is the "secure energy source" for many countries:

> Coal is not going to drop off the radar for developing or developed economies. Coal is going to be used for decades to come. (interview)

Many IEA insiders saw coal as a fuel of the future. A rapid transition away from coal was a dim prospect. The answer to the emissions problems of coal was for states to develop carbon capture and storage (CCS) technologies. One line of thinking in the IEA was to interest China in developing CCS. The hope was that China would pay the cost of development and then benefit by exporting CCS technologies to other markets. There was another potential gain. If China burned more of its coal, so much the better for world energy security.

Yet in the years that followed, as our interview data show, while many saw CCS as a good idea in principle, the likelihood of cost-effective CCS technologies being delivered in anything like the time required was thought to be more or less zero. Policy networks were publicly communicating one thing about CCS, but privately gloomy about its viability. The next section explores this issue in more detail.

The Myth of CCS

Three basic stages are involved in CCS: the capture of CO_2 from a source such as a coal-fired power station, its compression and transportation (for example, by pipeline), and its storage in some stable geological site.[20] The IEA was able to expand its policy-legitimating work on CCS because Australia, one of the world's largest coal exporters, made a "generous" contribution of around €10 million to the work program of the IEA's Working Party on Fossil Fuels (IEA interview 2009). This was part of a busy and broader agenda of Australian support for the development of CCS. Then–prime minister Kevin Rudd in 2009 gave a speech at the inaugural meeting of the Global Carbon Capture and Storage Institute, something Australia had worked hard

---

[20] International Energy Agency, *World Energy Outlook 2017*, OECD/IEA, Paris, 2017, (hereinafter WEO 2017), 216–217.

to establish.[21] Rudd suggested it was vital to find out if CCS could be made to work. As he pointed out, there was not one example of a fully integrated industrial-scale CCS project anywhere in the world.

What we do not know and probably never will is just how many people in the coal business thought that CCS was ever likely to work. Back in 2004 the IEA had been upbeat about the possibility of CCS, seeing it as a "promising emission reduction option."[22] In 2009 our IEA interviewees described four major CCS projects in the world (two in Norway, one in Canada and the United States, and one in Algeria). However, many more demonstration plants were needed in order to assess the costs of CCS. "Talking about the cost is a little theoretical at the moment" (IEA interview). What was clear was that CCS would dramatically add to the costs of coal plants. The capital costs of building a CCS demonstration plant were thought to lie somewhere between $500 million and $1 billion.[23] There was, in the words of one interviewee, a "commercial gap" when it came to financing CCS.

Three years later in its *World Energy Outlook 2012*, the IEA described progress on CCS as "highly uncertain." When we spoke to utilities in the United States in 2014 about CCS, their assessment of its prospects was more or less derisory. They had seen close up the fate of CCS research.

In 2003 the US Department of Energy had announced the FutureGen program. Its aim was to build the world's first zero-emissions coal-fired power plant.[24] About 76% of the $1 billion estimated cost was to be met by the Department of Energy and the rest by a consortium of coal producers and power companies known as the FutureGen Industrial Alliance. Worried by cost blowouts, the Department of Energy decided not to continue its arrangement with the consortium and moved to restructure the FutureGen program. Under the Obama administration FutureGen 2.0 was launched, but in 2015 the Department of Energy pulled out for a second time, citing issues about completion and private investment in the venture.[25]

---

[21] See the speech at https://pmtranscripts.dpmc.gov.au/release/transcript-16501.

[22] International Energy Agency, *Prospects for CO₂ Capture and Storage*, OECD/IEA, Paris, 2004.

[23] International Energy Agency, *World Energy Outlook 2007*, OECD/IEA, Paris, 2007 (hereinafter WEO 2007), 218.

[24] Details of the FutureGen project are to be found in United States Government Accountability Office, *Clean Coal: DOE's Decision to Restructure FutureGen Should Be Based on a Comprehensive Analysis of Costs, Benefits, and Risks*, US Government Accountability Office, Washington, DC, February 2009.

[25] Jeff Tollefson, "US Government Abandons Carbon-Capture Demonstration," *Nature News*, February 5, 2015, https://www.nature.com/news/us-government-abandons-carbon-capture-demonstration-1.16868.

Southern Company, one of the largest electricity utilities in the United States, did finish a CCS project: the Kemper County project, a 582-megawatt integrated gasification combined cycle plant. Those close to the project were circumspect about its scalability:

> Even the Mississippi plant will require further testing for five years, to 2020. Then you have to test this technology on one, two, or three new plants. And that is five years for each of those plants. (interview)

Insiders in the coal industry and the utility business probably knew or had a very good idea that CCS would simply not result in cost-competitive electricity. According to some of our interviewees, building plants with CCS would increase costs by 50% to 100% and reduce the efficiency of any such plant by 6% to 10%.[26] Cost blowouts stalk these kinds of projects. One estimate of the Kemper County project put it at $5.6 billion, more than double the original cost estimate. Basically in order to capture the CO_2 it is producing, a plant has to expend energy by burning more fuel, and so reducing its thermal efficiency—more energy to produce the same kilowatt hour of electricity. From a commercial point of view this is a "parasitic" operation in which "you are chasing your tail" (interview). Little wonder that some of our interviewees thought that CCS would "kill coal."

The only cases where CCS looked viable were those in which the plant could easily pipe the CO_2 to an oil company that could use it to help pump oil out of the ground. For example, the Kemper County project was able to sell its captured CO_2 for enhanced oil recovery operations at depleted oil fields in Mississippi.

Whatever its business merits, this is not a strategy for dealing with climate change. Extracting CO_2, using it in a pumping operation to extract another fossil fuel for burning, and then having to store the pumped CO_2 in a geological site for hundreds of years (for a given quantity of CO_2, about 15% to 40% will be present in the atmosphere 1,000 years after its emission[27]) is not an emissions reduction strategy, a low-risk strategy, or as has become very clear, a low-cost strategy.

---

[26] WEO 2007, 217, states that CCS reduces thermal efficiency in range of 8% to 12%.

[27] IPCC, *Climate Change 2013: The Physical Science Basis. Contribution of Working Group I to the Fifth Assessment Report of the Intergovernmental Panel on Climate Change*, Cambridge University Press, Cambridge, 1106.

The Lost Decades

When the history of climate change is written some time from now, the two decades from the 1990s will probably be seen as something of a lost opportunity when it comes to managing the trilemma. As we saw earlier, the coal industry in the 1980s had integrated itself into the IEA. Coal became a part of the IEA's strategy for managing energy security. The IEA in turn helped to turn dependence on coal into a self-fulfilling prophecy. National energy departments fed the IEA with data, and the IEA produced forecasts pointing to the long-term importance of coal, leading national governments to develop policies based on those forecasts. Those policies were influenced by the IEA's projections on the central role of coal, with renewables playing a more peripheral role.

The IEA was key to producing a "modelthink" about the future of coal and energy. The European Commission, which reviewed the IEA's reports, was part of a process of policy echoes on coal. Modelers of energy production and consumption in the commission were hardly likely to want to attract attention to themselves with radically different outcomes from the IEA, which, after all, had the status. Everyone was and wanted to be part of the same in-group. The energy people in the commission, when asked, reported not being "very distant from their [IEA] views." What was true of the commission was true of energy departments around the world. Whether their countries were members of the IEA or not, radical dissent by these energy departments from the views of a globally influential agency seemed too chancy. Everyone was in a self-reinforcing forecasting loop. National energy agencies would feed the IEA with detailed data on fossil fuel, and the IEA would make global projections that affected how national energy agencies thought about the future. As the 20th century drew to a close, the IEA continued with projections based on a business-as-usual framework. Coal, oil, and gas would dominate the fuel mix in 2020, it concluded in 1999, and carbon emissions would continue to rise.[28]

The coal industry, with its well-established lobbying networks, was highly effective in winning ground games when it came to decisions about the financing of research on CCS. National coal industries are old industries. They are not simply lobbying groups but rather networks with deep

---

[28] International Energy Agency, *World Energy Outlook: Looking at Energy Subsidies: Getting the Prices Right*, IEA, Paris, 1999, 37.

roots in governments and the IEA. *Lobbying* as a term does not really capture the work of the coal industry. Industries like coal are better thought of as old networks made up of people from the industry, government, and research institutions—networks that work constantly to help the industry adapt to new contexts such as air pollution legislation, demands to improve efficiency, or a climate crisis. These networks turn the industry into an institution. They integrate the industry into its surrounding political and social systems. Once an industry network embeds itself as an institution, its quick excision becomes extraordinarily difficult. The coal industry has acquired, as Julie Ayling argues, legitimacy with different groups such as local communities and politicians, requiring its critics to enter into amorphous legitimacy contests.[29] Coal's competitors understand this entrenchment effect best. "Fossil fuel is the government," as one wind-energy lobbyist put it. When it comes to competing with coal for finance and support from government, a comparatively young industry like wind energy has fewer lobbyists, fewer models and forecasts with which to question the gestalt of coal, and less representation in the policy webs that steer energy policy. For governments, the most important consequence is that they have to confront a powerful and globally connected institution. Managing an industry out of existence is hard. Extinguishing an institution is far harder.

It is important to be clear about the nature of the lost opportunity during these two decades. What was needed to manage the trilemma was radical technological and institutional innovation amounting to more or less the replacement of the existing energy system. Adding some wind or solar energy units to the existing grid architecture was not going to be enough. By 1990 the evidence was pointing to the existence of a worsening climate emergency. On any standard computation of risk involving the probability of an event and its consequences, the global magnitude of climate change consequences should have resulted in states moving with the speed of a Kissinger handling an OPEC oil crisis. The first priority should have been the thermal coal market (the power generation market), and the second the metallurgical

---

[29] Julie Ayling, "A Contest for Legitimacy: The Divestment Movement and the Fossil Fuel Industry," *Law & Policy*, 39 (2017), 349–371.

coal market (the use of coking coal in steel making). We know that charcoal made from sustainable organic resources can be used to replace significant portions of coking coal in metal production processes.[30] Greener ways of making steel could have arrived much earlier.

As we know, nothing like the required speed was achieved. After the UNFCCC was completed in 1992, states lurched into the Kyoto Protocol negotiations, which after years of haggling produced a commitment period starting in 2008.

Some governments in Europe were giving economic incentives to producers of solar and wind energy, as the introduction of Germany's feed-in tariff in 2002 shows. The aim of these tariffs was to scale the use of existing innovations. At the same time, this economic incentive for producers should have been complemented by large levels of public funding of research into technologies such as battery storage, as well as into architectural solutions such as digitally regulated grids for the delivery of renewable energy. Battery storage would have stopped coal lobbyists from characterizing wind and solar as the intermittent and unreliable friends of energy security. The levels of public research money needed to manage the trilemma never materialized. Government R&D spending on energy among IEA member states hit its height a few years after the OPEC crisis and then went into decline.[31] Other data shows that global public R&D money for renewable energy increased from $5 billion in 2004 to about $12 billion in 2013.[32] These are modest sums at best and hardly consistent with a global emergency response. Partly as a result of the IEA's influence, states channeled too much public money into CCS research.

There were other reasons for why the IEA was and remains fundamentally inappropriate for helping states manage the geo-energy trilemma. The rational management of a global climate emergency requires states to have easy access to an international energy organization to help them coordinate solutions. Easy access has not been a hallmark of the IEA.

---

[30] See   https://www.csiro.au/en/Research/MRF/Areas/Community-and-environment/ Responsible-resource-development/Green-steelmaking.

[31] Technology Executive Committee (UNFCCC), *Enhancing Financing for the Research Development and Demonstration of Climate Technologies*, Working Paper, UNFCCC, November 2017, 10.

[32] UNFCCC, *Enhancing Financing for the Research Development and Demonstration of Climate Technologies*, 11.

The Club within a Club

The IEA is really a club within a club. Before one can join the IEA one has to be an OECD member. Accession to the OECD is a major step for a state to take since the applicant state has to send strong signals about its intention to travel down the path of trade, market, and financial liberalization. It helps if one is a convert to neoliberalism. The state also has to accept the obligations in the OECD Code of Liberalisation on Capital Movements and of the OECD Code of Liberalisation of Current Invisible Operations in a range of sectors such as industry, insurance, and banking and finance. OECD membership does not automatically mean IEA membership because a state has to be able to meet the requirements of the IEA's emergency oil mechanism. Membership in the IEA has not swelled dramatically since its establishment by 16 founding members in 1974. In 2019 there were 30 members. Eight nonmembers, including Brazil, China, and India, have signed association agreements with the IEA.

From the point of view of managing the geo-energy trilemma, the real problems with the IEA have lain in the use that IEA members have made of it in climate change negotiations. The secretariats of the OECD and IEA serviced the Annex I Expert Group (created in 1994), the members of this group comprising government delegates from the OECD and other industrialized countries. In effect, the two secretariats were acting as a "resource for negotiators of Annex I countries" (IEA interview). Both the IEA and the OECD were in various ways reaching out to the large developing country emitters. India and China were sometimes invited to meetings of the Annex I Expert Group.

The problem lay in the closed-door meetings the IEA and OECD were having with their members. In the climate change negotiations, states did not shed a win-lose mentality. They still wanted to make gains or avoid losses. The work of the IEA was pointing in the direction of developing countries having to take on mitigation targets, a position these countries were keen to avoid. During the pivotal first decade of the 21st century, both the IEA and OECD served as analytical clubs for their members. When major developing countries were not invited to the crucial closed-door sessions or the important breakfast meetings, they predictably hardened their own positions and took a more skeptical view of the negotiating positions of developed countries.

Obviously the failure of international organizations to maximize trust among states in a climate emergency is a deep problem. The OECD for decades helped its members come to international negotiations with superior information, enabled them to set the agenda and eventually triumph (albeit with the use of some hard power) in negotiations over big issues like trade or intellectual property. By the late 1990s the countries known by the acronym of BRICS (Brazil, Russia, India, China, and South Africa) were no longer satisfied with waiting in corridors for the closed session from which they were excluded to come to an end. The corridors of international negotiations are often not places of power, but rather waiting areas for the weak. Developing countries wanted entry into the closed rooms of power. It was a matter of status and respect. Their own growing economies were changing the balance of global economic power. Small economies like the Czech Republic and Finland were members of the IEA with all the privileges of membership, and China and India were not.

No doubt this diplomatic pirouetting around face and status in a time of existential crisis will come to be seen as basically stupid. But the pirouetting mattered to its participants. The IEA and OECD did, during the period of the 1990s and 2000s, launch various initiatives of engagement with developing countries such as Brazil, China, and India. The OECD, for example, had an Enhanced Engagement process aimed at Brazil, China, India, Indonesia, and South Africa. But despite all the relationship building with developing countries, one basic reality held during this period. The IEA and OECD were organizations helping their members "to think" about wins and losses in climate negotiations. Those on the outside of the closed-door sessions knew that the OECD's and IEA's technical and analytical expertise was at various stages being harnessed to achieve negotiating wins.

The IEA/OECD officials we interviewed saw the line that travels from exclusion to loss of face to loss of trust. They spoke of the need for more open groups and for creating paths of integration into the OECD and IEA. There was a danger in not doing this: "You don't open doors, you become obsolete" (OECD interview). As the decade from 2000 wore on, China in particular would show a capacity to create new forums and grand initiatives.

Germany and IRENA

The IEA's views on energy security were a source of concern to Germany. The IEA was simply failing to elevate the importance of international cooperation on renewable energy. What was needed was a new narrative about renewable energy, new models to contest those being pumped out by the IEA.

Establishing an international body for renewable energy was an idea that had been kicking around in the UN system since the early 1980s.[33] But the 1980s was also the period in which the United States, under Reagan's two terms in office, rethought its engagement with the United Nations, opposing the new international economic order agenda that key developing countries had pushed through the UN system during the 1970s. The 1980s did see the beginnings of a new international economic order, but the architects of this order were the United States and its multinational companies. Through their domination of the Uruguay Round of trade negotiations they produced the World Trade Organization (WTO) and fulfilled some of the market access and intellectual property monopoly dreams of US multinationals.[34] There was little enthusiasm in the United States for funding an international agency on renewable energy, especially one dedicated to finding ways to transfer technologies and funds from developed to developing countries. In practical terms this left the IEA to drive international energy coordination during the 1980s and 1990s.

It was not that the IEA plotted against renewables, but rather that its mode of data collection plotted a path in which renewables did not displace the fossil fuel system. The IEA was treaty bound to develop databases in cooperation with the oil industry. National energy agencies knew they had to collect detailed data on their use of oil and coal. This detail enabled the IEA to develop the databases that underpinned its influential world energy reports. A market in third-party data providers on the use of fossil fuels grew, because there was demand for fine-grained data analytics around movements and prices in fossil fuels, especially oil. National energy departments developed some in-house expertise in these fields, and they made use of third-party data providers when they wanted more detail. Step by data step, a path to the future was laid in which fossil fuels would for many decades be the primary source of the world's supply of energy. Renewables, the projections showed, would be peripheral players. In short, there was a highly evolved and sophisticated market in data and its interpretation for fossil fuels and an ignorant market for renewables.

---

[33] See United Nations Conference on New and Renewable Sources of Energy, A/RES/36/193, December 17, 1981.

[34] Peter Drahos and John Braithwaite, *Information Feudalism*, Earthscan, London, 2002.

Those in the renewables industry realized the need for their own data and analytics champion. They had to create their own data path to a future for renewables. The idea for an international agency to help coordinate a push on renewables flickered on like a weak candle during the 1980s and beyond. The European Association for Renewable Energy, which had been formed in 1988, became a strong advocate for an international renewables agency, leading a campaign for such an agency for some 19 years.[35] In 2008 there were some preparatory conferences held in Germany and Spain. At Germany's invitation and with support from Spain and Denmark, a foundation conference to establish the International Renewable Energy Agency (IRENA) was held in January 2009 in Bonn, Germany. The Statute of IRENA was opened for signature, with 75 of the 124 states attending signing it.[36] Finally, renewable energy, which in the words of the Danish delegate had been "homeless in the international family," had found an agency home.[37]

People we interviewed in the renewable energy industry in 2009 welcomed IRENA because the IEA had, in the words of one, "failed to deliver on renewables." Some interviewees suggested that the IEA might not be especially happy with the new renewables kid on the block since this kid might "cut into its traditional work."

Today IRENA has some 149 members, including China and the United States. To the outside eye there is one oddity. IRENA's secretariat has been given a roof over its head by the United Arab Emirates, an OPEC country and one of the world's largest exporters of oil. The UAE had competed hard with Germany for the right to host the secretariat, perhaps because it saw a need to be serious about diversifying its economy. Whatever the reason, IRENA is to be found nestled in the Persian Gulf amid countries whose economies depend largely on the export of oil and gas.

---

[35] On the role of EUROSOLAR, see http://eurosolar.de/en/alt/index.php/publications-mainmenu-54/books-mainmenu-7/357-the-long-road-to-irena.

[36] See Report of the Conference on the Establishment of the International Renewable Energy Agency, http://www.irena.org/Assembly/index.aspx?mnu=Pri&PriMenuID=44.

[37] See http://www.irena.org/DocumentDownloads/Foundconf/Statements/StatementDenmark.pdf.

5

"Winners" and "Losers" in Hotter Worlds

Why 2°C or Less?

The Australian bushfires of 2019–2020 burned an area roughly the size of South Korea. Thousands of buildings were destroyed. Others were left standing. No one spoke of winners and losers from this climate event.

But industries continually whisper to their governments about winners and losers when it comes to climate policy. However, as the science makes clear, the changes in biophysical systems flowing from climate change are likely to be so great that there will only be survivors and losers. Radical biophysical changes incompatible with mammalian life were initially associated with global temperature increases of 5°C or 6°C. We know now that these changes will arrive at lower levels of increase.

In 2001 the Intergovernmental Panel on Climate Change (IPCC) presented a synthesis of the likely relationships between global temperature increases and their effects.[1] It was an exercise in simplification aimed at helping readers arrive at a judgment about what might constitute dangerous climate change. The approach taken was to identify areas in which, if there were changes, there would be reasons for concern that the climate system was heading into dangerous territory. Five reasons for concern were identified: the loss or damage of unique or threatened systems (for example, coral reefs); the geographical distribution of climate change impacts; the global impacts such as number of lives lost; the incidence of extreme weather events; and the likelihood of single large-scale events (tipping points) such as the collapse of the West Antarctic ice sheet.

Likely changes in these areas were linked to increases in global temperatures. As part of the simplification exercise, temperature increases were grouped into small (no more than 2°C), medium (between 2°C and

---

¹ Intergovernmental Panel on Climate Change, "Vulnerability to Climate Change and Reasons for Concern: A Synthesis," in *Climate Change 2001: Impacts, Adaptation, and Vulnerability*, Cambridge University Press, New York, 2001, 915–967.

3°C), and large (more than 3°C). The temperatures were not thresholds, but approximations of where processes might shift. Below 2°C was not seen as providing a safe zone. Coral reefs, mangroves, biodiversity, and tropical glaciers are examples of systems that could all be badly affected by small temperature increases. As the IPCC pointed out in 2001, an increase of 2°C from 1990 to the end of the 21st century would be the greatest experienced by any human civilization. Increases characterized as small could still produce effects of great magnitude. Each of these reasons for concern was updated in the IPCC's Fourth Assessment Report (2007), this report being expressly drawn upon by the states that agreed on the Copenhagen Accord at the UN Climate Conference in Copenhagen in December of 2009.

The Copenhagen Climate Change Conference of 2009 did deliver, in the form of an accord, a consensus among states on the need to keep the global temperature increase below 2°C; too many risks were associated with temperature increases of more than 2°C. The accord also had a scale of agreement that the Kyoto Protocol did not. It saw China and India formulate targets for themselves. These were submitted to the United Nations Framework Convention on Climate Change (UNFCCC) as nonbinding pledges. China did not promise an absolute reduction in emissions, which is what is required of developed countries under the Kyoto Protocol, but rather said it would it lower its CO_2 emissions per unit of GDP by 40% to 45% by 2020, using 2005 as its baseline. India took on an emissions intensity target of 20% to 25%, also using 2005 as its baseline. In promising these targets, China and India— the two biggest developing country emitters—were recognizing that without their help, developed countries would have no chance of staying below a 2°C limit. Everybody was in the same lifeboat.

After Copenhagen, the science continued to reveal the likelihood of greater biophysical changes at smaller levels of temperature increase. In the case of risks to unique and threatened systems, there was evidence of substantial impacts at existing temperatures and potentially severe impacts at 1°C. Much the same conclusion applied to extreme weather events such as cyclones, floods, heat waves, and droughts.

Faced by mounting evidence of the dangers of a 2°C world, states at the Paris climate conference of 2015 recognized the wisdom of turning down even further the anthropogenic control knob on emissions. The Paris Agreement reinforced the 2°C limit but also added the aim of "pursuing efforts" to keep the global temperature increase to below 1.5°C. By the time of the IPCC's Special Report on Global Warming of 1.5°C in October 2018, human-induced warming was hovering around 1°C.[2]

Debates over what amounts to dangerous interference in the climate system, which over the decades have wasted precious time, will probably fade away as it becomes clear that the world capitalist system is now operating within earth system dynamics that are full of risks for the survival of capitalism. The science will, of course, continue to focus on feasible paths to a world of no more than 1.5°C and then, if that looks infeasible, to a world of no more than 2°C and so on and so forth. States will likely begin to invest in strategies of survival governance.

The Feasibility of a 1.5°C World

The shift to renewable energies and a zero-emissions world is sometimes described as unstoppable. However, there is an important question: Will this unstoppable transition scale at speed? We cannot, based on the evidence, risk a slow transition. It is not enough if only some major emitters achieve a rapid transition. Scaling at speed holds the key to staying in a world of less than 2°C.

If it looks to be a many-decades-long transition, then fossil fuel companies face less risk to their future income streams and so can mount an investment case to their present-day bankers such as JPMorgan Chase and Wells Fargo. Global capital markets are deep. Some investors may well calculate there is a positive return to be made on capital invested in the fossil fuel industry. Where, however, investors are given sharp, clear signals of a rapid transition to renewable energy, their calculations about the present value of future returns on fossil fuel investment will be different.

The world of global climate policy and treaty negotiation should be a world of harmonized sharp signaling, not just at the level of national policy but also at the level of global regulation. It is not. Forums come and go. George W. Bush forms the Major Economies Meeting. Obama creates the Major Economies Forum. Trump decides to pull the United States out of the Paris Agreement. These events all signal different degrees of divergence or convergence of position with other key players such as the European Union.

---

[2] Intergovernmental Panel on Climate Change, *Global Warming of 1.5°C: An IPCC Special Report*, World Meteorological Organization, Geneva, 2018.

High-level diplomats attending these meetings rake over the details and make linear projections on the state of play that a little later are shown to be worthless.

One can, of course, build the case for an unstoppable trend toward a low-emissions world, but as I have just argued, the far more important issue is whether states can scale to this world at speed. On speed of transition, states have generated a world of equivocal signaling. Even more damagingly, states have, at least to some extent in the eyes of the oil industry, dissembled about how much they really care about the risks of climate change. The oil industry, as I show later in this chapter, pays more attention to what states do than to what states promise or pledge. Our interviews with oil industry figures revealed an industry more confident about a slower transition than not. Some International Energy Agency (IEA) energy scenarios back this confidence, predicting an overall rise in demand for oil because of a growth in demand in sectors such as aviation and shipping.[3]

Aviation provides a good example of how urgent action by states is delayed in sectors where their industries are asked to bear relatively modest costs of climate action. In an important step, the European Union in 2012 included aviation in its emissions trading scheme, but then reduced its scope to flights within Europe because of resistance from non-European countries, including the United States and China. Following on from the European Union's aviation initiative, the International Civil Aviation Organization developed a Carbon Offsetting and Reduction Scheme for International Aviation in 2016, the aim being to stabilize aviation emissions at 2020 levels. Pilot exercises and voluntary participation during the first half of the 2020s characterize this scheme. For the moment the regulation of the aviation sector is not consistent with the goal of keeping the global temperature increase to 2°C, even though the industry is responsible for an estimated 4% to 5% of greenhouse gas emissions.[4] The oil industry is betting on the aviation industry being able to resist the single most effective form of emissions regulation in the shape of steep taxes on aviation fuel.

If we step back from the intense detail of three or so decades of climate change negotiations, the upshot is a world of mixed signaling. Negotiations on the UNFCCC started in 1991, with the treaty coming into operation in

[3] International Energy Agency, *World Energy Outlook 2017*, OECD/IEA, Paris, 2017 (hereinafter WEO 2017), 94.

[4] Jörgen Larsson, Anna Elofsson, Thomas Sterner, and Jonas Åkerman, "International and National Climate Policies for Aviation: A Review," *Climate Policy*, 19 (2019), 787–799.

1994. Negotiations over the Kyoto Protocol started in 1995, with the protocol coming into operation in 2005. The protocol set up a period (2008–2012) of binding emission targets for developed countries. A second period of commitment (2013–2020), referred to as the Doha Amendment to the Kyoto Protocol, was agreed upon in 2012, but has not yet become legally binding. When or if it does, it will bind those developed countries that have agreed to be bound. The number of countries with binding targets in the second period is smaller than under the first, with the European Union and its member states being the most significant group. Canada has withdrawn from the protocol, and some countries have decided not to enter this second period (Japan, New Zealand, and Russia). The United States has not ratified the Kyoto Protocol. Developing countries may continue to make voluntary commitments in this second period. The countries with potentially binding commitments in this second Kyoto phase are projected to account for about 10% of world greenhouse gas emissions by 2020.[5]

The Paris Agreement is an example of more rapid action in terms of treaty text. A draft text was produced in Paris in December 2015 and entered into force in November 2016. However, the Trump administration in 2017 announced its withdrawal from the agreement. If nothing changes, the United States would leave toward the end of 2020. The Paris Agreement represents progress in treaty terms, but in climate system terms it is not enough. The Climate Tracker website, which monitors the Paris Agreement commitments of individual states, keeps on finding gaps between the commitments of some states and the policies needed to meet them. Even states meeting their Paris commitments will not be enough to hold temperature increases below 2°C.

Climate negotiations have over time produced more aspirational language and more ambition in terms of temperature goals. However, the climate system does not respond to textual emissions. It responds to greenhouse gas emissions. The decade up to 2010 produced the highest total of greenhouse gas emissions in human history.[6] Not even the global financial crisis was able to stop this record emissions run.

As the Copenhagen Accord of 2009 acknowledged, "Deep cuts in global emissions are required." This was blunt and clear language. Making cuts

---

[5] International Energy Agency, *Redrawing the Energy-Climate Map*, OECD/IEA, Paris, 2013, 19.

[6] Intergovernmental Panel on Climate Change, *Summary for Policymakers in Climate Change 2014: Mitigation of Climate Change, Contribution of Working Group III to the Fifth Assessment Report of the Intergovernmental Panel on Climate Change*, Cambridge University Press, Cambridge, 2014, https://www.ipcc.ch/site/assets/uploads/2018/02/ipcc_wg3_ar5_summary-for-policymakers.pdf, 6.

early reduces the need to make very large cuts later, as well as lowering the risk of facing cuts of infeasible magnitude. The global motto and practice for achieving a world of less than 2°C should be "Go early, go deep." The actual practice, however, is more consistent with the motto of "go late, go shallow." In 2013 the IEA warned of a "growing disconnect" between the world's actual emissions trajectory and the desired limits.[7]

The evidence of this disconnect has led to the development of later-action mitigation scenarios in which large cuts to emissions are made after 2030. Later-action scenarios require reductions of around 6% to 8.5% per year after 2030.[8] Are the reductions demanded by later-action scenarios achievable? Belgium, France, and Sweden in response to the oil crisis of 1973 used nuclear power to achieve reductions of around 4% to 5% per year for a decade or more.[9] However, while we can point to individual country reductions that begin to approximate what is required in later-action scenarios, a global reduction of this magnitude has not been seen. The global financial crisis of 2007–2008 produced a decline in global carbon dioxide emissions from fossil fuels and cement of 1.4%,[10] but this was followed by a rapid rebound in which emissions increased by about 3% between 2010 and 2011.[11] The reduction produced by the global financial crisis was short-lived compared to the reduction in emissions produced during the oil crisis of the 1970s because the latter crisis produced structural reforms in national energy systems in which countries set about finding efficiencies and substitutes for oil consumption. Progress on decoupling emissions from economic growth is patchy, with some leveling between 2014 and 2016 but then a rise in 2017, leading to what the IEA described as a "historic high" in 2018.[12]

Big reductions in emissions from 2030 imply rapid changes in energy systems. For the moment at least we are not seeing this, but rather incremental progress. For example, in the US coal power plants are being retired and more natural gas is being used in electricity generation, but coal and gas together

[7] International Energy Agency, *World Energy Outlook 2013*, OECD/IEA, Paris, 2013, 59.

[8] United Nations Environment Programme, *The Emissions Gap Report 2013*, UNEP, Nairobi, 2013, 20.

[9] G. P. Peters, Robbie M. Andrew, Tom Boden, Josep G. Canadell, Philippe Ciais, Corinne Le Quere, Gregg Marland, Michael R. Raupach, and Charlie Wilson, "The Challenge to Keep Global Warming below 2°C," *Nature Climate Change*, 3 (2013), 4–6.

[10] G. P. Peters, Gregg Marland, Corinne Le Quere, Thomas Boden, Josep G. Canadell, and Michael R. Raupach, "Rapid Growth in CO_2 Emissions after the 2008–2009 Global Financial Crisis," *Nature Climate Change*, 2 (2012), 2–4.

[11] IPCC, *Summary for Policymakers in Climate Change 2014*, 11.

[12] International Energy Agency, *Global Energy and CO_2 Status Report*, OECD/IEA, Paris, 2019, https://www.iea.org/geco/emissions/.

still provided 63% of US electricity generation in 2018.[13] Planning for late-action scenarios will have to contend with price-optimizing games from fossil fuel investors. By way of example, biofuel subsidies, on some models, may hasten the extraction of fossil fuel over a period of time sufficient to offset the gains of the subsidies.[14] These kinds of models are part of the green paradox argument in which fossil fuel owners confronted by the prospect of unfavorable future profits extract more resources in order to take advantage of more favorable present conditions.[15]

The fossil fuel industry can make rapid supply decisions because it has the infrastructure of extraction and distribution at its disposal. Fracking technologies give the industry even more flexibility of supply. Later-action scenarios, which essentially require a doubling of the rate of emissions reduction after 2030, underestimate the continuing impact of the scale of the existing infrastructure for fossil fuels.

There is, as the IPCC notes in its Special Report, no simple yes or no answer to whether a 1.5°C world is feasible. As I indicated in chapter 1, limiting warming to less than 2°C is now dependent upon a state-organized exogenous shock. Why do I place so much emphasis on the state, when much of the work on new environmental governance in the last decade or so has pointed to the importance of non-state actors in the delivery of environmental goods or looked to market-trading schemes to deliver environmental outcomes?

Two capacities of the state matter to the answer to this question. The state continues to be able to issue commands with structural effect in the economy, and the state can create money on a vast scale. These two capacities were used, for example, by the US government when in 2008 the George W. Bush administration began what would prove to be a multibillion-dollar bailout of the US car industry. Under the Obama administration the US Treasury purchased stock in General Motors and Chrysler. Regulation was used to push the US car industry to do more on energy efficiency and electric vehicles. As the European Union has shown with its various directives and regulations on the disposal and recycling of packaging, batteries, construction waste, vehicles, electronic equipment and many other forms of waste, the state can,

---

[13] The US Energy Information Association (EIA) forecasts that renewables will be the fastest-growing source of electricity generation. See https://www.eia.gov/todayinenergy/detail.php?id=38053.

[14] R. Quentin Grafton, Tom Kompas, and Ngo Van Long, "Biofuels Subsidies and the Green Paradox," CESifo Working Paper No. 2960, 2010.

[15] H. W. Sinn, "Public Policies against Global Warming: A Supply Side Approach," *International Tax and Public Finance*, 15 (2008), 360–394.

through regulation, alter capitalism's patterns of consumption and waste in fine-grained ways.

Shifting world capitalism away from trajectories that land it in worlds of 2°C or more requires the transformation of most of its existing global circuits of commodity circulation. Transformation is something of a euphemism here since existing circuits, most obviously those created over the last 100 years or so by fossil fuel capital, will have to be extinguished quickly and replaced by new circuits. Without the incentive of new circuits, insufficient levels of global capital will shift to support radical innovation. Incremental innovation will keep fossil fuel capital in play, and the world system will steam on into warmer worlds. State power, then, is fundamental to the feasibility of a world of less than 2°C . Only state power can deliver the shock of a green financial system that will cause an exodus from fossil fuel and an entry into green financial assets. As I argued in chapter 2, China could harness its pressure driving mechanism to deliver this green financial shock on a global scale.

State power, however, cuts both ways. States dependent upon the rents of fossil fuel extraction are hardly likely to sit idly by applauding capitalism's adaptability in switching away from fossil fuels. As the next section shows, these states have worked to slow the transition and have incentives to continue to do so. The fossil fuel industry will, as the green paradox literature suggests, continue to react in supply and pricing terms.

Another problem is that China itself is part of the fossil fuel empire, something I expand on in the last section of this chapter. It has among the world's largest coal and shale gas reserves and has in different ways enmeshed itself in the global oil industry. For example, after Ecuador's bond default of 2008 China became a source of lending. This relationship deepened in other ways as Petroecuador agreed to sell oil to Petrochina on a longer-term basis. By 2013 Ecuador was placing more than 80% of its oil export under the trading control of Chinese companies—from where more of it ended up being sold into the United States, the principal market for Ecuador's oil exports, rather than being imported into China.[16] Nevertheless, of all large fossil fuel states, China has the greatest incentive to lead a transition, an argument I develop in more detail in chapter 6.

---

[16] J. Schneyer and N. Medina Mora Perez, "How China Took Control of an OPEC Country's Oil," *Reuters*, November 26, 2013, http://www.reuters.com/article/2013/11/26/us-china-ecuador-oil-special-report-idUSBRE9AP0HX20131126.

What Does a 2°C Limit Mean for Fossil Fuel Producers?

In 2015 McGlade and Ekins explored the issue of how much of the world's reserves of coal, gas, and oil would have to stay in the ground if states wanted a better than 50% chance of meeting the 2°C limit.[17] According to their estimates, "A third of oil reserves, half of gas reserves and over 80 percent of current coal reserves" could not be used.

In a world where countries take the 2°C limit seriously, all regions have to keep some of their fossil fuel income and investment prospects buried, but for each fuel there are major regional losers when it comes to not using their reserves:

Oil: The Middle East (by far the largest loser), Central America, South America, and Canada

Gas: The Middle East (by far the largest loser), former Soviet Union states, Central America, and South America

Coal: The United States, former Soviet Union states, China, Australia, and India

In 2012 the IEA performed a similar calculation in which it concluded that if the world wanted a 50% chance of staying under 2°C by 2050 four regions or states—North America, the Middle East, China, and Russia—alone had reserves that they would have to keep in the earth.[18] Government-owned companies were estimated to hold 74% of all fossil fuel reserves. It is a picture of surprising regional and government concentration.

Oil and gas resources are often divided into proved reserves, economically recoverable resources, technically recoverable resources, and remaining oil and gas in place.[19] How much ends up in each category in a given period depends on market demand and innovation in extractive technologies as well as substitute technologies.

The scale of advances in the United States for the extraction of shale gas and oil has been described as an "energy renaissance," a little odd given that the word *renaissance* is generally not associated with a climate apocalypse.[20]

---

[17] C. McGlade and P. Ekins, "The Geographical Distribution of Fossil Fuels Unused When Limiting Global Warming to 2°C," *Nature*, 517 (2015), 187–190.

[18] International Energy Agency, *World Energy Outlook 2012*, OECD/IEA, Paris, 2012, 259.

[19] See http://www.eia.gov/todayinenergy/detail.cfm?id=17151.

[20] WEO 2017, 69.

Ten years ago the United States was a massive importer of oil and gas. In 2017 it was moving toward being a net exporter of gas and likely to be a net exporter of oil by the end of the 2020s. Importantly, this speed of output growth has been achieved during a period of lower prices. Under some projections, by 2025 "nearly every fifth barrel of oil and every fourth cubic metre of gas in the world" would have been drilled in the United States.[21] Not even Saudi Arabia for oil or the former Soviet Union for gas at their respective heights of production growth exceeded this increase in output. US capital investment to back this escalation has, since 2010, climbed to almost $1 trillion.[22] Through energy investment measures, the United States has lowered its domestic demand, increasing the need for its producers to export. In 2015 the United States moved to full export liberalization of its crude oil, allowing producers to export without a license. Under IEA projections, the United States will likely end up as the world's largest exporter of carbon emissions. In terms of the geo-energy trilemma the United States has prioritized, perhaps even locked in, the energy security and the military/economic prongs of the trilemma.

It is worth taking a few moments to see how the United States was able to reverse an energy dependency that many, if not most, thought irreversible, because it helps to understand why the United States is not likely to manage its fossil fuel industry out of existence as quickly as is needed. Through consistent incremental innovation, the US gas and oil industries have turned resources into reserves. Fracturing oil wells goes back to the mid-19th century in the United States, when miners began experimenting with different ways to stimulate well flows, including the use of nitroglycerin.[23] Over the following decades, techniques improved. Hydraulic fracturing (fracking) technologies were developed for commercial use in the United States during the 1940s. These involved the pressurized injection of a mixture of chemicals and sand into the rock formation around the well, causing it to fracture and allowing the trapped oil or gas to flow. In the search for improvements to the process, novel approaches continued to be suggested, including the use of nuclear explosions in oil shale.[24]

---

[21] International Energy Agency, *World Energy Outlook 2018*, OECD/IEA, Paris, 2018, 2.

[22] WEO 2017, 69.

[23] Carl T. Montgomery and Michael B. Smith, "Hydraulic Fracturing: History of an Enduring Technology," *Journal of Petroleum Technology*, 62 (2010), 26–32.

[24] See the description of Project Bronco at https://www.osti.gov/biblio/6086597/thumbnail.

During the 1980s and 1990s hydraulic fracturing technologies were being applied to coalbed methane and oil. The application of fracking to gas in shale rock was thought to be too risky and expensive. But an independent prospector, George Mitchell, had other ideas.[25] In the wildcatter tradition he and his engineers persisted for years in experimenting with fracking the Barnett Shale, an area in North Texas. By 1997 they had discovered that, by using millions of liters of water and a comparatively small amount of chemical additives, shale could be efficiently cracked. What is sometimes called *slickwater fracking* has turned trillions of cubic feet of gas resources into reserves. The number of gas wells in the United States went from around 262,000 in 1989 to a little over 482,000 in 2012.[26]

Once the processes for extracting unconventional oil and gas had been demonstrated, a combination of learning and continuous improvement led to reductions in production costs. Extracting unconventional oil and gas became much more price competitive and continues to remain so, making the global fossil fuel market more competitive.

Because the earth's total fossil fuel resources are not known, a guessing game has taken place over the application of Hubbert's famous models of peak and decline. The guessing game has had a pessimistic bias, with many experts and models proving to be wrong about the time of peak and decline.[27] The success of fracking has even led to an optimistic bias with some seeing oil as having entered an age of abundance.[28]

The peak that matters the most is the one on the global emissions curve. Every year in which we fail to peak emissions increases the risk of entering a 2°C world, then a 3°C world, and so on. In order to avoid these hotter worlds, vast oil and gas resources will have to stay in the ground. For the fossil fuel industry, peaks based on the geology of finite supply now probably matter less than potential regulatory peaks that states will have to impose to avoid moving into climate red zones. State leadership in delivering those regulatory caps is urgently needed, as many climate reports make clear. But it is hard to see this leadership coming from the United States. US oil and gas innovation has created incentives for it not to lead a rapid and global

---

[25] See D. D. Hinton, "The Seventeen-Year Overnight Wonder: George Mitchell and Unlocking the Barnett Shale," *Journal of American History*, 99 (2012), 229–235.

[26] See http://www.eia.gov/dnav/ng/hist/na1170_nus_8a.htm.

[27] See Michael C. Lynch, "Forecasting Oil Supply: Theory and Practice," *Quarterly Review of Economics and Finance*, 42 (2002), 373–389.

[28] Steve Levine, "The Era of Oil Abundance," *Foreign Policy*, July 17, 2012, https://foreignpolicy.com/2012/07/17/the-era-of-oil-abundance/.

transition to a low-carbon world. From this innovation the United States has a level of energy security not thought possible even a decade ago. It also has more jobs, growing export dollars in liquefied natural gas markets, large investments in the US petrochemical industry, and lower costs of US manufacturing. There is also the geopolitical influence that comes with being a global energy exporter. US shale gas and oil represent an innovation success story.

No other region, based on McGlade and Ekins's estimates of forgone fossil fuel reserves and resources, houses the kind of effective resistance capable of being mounted in the United States, if the nation decided to limit its use and export of fossil fuel reserves. Saudi Arabia would, of course, be a huge loser if the world acted swiftly to limit emissions. It depends on oil and gas for about 85% of its export earnings. Saudi Arabia is a low-cost producer with vast reserves, which allows it, at least in theory, to play a predatory pricing game—dropping prices, below the cost of production if necessary, in order to drive other competitors out of the market or to obtain a greater share of the market in an environment where the price of oil remains persistently low. Iraq, another large oil producer, might also find ways to hang on. In a world of declining demand for oil, the producers most likely to stay in the game the longest are the Saudis. The other regions—Central and South America and Canada—would probably be unable to compete for a large slice of this declining demand because they are higher-cost producers. Venezuela faces political and economic uncertainties about the possibility of scaling up production even though it has large reserves.

In the case of gas, aside from the United States, the regions that would have to leave the most resources in the ground in order to keep within the 2°C limit are the Middle East and countries from the former Soviet Union. Gas and oil have been central to Russia's economy for many decades. Whenever gas and oil prices have fallen, as they did in the mid-1980s and then again in 1998, the resulting drop in revenues quickly affected Russia and the former Soviet states. Russia's export dependence on oil and gas is stark, forming 66% of exports in 2014 and 62% in 2015.[29] A fast transition to a world dominated by renewable energy would send Russia into a cycle of debt and recession. Few would mourn the Russian bear trapped in a rapidly declining economy. Ironically, Russia's influence in the world depends heavily on US fossil fuel networks slowing a transition to a world of renewable energy. So long as the

---

[29] World Bank, *Russia Economic Report*, no. 351, 2016, 55.

world moves sluggishly on fossil fuels, Russia with its vast reserves will remain a player in the global market.

In the case of coal, three things need to happen. China has to leap in the direction of dismantling its coal-based energy system, India has to avoid scaling up its coal-based energy system, and the United States has to reduce its coal demand.

As I explain in chapter 6, China's economic growth has been underpinned by a remarkable coal-based electrification of its economy during the 1990s and the early part of the 2000s. India has taken longer than China to electrify its economy. Any geo-political path that limits warming to 2°C has to offer some plausible account of why China and India decide not to use their vast coal reserves and close down the comparatively young energy infrastructure they have built to exploit them. In 2015 coal consumption did decline in China by 1.5%, but rose in India by almost 5%.[30] China has taken a quiet but significant step if one keeps in mind that during the 2000s its coal use grew by an average of 9.5%.[31]

In the United States, demand for coal has dropped by 23% from its peak in 2005. While the US coal industry has been better served by the Trump administration, it faces competition from gas. In 2016 more electricity was generated in the United States from gas than from coal.[32] A large part of the growth in coal demand, according to the IEA, is expected to come from India. For the world to stay within the bounds of a 2°C limit, the giant leap required from India is into renewables and not coal. I take up the plausibility of such a leap in chapter 9.

The geography and geology of fossil fuels provide us with a rough guide as to those states with interests in finding ways to delay a rapid transition to a zero-emissions world. Geological luck (or bad luck) has played a part in helping to accelerate the US shale gas revolution. China, like the United States, has abundant shale gas resources. However, as one US expert put it, "The shale is better in America" (interview, 2014). The geological formations in the United States are much easier to access, more like a wedding cake, with smooth layers of sponge stacked upon each other, making horizontal drilling so effective. China's geology makes fracturing much more complex and costly, decreasing its chances of a fracking-based "energy renaissance."

---

[30] BP, *BP Statistical Review of World Energy 2016*, London, 2016, 4.
[31] IEA, *World Energy Outlook 2015*, OECD/IEA, Paris, 2015, 272.
[32] WEO 2017, 204.

Large reserves of gas and oil are concentrated in the Middle East among comparatively low-cost producers. Their costs of production will allow them to compete with the innovation and price drops being delivered by the US oil and gas industry. Playing price and supply games is really the only strategy available to fossil fuel–rich states that are also middle or small powers.

The opportunity for the Saudis to delay action on climate change was the greatest during the 1990s and 2000s when the major powers such as the United States, the European Union, and China were divided on climate. China during this period was building an energy infrastructure dominated by coal. Taking the lead on carbon mitigation was not a role it wanted to assume. The Saudis set about helping the world to lose opportunities to act on climate change by hiring US legal talent skilled in the arts of text drafting and adversarial tactics (interview data).

A well-organized inner circle (in this case, the Saudis and Gulf states) with the aid of an outer circle (other Organization of the Petroleum Exporting Countries [OPEC] members) can achieve much of its agenda, especially if it is focused on slowing things down rather than moving them along. The support of a secretariat is important since it tracks developments between the various negotiating conferences. The Saudis were able to use the OPEC Secretariat in Vienna to support their planning. If an OPEC member volunteered to chair the G77, it would have the benefit of the secretariat's detailed work, a secretariat largely funded by the Saudis. Under these conditions, middle powers can have a strong influence on the course of the negotiations. But this influence is dependent on the space created by an absence of leadership by the major powers and a capacity of the middle powers to organize and focus their own influence. Backed by the resources of the OPEC Secretariat, an OPEC chair of the G77 would be able to speak as if there was an agreed-upon position of the group, when in reality, with a group of over 130 countries, very often there is none.

In summary, US-centered oil and gas networks probably represent the single biggest obstacle to a rapid transition away from fossil fuels. The resilience and innovative capacity of the US oil and gas industry, something that has been demonstrated during periods of low prices, is a major stumbling block to paths in which global warming stays under 2°C. The oil industry's business model is not so much affected by the decline rates of wells as the prospect of access to oil. Innovation has delivered this access. This is a reason for at least some banks and large investors to support long-term borrowing by the oil and gas industry. The price volatility of oil has over the years been seen by some investors as a chance for profit because of the capacity of the oil price to surge back to high levels. Riding these waves of volatility and making the case to investors that they still represent a good bet is something the oil majors in particular have a lot of experience of. Through delivering energy security and competitiveness, the industry has extended its influence in US political circles, allowing it to portray the United States as being a loser from radical action on climate change.

China and India might also be characterized as "losers" if they do not make use of their large reserves of coal in particular, but a global increase of even 1°C represents the mean of very different regional temperature rises. China and India, the evidence increasingly suggests, will be on the receiving end of higher regional rises with likely devastating impacts on their large populations. By way of example, a global mean temperature rise of 1.5°C would see a significantly higher rise in the Hindu Kush Himalaya region, producing, among other things, declining glacier volumes.[33] There would be major adverse consequences for the 10 river basins fed by this mountain system and the 1.9 billion people living in those river basins. Eight countries are linked by the Hindu Kush Himalaya region, including India and China. They have incentives to push for a postcircular economy (see chapter 7). The oil industry, as the next section shows, sees the likely behavior of states as being different from what one might suppose.

Oil in Tropical Eden, or What the Oil Industry Pays Attention To

Some of the oil executives we interviewed reminisced about their early days in the industry in places such as Ecuador. Oil companies have been present in Ecuador for decades, going back to the 1930s when Shell began exploring the Oriente region. The oil company executives who made the trip to the remote parts of Ecuador's forests saw a natural beauty only lightly touched by its small populations of indigenous people. Oil companies have had a heavier touch.

---

[33] Philippus Wester, Arabinda Mishra, Aditi Mukherji, and Arun Bhakta Shrestha (eds.), *The Hindu Kush Himalaya Assessment: Mountains, Climate Change, Sustainability and People*, Springer, Switzerland, Cham, 2019.

The phrase *minimum-impact development* sounds good, especially in the hands of mining giants. The executives who handle negotiations with cash-hungry governments know, in the words of one, that you can "almost sell any garbage if you package it right."

Minimum-impact development has not quite worked out in Ecuador. After a major discovery in 1967 in the tropical rainforests of Ecuador's Oriente region, oil companies extracted more than two billion barrels of oil. Along the way they used the tropical rainforests to dispose of their chemical garbage. By 1993 some 30 billion gallons of oil and toxic waste had been released into the waterways and land of the Oriente.[34] This contamination led to elevated rates of cancer for the people living close to the oil fields. In 2013 a broken pipeline spilled 400,000 gallons of oil into the Quijos River. Sliding along Ecuador's interconnected river system, the oil slick made its way toward the Peruvian Amazon region of Loreto.[35] Wherever the slick traveled, the towns and communities on the rivers lost their water supply and had to rely on bottled water.

Ecuador proved significant in another way for the oil and gas industry. In 2006 Petroecuador, the national oil company, discovered oil in Yasuni National Park. For Ecuador, the find was estimated to be about 20% of its existing reserves and thus worth billions. But Yasuni's forests were also full of precious biodiversity. By now no one much believed the low-impact rhetoric. The president of Ecuador, Rafael Correa, offered the world a simple deal. If countries really wanted to keep this tropical paradise they could help by paying Ecuador not to mine it. Correa asked the rest of the world to contribute $3.6 billion by 2024, about 50% of the then net present economic value that Ecuador would be giving up by not allowing mining. Ecuador would use the money to invest in renewable energy and sustainable development for its indigenous groups. There were clear global benefits, including avoiding the CO_2 emissions that would have come from extracting the oil and destroying Yasuni's forests, as well as the carbon sink and biodiversity benefits of preserving those forests.

---

[34] Anna-Karin Hurtig and Miguel San Sebastian, "Geographical Differences in Cancer Incidence in the Amazon Basin of Ecuador in Relation to Residence Near Oil Fields," *International Journal of Epidemiology*, 31 (2002), 1021–1027.

[35] See http://ens-newswire.com/2013/06/11/oil-spilled-into-ecuadors-rivers-reaches-peru/.

The Yasuni ITT Trust Fund was set up in 2010 and administered by the United Nations Development Programme (UNDP). The fund's annual reports revealed modest progress. There were commitments of funding; technical cooperation was promised; and Italy and Ecuador signed in September 2012 a $44 million debt-swap deal to be done in tranches. But when all was said and done, the end of 2012 saw the Yasuni Trust Fund holding $6.5 million.

In 2013 Ecuador abandoned its trust fund plan, and the National Assembly voted to send the miners into its tropical Eden. Correa promised that Yasuni would be low-impact development. The Yasuni Trust Fund was closed, and the UNDP began handing back the $10 million it had received in contributions.[36]

Ecuador's trust fund model was an attempt to find a collective path away from oil extraction and toward climate stability and biodiversity preservation. Its failure led to a blame apportionment game in which some blamed Correa for a confusing public rhetoric. The bigger lesson here, though, was that despite the warm support from UN officials and the environmental movement, states and investors had not backed Ecuador's plan. Perhaps Ecuador's long track record of debt default, including a major default in 2008 on sovereign bonds, played a part in this.

For oil executives there was only one conclusion to draw: new oil fields were more important to global investors than the climate or respecting the sovereignty of the indigenous cultures in the Amazon basin. Ecuador is one example of many. The European Union's emissions trading scheme ended up being very generous when it came to allocating free emissions permits to companies. These free allocations, along with the importation of carbon credits from outside of the European Union, has seen its carbon market produce prices that are generally thought to be too low to produce the big shifts in firm behavior that are required. It has not stopped the oil and gas industry from investing in their core business. In Australia, the carbon pricing scheme that became law in 2011 was repealed by the conservative government that came to power in 2014.

In short, for many in the oil industry, understanding the behavior of states when it comes to fossil fuel consumption is a straightforward application of revealed preference theory.

---

[36] See http://www.undp.org/content/undp/en/home/presscenter/articles/2014/02/26/undp-statement-on-decision-by-government-of-ecuador-to-conclude-yasun-itt-initiative/.

China: The new Fossil Fuel Empire?

Contrary to the line of thinking being explored in this book, some in the oil industry see China's huge demand for energy as being the industry's best bet. No country imports more oil than China.[37] China is the world's biggest producer of fossil fuels and the biggest importer.[38]

The oil and gas industry has, through innovation such as fracking, made it easier for China to manage the complexity of supply. In 2017, for example, the United States sent 7% of its petroleum exports to China.[39] Diversity of supply matters to China's oil security. For example, Libya, Sudan, and South Sudan combined were at one point meeting about 8% of China's oil import needs, but by 2011–2012 this had declined to probably less than 3%. China's long relationship with the Gaddafi regime in Libya came to an end as various rebel forces took over the country in 2011, killing Gaddafi in the process.[40] Sudan was in the early 2000s supplying a little over 9% of China's oil imports.[41] Civil war changed this. When South Sudan seceded from Sudan in 2011, it also assumed control over the majority of the oil fields, although the pipeline to Port Bashair on the Red Sea remained under Sudan's control. In 2013 South Sudan slid into civil war. Sudan and South Sudan in 2011 together accounted for 5% of China's imports, but in 2013 this had fallen to 2%.[42]

In a world of complex interpenetrating systems, every key player has a strategy and is planning apace. Some of the oil majors "have a huge plan for China" (interview). The plan is simple enough. It consists of drilling many more wells. A Shell publication makes this perfectly clear: "If oil and gas companies are going to provide the energy that the world needs, they will have to drill a lot of wells."[43]

---

[37] WEO 2017, 474

[38] WEO 2017, 486.

[39] See US Energy Information Administration, https://www.eia.gov/tools/faqs/faq.php?id=727&t=6.

[40] In 2010 China imported about 3% of its oil from Libya. See http://www.eia.gov/todayinenergy/detail.cfm?id=590.

[41] Daniel Large, "China and the Contradictions of 'Non-Interference' in Sudan," *Review of African Political Economy*, 35 (2008), 93–106, 97.

[42] US Energy Information Administration, *Country Analysis Brief: Sudan and South Sudan*, Washington, DC, September 3, 2014, https://www.eia.gov/beta/international/analysis_includes/countries_long/Sudan_and_South_Sudan/sudan.pdf, 11.

[43] See "Creating Value from Wells," 1, https://www.shell.com/careers/life-at-shell/importance-of-innovation/shaping-the-future-of-wells-today/_jcr_content/par/textimage.stream/1440096451843/d28347d16728ce4bc83f4e656303809914f9c7744db26df99f004ee71139e4a/wells-brochure.pdf.

The big lesson of the US shale experience is that thousands rather than hundreds of wells have to be sunk. In 1995 there were a little over 730 rigs in the United States. In 2003 the number was over 1,000, and in 2011 it hovered around the 2,000 mark.[44] The oil and gas majors did not start the fracking revolution in the United States. Independents like George Mitchell can claim the credit for this. The majors would drill one well and then "contemplate their navels," in the words of one interviewee. The independents took the risk of drilling hundreds.

The rest of the industry has studied the success of independent producers in the United States. If the world is to follow the United States into unlocking hydrocarbons from tight spaces, drilling technology has to reach new heights of automation and efficiency. Dropping the cost of drilling is vital for oil and gas majors. They have to remain competitive against the falling price of renewable energy sources. Too high a price for oil and gas reduces demand, spurs on renewable energy innovation (as it did briefly after the OPEC oil crisis), and ultimately prevents the value of their assets being realized.

An early example of a joint venture to lower the cost of drilling is the one between Shell and the China National Petroleum Company in 2011.[45] China's low-cost mass production capabilities made it a natural partner. The goal was to develop well systems with a high degree of automation, making drilling less vulnerable to labor market shortages in boom times. Software would capture the best of human performance. The old rigs were a little like Swiss Army knives, designed to carry all that was needed for the terrain and requiring a local workforce. They would be replaced by automated fleets of specialist rigs, working smoothly across fields guided by algorithms. Drilling thousands of vertical and horizontal wells, these fleets would be monitored remotely by small teams of engineers rather than a large onsite labor force.

Some eight years later, well automation technology has arrived in the oil and gas industry. Innovation shows no sign of slowing down as the industry improves its big data analytics, applies machine learning to that data, and continues to improve the automation of its operations.[46] The plan is to continue to deliver fossil fuel energy to the world based on fleets of smart drilling automatons.

---

[44] This data is taken from the Baker Hughes North American Rig Count. See http://www.bakerhughes.com/rig-count.

[45] The joint venture eventually took the form of Sirius Well Manufacturing Services. See http://www.swmsglobal.com/about.

[46] David G. Victor and Kassia Yanosek, "The Next Energy Revolution: The Promise and Peril of High-Tech Innovation," *Foreign Affairs*, 96(4) (July/August 2017), 124–131.

Innovation and discovery are everything for the industry. Even if a major company has a decline rate of 6% to 8% in its oil fields, that is not in itself a problem if investors are convinced it has growth prospects. Innovation that brings access to oil is key to persuading investors that it is all not a house of cards and companies are not simply "hamsters on wheels" (interview).

The oil people we interviewed were more confident about the future of the industry than we had anticipated. They understood much better than we did just how innovative the industry had been over the last few decades: "oil has capital and smart people" in the words of one. The industry sees itself as being in an innovation race with renewables. But, one might ask, haven't companies like Shell made some investments in renewables, as well as exotic technologies such as the conversion of oil from algae into biofuel? Those investments into technology exotica, however, have to stack up against the profitability of oil and gas drilling. This is a core business the oil giants know. Companies like Shell, Mobil, and Chevron have company histories going back over 100 years. They are old incumbents with lots of capital and networks of regulatory influence. They know what the returns will be if they spend hundreds of millions of dollars improving their drilling rigs. They know less about oil from algae.

Innovation in drilling and platforms has always been part of the industry's history. Different parts of the industry have taken on different risks. The majors have taken on the risks of deep offshore drilling for oil and gas. Independent producers have taken on the experimental approaches needed to develop fracking technology. With some of the majors like Shell and ConocoPhillips moving into cheaper shale drilling, their capital can keep the shale revolution going for a long time. These majors deal with an offshore drilling world where a rig can cost $500 million to $600 million. In the United States they do not worry about a ban on fracking. The fracking train "has well and truly left the station" (interview with oil major executive). Through process and price innovation the oil and gas industry has turned more and more of the planet's recoverable resources into economically recoverable resources. Of course, the industry needs time horizons of 30 and 40 years in which to capture the economic benefits of its investments in the planet's vast carbon resources.

The industry no longer worries about Hubbert's models of peak and decline. "We run the risk of cooking the earth before peak oil," as one senior executive put it. Regulatory peaks and declines are another matter, however. China could rob the industry of the time it is counting on if the nation moves aggressively to limit global warming. Some we interviewed thought it very unlikely that China would retire its carbon capital prematurely. Nevertheless, China, much more than the United States, is the key to the oil and gas industry's future.

In China's cities there is everything to play for. Cities could form the basis of an organized exogenous shock that shortens the life of the oil and gas industry. The electric vehicle market provides one source for organizing such a shock. Chinese households have yet to consume energy along the lines of their Western counterparts.[47] China's domestic market for vehicle sales is now bigger than the United States, Germany, and Japan put together.[48] For the oil industry, this represent a colossal source of potential transport demand. The industry's hope is that the existing infrastructure for oil and gas will dramatically slow down the transition to electrical vehicles. But it may turn out differently. The IEA has a Low Car Ownership–High Electrification case for China in which global demand for oil hits a ceiling by 2030.[49] Well before the IEA began factoring electric vehicles into its scenarios, the Chinese government began to implement a strategy for its future electric vehicle market. In 2009 it initiated the Ten Cities, Thousand Vehicles Program.[50]

Regulatory models for ratcheting up the penetration of electric vehicles also exist in Europe. Norway is the most talked-about example, with a ban on the selling of internal combustion engines to come into effect in 2025. This—along with a raft of other policies such as the absence of import taxes, toll-free driving, and no annual road tax—saw electrical vehicles and plug-in hybrids constitute almost 40% of the market in 2017.[51] Germany has a ban on fossil fuel engines for cars that comes into effect in 2030, and France and the United Kingdom have bans in place for 2040. But these are much smaller markets than China's market, and these nations are moving at a slower pace than the rapid exogenous shock that is needed.

[47] WEO 2017, 479.

[48] WEO 2017, 523.

[49] WEO 2017, 530.

[50] World Bank and PRTM Management Consultants, *The China New Energy Vehicles Program: Challenges and Opportunities*, World Bank, Washington, DC, 2011, siteresources. worldbank.org/EXTNEWSCHINESE/Resources/.

[51] See Thomson Reuters, "Will Electric Vehicles Really Create a Cleaner Planet?," https://www. thomsonreuters.com/en/reports/electric-vehicles.html.

Fossil Fuel Logic: The Case of Norway

Norway also represents a good example of how fossil fuel states and their industries cling to short-term calculations of "winning" from fossil fuel, unable to free themselves from the flows of its wealth. Norway has clung to these fossil fuel profit calculations for decades.

Oil was discovered in the Norwegian continental shelf in the early 1960s. The Norwegian state used different policy tools over the decades, such as protectionism, tax breaks, and privatization, to help build a strong export industry in terms of oil and gas sales and a strong oil and gas service industry.[52] The state was a crucial partner in the expansion of the Norwegian Petroleum Innovation System, helping Norway's companies to become international and integrated actors in the global oil and gas system.[53] The Norwegian case is also a good example of oil industry innovation. By adopting open innovation, the industry has created solutions to reduce costs in high-cost areas such as offshore shipping.[54]

Norway's sovereign wealth fund for many years made big investments in the oil, gas, and coal sectors.[55] It has been a "relatively passive money-making machine" (interview). More recently, it has begun to factor climate risk into its investment strategy, but there is no sign it will pull out of all fossil fuel investment. Norway's fund is about managing the risks to its oil and gas money, not managing the risk of climate change. For a time the Norwegian oil company Statoil invested in Canada's controversial oil sands project, withdrawing in 2016.

When we look at Norway we can see that it has for many years "spoken with two tongues" (interview). One has been as an oil and gas exporter and the other as the sincere climate negotiator and trustworthy partner, willing to do its share on climate change. Norway is a good example of the forked rationality that bedevils the climate change problem. All of the bureaucrats we

[52] Helge Ryggvik, "A Short History of the Norwegian Oil Industry: From Protected National Champions to Internationally Competitive Multinationals," *Business History Review*, 89 (2015), 3–41.

[53] Ole Andreas H. Engen, "The Development of the Norwegian Petroleum Innovation System: A Historical Overview," Centre for Technology, Innovation and Culture (TIK) Working Paper on Innovation Studies No. 20070605, University of Oslo, 2007, https://www.sv.uio.no/tik/InnoWP/EngenTIKpaper%20WPready.pdf.

[54] T. Iakovleva, "Open Innovation at the Root of Entrepreneurial Strategy: A Case from the Norwegian Oil Industry," *Technology Innovation Management Review*, 17 (2013), 17–22.

[55] Martin Skancke, Elroy Dimson, Michael Hoel, Magdalena Kettis, Gro Nystuen, and Laura Starks, *Fossil-Fuel Investments in the Norwegian Government Pension Fund Global: Addressing Climate Issues through Exclusion and Active Ownership*, A Report by the Expert Group Appointed by the Norwegian Ministry of Finance, Oslo, 2014, 25.

interviewed in Norway recognized the rationality of global action on climate change, extolling the virtues of cap and trade, emphasizing how Norway was "willing to pay handsomely for action."

Behind this giving of alms is a deeper and more practical calculation. It factors in the substitution of gas for coal, the fact that buyers of fossil fuel rather than exporters will pay the carbon emissions cost, the likely effects of OPEC's price policy on Norway, and the likelihood of a tough international agreement on climate action to which Norway could not adapt. This calculation (backed by a lot of internal modeling) points to continuing investment in gas and oil. It shows the rationality of continuing to operate as a smart and innovative petroleum state, pushing on with oil and gas extraction from the oceans. It shows profit, lots of profit. It is the same rational egoism of indifference to deep ecology that drives petrodollar networks everywhere. Since reputation matters in international negotiations, Norway also buys a "nice international profile" (interview) by putting money into REDD (reducing emissions from deforestation and forest degradation) mechanisms.

Norway's logic is the same as we found in other parts of the oil and gas industry. It is not just to continue with business as usual, but rather to continue innovating and investing as usual on the assumption that 2050 (the year in which Norway has said it will achieve carbon neutrality) is some time off. We will all be in a very different world by then.

To conclude, as I hope is clear from this chapter, not much can be expected of the United States in terms of rapid action on limiting global warming. Too many of its political, policy, and lobbying networks see the United States as a winner from its fracking revolution. For many on Capitol Hill, renewable energy industries are a little like Oliver Twist, always wanting more in the form of tax credits. For these networks, the oil and gas industry has put the United States in the driver's seat of global energy supply. China's incentives, however, are different. We turn to those in the next chapter.

6

China's Limits to Growth

A 1972 Model

China's rapid growth has taken it closer to the frontiers of ecological collapse. As I argued in my opening chapter, avoiding the rapid breakdown of ecosystems drives survival governance. China, more than the United States, has reasons to lead the reorganization of global capitalism's energy infrastructure. As this chapter shows, China's industrialization began from a low base in the 1940s and was underway well before 1978, the year used to mark China's decision to accelerate its development through an open-door policy. China electrified its economy with astonishing speed, drew in vast flows of foreign investment, and built an export manufacturing base in two to three decades. However, the price of this investment and export success was growing social inequality and a modest to small share of the profits to be made from the value chains of which Chinese factories were a part, a share made even smaller by the growing costs of China's severe environmental contamination. Mounting pollution problems have led China into a search for more sustainable models of economic growth, the circular economy model being one prominent example.

Warnings about the probability of a world systems collapse are to be found in the 1972 report *Limits to Growth* (LG).[1] Despite its reliance on what is, by today's standards, ancient computing technology, LG captured something important about the longitudinal relationships among its five variables—world population, industrialization, pollution, food production, and resource depletion.

In 2008 Graham Turner published a paper in which he compared three key LG scenarios with independently obtained historical data for the 1970–2000 period.[2] Of the three scenarios, the scenario LG described as the standard

---

[1] Donella H. Meadows, Dennis L. Meadows, Jorgen Renders, and William W. Behrens, *The Limits to Growth: A Report for the Club of Rome's Project on the Predicament of Mankind*, Universe Books, New York, 1972.

[2] G. M. Turner, "A Comparison of the Limits to Growth with 30 Years of Reality," *Global Environmental Change* 18 (2008), 397–411.

run (where the world system follows a business-as-usual path) lined up well with the actual historical data. In the standard-run scenario, food production, industrial output, and population grow exponentially, consuming non-renewable resources to the point where resource extraction consumes too much investment. The industrialized food system collapses, bringing about eventual population decline. Even when the amount of known available resources for consumption was doubled, the standard run ended in world collapse. Doubling the resources produces much higher levels of industrialization, leading to negative feedback in terms of higher pollution, which in turn eventually produces higher death rates and declining food production.

Lying at the core of the LG analysis were exponential scaling and system feedback loops. Exponential population increase combined with increasing rates of personal consumption would see the need for states to find substitutes for chromium, cobalt, mercury, tin, tungsten, and zinc, as well as fuels such as coal, petroleum, and natural gas. A standard economic counter to the problem of resource depletion is to say that, as prices of resources rise, the incentives for the discovery of new resources or for the invention of substitutes will also rise. This price-incentive response, however, underestimates the problem of exponential scaling. So, for example, a discovery that doubled the known reserves of chromium would, under the assumptions the LG model made about conditions of exponential growth, only increase feasible economic use of the resource by about 20 years (from 125 to 145 years).

Exponential growth makes relatively short work of even the largest resource discoveries. In other words, states cannot expect to stay ahead of resource depletion through finding new resources. They have to invent and innovate their way out of the constraints of the LG world. Innovation means industrial restructuring, which produces strong resistance from losing industries.

What Really Rapid Growth Looks Like

China announced its first Five-Year Plan (1953–1957) in 1952, at a time when its industry was responsible for 10% of national production, 5% of which came from its handicraft industry.[3] The hurdles to China's industrialization were high. There were shortages of capital and a skilled workforce. China's

---

[3] Robert M. Rosse, "The Working of Communist China's Five-Year Plan," *Pacific Affairs*, 27 (1954), 16, 19.

existing plants and machinery were foreign built and aging. The Korean War meant that China's access to Western sources of development aid had largely dried up, and there was a shortage of electricity to drive industrialization. China turned to the Soviet Union for help. In the 1950–1955 period, China and the Soviet Union signed agreements relating to 156 major projects of industrial and military significance.[4] There was in this period, as there had been in the Soviet Union, an emphasis on heavy industries because of their importance to military development. These 156 projects were intended to ground the infrastructure of China's development over the next few decades. With the help of Soviet soil scientist V. A. Kovda, who was advising the Chinese Academy of Sciences, Chinese officials also drafted a 12-year plan (1956–1967) for science and technology development.

China's heavy industries started from pitifully low bases. In 1949 its production of fertilizer was essentially nonexistent.[5] In the same year, estimates put its crude steel production at 158,000 tons.[6] From these levels of production China could only head upward, and that is what happened. At different points in time it chugged past other countries to become the world's main producer of these commodities. In 1985 it became the world's biggest cement producer. In 1996 it became the world's largest steel producer.[7] The fertilizer products of primary importance to agriculture around the world are nitrogen, phosphorous, and potash. In 2010 China became a net exporter of nitrogen and phosphorous fertilizers but remained a net importer of potash.[8]

In growing these heavy industries China had done a little more than simply edge past US and European industries. In 2010 China accounted for more than 50% of world cement production. On a per capita basis the demand for cement in China in 2013 was 1,500 kilograms, about three times the global average.[9] Its output of steel in 2003 was more than the combined output of Japan and the United States.[10]

[4] Zuoyue Wang, "The Chinese Developmental State during the Cold War: The Making of the 1956 Twelve-Year Science and Technology Plan," *History and Technology*, 31 (2015), 180–205, 180.

[5] Yuxuan Li, Weifeng Zhang, Lin Ma, Gaoqiang Huang, Oene Oenema, Fusuo Zhang, and Zhengxia Dou, "An Analysis of China's Fertilizer Policies: Impacts on the Industry, Food Security, and the Environment," *Journal of Environmental Quality*, 42 (2013), 972–81, 976.

[6] R. Tang, *China's Steel Industry and Its Impact on the United States: Issues for Congress*, Congressional Research Service, Washington, DC, 2010, 2.

[7] Tang, *China's Steel Industry and Its Impact on the United States: Issues for Congress*, 4.

[8] Yuxuan et al., "An Analysis of China's Fertilizer Policies," 976.

[9] See http://www.worldcement.com/asia-pacific-rim/26022013/Cement_China_industrialisation_investment_Taiwan_03113/.

[10] Tang, *China's Steel Industry and Its Impact on the United States: Issues for Congress*, 4.

The development of China's industries had at various stages been heavily dependent on the rapid proliferation of small plants in some sectors. For example, these were used extensively in the 1960s for the production of nitrogen and phosphate fertilizers. By 1972 they accounted for about 60% of national output. China could quickly and cheaply build these types of plants throughout the country.[11] Because of their simplicity they could be run by comparatively unskilled labor. The small-plant strategy was also accompanied by a parallel strategy of large plant development. Beginning in the 1960s, China began importing the equipment for large plants from Italy, Japan, Britain, and the Netherlands. In the 1970s this strategy went into high gear as contracts were given to foreign firms to build the biggest plants of their kind in the world. Building this indigenous capacity in fertilizers worked out well, because the oil crisis of the 1970s hugely drove up the cost of importing fertilizers.

The 1970s laid the foundations for giant manufacturing capacity, and from there the fertilizer industry moved in stages to a market system. Manufacturers were allowed to sell surpluses at a market price once they had met their quotas and price targets. In the late 1990s this system was switched to one in which manufacturers operated in a market but with price caps, which were removed in 2009. However, various subsidies for manufacturers remained in place.

A goal of urban policy during the 1980s was more growth and development of China's small to medium-size cities. A system of household registration (the *hukou* system), which made it difficult for people to change their rural status, was modified so that labor could more easily flow into the cities. During the second half of the 1990s the idea of urban clusters with large cities at their heart began to gain more policy prominence. These large cities in turn formed the basis for urban clusters through which ran many of the supply chains of the world's biggest companies. In these cities' factories, China's workers assembled products for export to consumers in the West. Clusters such as the Yangtze River Delta, the Pearl River Delta, the Beijing-Tianjin cluster, and the Shandong Peninsula became the main contributors to China's GDP. Building these urban clusters depended on power-hungry heavy industries such as cement, fertilizers, iron, and steel. Globally these industries were heavy but stable emitters of CO_2. This changed around 2000,

---

[11] Kang Chao, "The Production and Application of Chemical Fertilizers in China," *China Quarterly*, 64 (1975), 712–729, 717.

when emissions from these industries began to increase as China and India invested in them.

Some sense of just how rapid China's growth was comes from World Bank data on China's GDP.[12] In 1980 it was estimated at $340.6 billion (the United States for same year was about $6.5 trillion). In 2000 China's GDP was around $2.2 trillion (compared to $12.6 trillion for the United States), and in 2010 it was $6 trillion (US GDP was $15 trillion).

Investment and Technology Spillovers

During the 1980s China was not a major recipient of flows of foreign direct investment (FDI). The decade had been dominated by the United States, the European Community, and Japan. It took until 1986 for the countries of East, South, and Southeast Asia to overtake Latin America and the Caribbean as a destination for FDI.[13] These first rays of an investment dawn in China were followed by a rapid rise. By the end of the 1990s China had become the biggest host nation for FDI in the Asia region. China by 2009 was second only to the United States as a recipient of FDI.[14] As a foreign investor, China moved into third place in 2012 with only the United States and Japan in front of it.

China's reason for encouraging foreign multinationals to build production facilities in China, as well as to enter into joint ventures with Chinese enterprises, was straightforward. It needed to build an innovation system. A good place to start was studying the advanced technologies of firms from other countries. This was an old practice and generally complemented by the equally old practice of industrial espionage. In the 18th century, Britain, having climbed up the ladder of technological capability, found itself the target of strategies to obtain its innovations and secrets, most notably by France. Early on in the century the French controller-general of finances organized a scheme to draw skilled British workers in industries such as iron and steel manufacture, naval design, lockmaking, and watchmaking to France. Alarmed by the scale of technology transfer to France, in 1719 Parliament passed a law aimed at deterring this migration of skilled

---

[12] The data reported here uses the World Bank's constant 2010 US$ measure. See https://data.worldbank.org/indicator/NY.GDP.MKTP.KD?locations=CN-US.

[13] United Nations Centre on Transnational Corporations, *World Investment Report 1991: The Triad in Foreign Direct Investment*, United Nations, New York, 1991, 12.

[14] United Nations Conference on Trade and Development, *World Investment Report: Overview—Investing in a Low-Carbon Economy*, UNCTAD, New York, 2010, 7.

workers.[15] Throughout history, countries going through stages of industrial development have sought to accelerate the process by finding ways to learn from the efforts of more advanced countries. In the 19th century, for example, Switzerland set up its patent law so as to make it impossible for pharmaceutical inventions to be registered, thereby favoring its own weaker industry. Japan, for a large part of the 20th century, set up its intellectual property laws to favor diffusion rather than exclusion of technological knowledge. And toward the end of the 18th century, the US government under the influence of Alexander Hamilton copied the French approach to industrial espionage by focusing on luring skilled technology workers from Britain.[16] Free-riding is a glass house in which every industrialized nation has lived.

The overarching bargain taking shape in the mind of Chinese authorities was market access for multinationals in exchange for the possibility of technology spillovers. These spillovers would in turn lay the foundation for the emergence of a model of economic growth based on human capital, knowledge, and innovation. China's first 12 year science plan (1956–1967) had identified several fields as crucial to its economic and military development: jet propulsion and rocket technologies, radio electronics, automation, and semiconductor and computing technology.[17] Western multinationals, which owned many core technologies in these fields, represented China's best bet of gaining access to the latest advances.

There was, however, one way in which the great global game around obtaining knowledge spillovers had become more difficult. In the 1980s some large US multinationals such as Pfizer, IBM, and Du Pont—taking advantage of the Uruguay Round of trade negotiations—had added some more rules to the game by globalizing a set of intellectual property standards for all countries that wanted to be members of the World Trade Organization (WTO). In essence these incumbents of the knowledge economy were trying to lock in their incumbency and lock others out by restricting access to knowledge and data for as long as possible. Slowing the diffusion of technological knowledge in key sectors such as computing, biotechnology, nuclear power, and aeronautics was also consistent with the interests of the US national security state. US military prowess rests on it dominating weapons innovation.

---

[15] For the history see J. R. Harris, *Industrial Espionage and Technology Transfer: Britain and France in the Eighteenth Century*, Ashgate, Aldershot, UK, 1998.

[16] Doron S. Ben-Atar, *Trade Secrets: Intellectual Piracy and the Origins of American Industrial Power*, Yale University Press, New Haven, CT, 2004.

[17] Wang, "The Chinese Developmental State during the Cold War," 195.

Even though China implemented its obligations under the WTO's Agreement on Trade-Related Aspects of Intellectual Property Rights, the tensions between the United States and China over intellectual property have not gone away. They have actually worsened to the point of producing in 2018 a trade war between the two countries. Combative relations over technological innovation between China and the United States has the potential to complicate—perhaps even wreck—the world's chances of keeping global warming under the 2°C mark. I explain the reasons for concern in the final chapter.

King Coal in China

For China, one of the lessons of US economic growth was the need for electricity. As Mowery and Rosenberg point out, once US households gained access to the grid they became consumers for many different kinds of products and services, creating a large domestic market for US manufacturers.[18] Those manufacturers gained experience in the setting of technical standards in the US market, experience they took with them as they moved into international areas. Something like this cycle may repeat itself through smart grids, which will shape supply and demand in the postcircular economy in many different ways.

As I mentioned in chapter 1, in a 25-year period beginning in 1980 China achieved an electrification rate of 99%, one of the great engineering feats of modern history. As the Chinese grid expanded, so did manufacturing. Manufacturing employment in China began to rise in the 1980s, reaching a peak in the mid-1990s. It declined in the late 1990s as publicly owned factories went through a period of privatization and reorganization, but then resumed its upward trend. By 2002 China's estimated 109 million manufacturing workers represented more than double the total of 53 million workers to be found in Canada, France, Germany, Italy, Japan, the United Kingdom, and the United States combined.[19]

It is hard to comprehend the speed at which China built an energy system based on coal. By 2006 China was producing the power equivalent to a coal

---

[18] David C. Mowery and Nathan Rosenberg, *Paths of Innovation: Technological Change in 20th-Century America*, Cambridge University Press, Cambridge, 1999, 105.

[19] J. Banister, "Manufacturing employment in China," *Monthly Labor Review*, 11 (2005), 11.

plant of about 500 megawatts every two days.[20] This would probably be enough for a US city of around 140,000 people.[21]

China's massive expansion into coal was based on its low-cost domestic supplies. Depending on production levels, China had reserves of at least 50 to 60 years. These reserves were often buried at depths of 400 meters or more, making life very dangerous for China's coal miners. But from an energy security perspective the logic of mining millions of tonnes of coal at these depths was straightforward. Turning to gas rather than coal would have required China to embark on a massive importation program because, based on estimates and technologies of the 1990s, China had only modest proven reserves of gas. The US fracking revolution was only just beginning, and the possibilities of fracking technology for China remained opaque.

Coal found its way into every major part of the Chinese economy. In 2007 China accounted for about 50% of the coal being mined in the world. Coal supplied 63% of China's primary energy supply and 80% of its electricity supply. It was a critical input into fertilizer and chemical production, the iron and steel industry, and cement production. Approximately 45% of China's consumption of coal went into its heavy industries.[22] Patterns of urbanization began to change in China. In 1949 about 11% of China's population lived in cities. By 2012 this had become 52%.[23] Much of this movement of people occurred from the early 1980s onward, triggered by the demand for factory workers in the cities.

Coal's full costs became evident over time. China's miners were among the first who paid for China's coal revolution. Coal mines in China became the most dangerous on the planet, averaging almost 6,000 deaths per year for the 1992–2001 period.[24] Hundreds of thousands of workers were diagnosed with a disease commonly known as black lung. Whatever official numbers were reported, no one thought they represented an overestimate of the true numbers.

In addition to generating electricity, depending on its size a coal plant also produces several million tons of carbon dioxide and thousands of tons of sulfur dioxide and nitrogen oxide, the latter two being major causes of acid

[20] International Energy Agency, *Cleaner Coal in China*, OECD/IEA, Paris, 2009, 50.

[21] See http://www.ucsusa.org/clean_energy/coalvswind/brief_coal.html.

[22] International Energy Agency, *World Energy Outlook 2013*, OECD/IEA, Paris, 2013, 156.

[23] United Nations Development Programme, *China Human Development Report. 2013: Sustainable and Liveable Cities: Toward Ecological Urbanisation*, Beijing, 2013, 15.

[24] T. Wright, "The Political Economy of Coal Mine Disasters in China: 'Your Rice Bowl or Your Life,'" *China Quarterly*, 179 (2004), 629–646, 631.

rain. Also on the list of emissions and waste are small particles, carbon monoxide, hydrocarbons, ash, and sludge, along with various toxic metals.

By the early 1980s, coal was the single biggest cause of air pollution in China, contributing to high levels of airborne particles and sulfur dioxide. Chinese scientists started warning about the rising air pollution and its effects on health, as well as heavy acid rain problems.[25] Aggregated epidemiological data from around the world showed that even low levels of air pollution raised morbidity and mortality in children, with coal burning being particularly risky.[26] None of these warnings made any difference. China had committed itself to coal-based growth.

China's plan for dealing with coal's many negative effects was to work toward picking up from countries such as France, Germany, the United Kingdom, and the United States the regulatory capacity and technologies needed to clean up the mining and burning of coal. Collectively these countries had hundreds of years of experience in managing their national coal industries. China was banking on acquiring what it needed from the West in terms of regulatory learning and "clean coal" technologies.

As a developing country China did not have specific emissions targets under the Kyoto Protocol. Developed countries were, in the words of the United Nations Framework Convention on Climate Change (UNFCCC), responsible for "the largest share of historical and current global emissions of greenhouse gases." China's coal industry did begin growing early in the 20th century.[27] But this growth did not match what was happening in Europe or the United States. This late start allowed it to promote the argument that the climate change problem was a problem for the rich West. After all, the West had industrialized in the 19th and 20th centuries using coal and oil. But as China's coal-based energy revolution spread to a monumental scale, the claim that the rich West alone was pushing the world into a climate catastrophe became less and less persuasive.

China kept on asking for clean coal technology in various forums. Chinese officials would at every opportunity press the International Energy Agency (IEA), as well as those working in US laboratories, for information about "magical technologies" relating to clean coal (interviews). However, as we

[25] Dianwu Zhao and Bozen Sun, "Air Pollution and Acid Rain in China," *Ambio*, 15 (1986), 2–5.

[26] D. V. Bates, "The Effects of Air Pollution on Children," *Environmental Health Perspectives*, 103 (supplement 6) (1995), 49–53.

[27] Tim Wright, "Growth of the Modern Chinese Coal Industry: An Analysis of Supply and Demand, 1896–1936," *Modern China*, 7 (1981), 317–350.

saw in chapter 4, technologies of carbon capture and storage were magical only insofar as they were illusory. As the first decade of the 21st century came to an end, it became clear to China that waiting for the arrival of magical technologies from the West was a bit like waiting for Godot. In any case, CO_2 emissions and air pollution were part of a longer list of environmental problems in China.

Water Pollution

Building the world's biggest fertilizer industry came with costs for China. It increased China's use of its own coal in the production process. Through a subsidy program Chinese farmers were given access to cheap fertilizers. Their price combined with a poor understanding about their proper levels of application led to overuse, especially of nitrogen fertilizers. This overuse contributed to an underuse of the vast amounts of soil-improving organic nutrients that China was producing. The pile-up of fertilizers and organic material in China's systems rapidly led to the pollution of China's waterways. Just as the models in *Limits to Growth* had assumed, exponential growth was creating huge and negative feedback loops in China's environment.

China's fertilizer production went into overdrive in the decade beginning in 2000, with China being responsible for almost 60% of the annual increase in world production.[28] China's river systems turned out to be one casualty of this march of heavy industry. Water pollution had reached levels where, in the chilling words of one researcher, "China represents an excellent context to investigate a causal association between contaminated water and digestive cancer."[29]

A New Model?

In broad terms, China has two types of incentive to reconsider its export manufacturing approach to growth: one economic and one environmental. As has become evident, China's export success is housed in something of a

---

[28] Yuxuan et al., "An Analysis of China's Fertilizer Policies," 976.
[29] Avraham Ebenstein, "The Consequences of Industrialization: Evidence from Water Pollution and Digestive Cancers in China," *Review of Economics and Statistics*, 94 (2012), 186–201, 186.

multilateral glass house in the form of the WTO. The rise of bilateral preferential wheeling and dealing outside of the WTO, which has been led by the European Union and the United States, is well documented. The United States has some 20 free trade agreements in force, while the European Union is estimated to have trade agreements in place covering some 70 countries.[30] Moreover, the WTO's enforcement mechanism, often depicted as the jewel in the crown of a rules-based trading regime, has become the focus of US veto politics. In 2016 the Obama administration opposed the reappointment of a South Korean judge to the WTO's Appellate Body. The Trump administration has picked up this baton of opposition, refusing to support the replacement of retiring members from the WTO's Dispute Settlement Body. If the United States continues with its blocking strategy, the WTO will cease to have an operating enforcement mechanism.

The evidence of climate change, along with the evidence of its own record of environmental disasters, provides China with another incentive to develop a new economic model. More than any other country in the world, China has the carbon-based industrial capacity to trigger the exponential feedback functions of world system collapse. China's CO_2 emissions in 1980 were a little less than 8% of the world total, but by 2007 it had become the world's biggest emitter, responsible for 20% of world emissions.

There is some evidence of a response from China's planners to these two incentives. In 2013 Ross Garnaut and his colleagues suggested it was time to speak of a new model of economic growth in China.[31] The characteristics of this new model include a slowing of China's GDP growth, more emphasis on consumption and the development of services, and more attention being paid to the environmental sustainability of growth. Progress with this new model has generally been slow, but importantly significant reductions have their place in the use of coal for energy and in the making of cement and steel. Perhaps, as Garnaut hints, the changes in coal demand taking place in China since around 2012 may represent larger turning points in China's carbon economy than are currently evident.

To this, I would add that China has been working hard to transform itself into an innovation leader. As a factory assembler of innovation owned

<hr>

[30] See https://ustr.gov/trade-agreements/free-trade-agreements and Dominic Webb, *UK Progress in Rolling Over EU Trade Agreements*, Briefing Paper 7792, House of Commons Library, London, April 26, 2019.
[31] Ross Garnaut, Cai Fang, and Ligang Song (eds.), *China: A New Model for Growth and Development*, ANU E Press, Canberra, Australia, 2013.

by others, China has grown by making a little bit on each of the products it assembles. It became the optimal assembly point for those multinationals coordinating global production and supply chains.[32] This model, with cheap labor rather than innovation at its core, is being rethought in China. Studies of China's share of prices for consumer electronics such as phones and laptops, the intellectual property in which is owned by multinationals like Apple, have revealed figures of less than 5%.[33] Modern economic theory has increasingly recognized the importance to economic growth of technical change, learning, human capital, and innovation. There is, from an economic growth perspective, a clear incentive for China to develop its own innovation and intellectual property. Within the United States there is a simple but widely believed narrative about China and intellectual property: China steals US innovation and intellectual property. Whether it is the 1980s, the 1990s, or the 2000s, one can find US companies and US political elites complaining about China when it comes to intellectual property practices. Washington's beltway has been full of initiatives aimed at targeting China on intellectual property. These are put into circulation through show commissions such as the Commission on the Theft of American Intellectual Property. One recommendation from the commission was to impose tariffs on Chinese imports to the tune of 150% of the estimated theft of US intellectual property by China in the previous year.[34] The Trump administration wasted no time in acting on some of these ideas for disciplining China on intellectual property.

If, as I argue, China represents the world's improbable but last chance for a trajectory consistent with limiting global temperature increase to 2°C or less, China would have to succeed in its innovation ambitions. To add to the improbability, it would also have to succeed in a directive way. To remind ourselves of a point made in chapter 1, China cannot, unlike the United States, be innovation-agnostic when it comes to fossil fuel. If it follows the United States in an embrace of the fracking revolution, China will simply tip the world into the worst of the climate scenarios.

---

[32] Richard Baldwin, *The Great Convergence: Information Technology and the New Globalization*, The Belknap Press of Harvard University Press, Cambridge, MA, 2016.

[33] Jason Dedrick, Kenneth L. Kraemer, and Greg Linden, "Who Profits from Innovation in Global Value Chains? A Study of the iPod and Notebook PCs," *Industrial and Corporate Change*, 19 (2010), 81–116.

[34] Commission on the Theft of American Intellectual Property, *The Report of the Commission on the Theft of American Intellectual Property*, National Bureau of Asian Research, 2013, 84, http://ipcommission.org/report/IP_Commission_Report_052213.pdf.

China's innovation ambitions and planning also have to run a geopolitical gauntlet. As the next chapter shows, my scenario requires China to become a leader in bio-digital energy technologies. The more China succeeds as an innovator, the more this will fuel US fears of its own decline. Innovation has been fundamental to US military and economic ascendancy, a point we revisit in chapter 10. After World War II, the US national security state assisted its firms in strategic defense areas such as aeronautics and computing through the funding of research and development and defense procurement contracts, precisely because it wanted to stay ahead in weapons innovation races.[35]

Intellectual property rights have been a matter of perpetual negotiation between the United States and China because they are a proxy for the ownership of intangible assets made concrete in our material world in forms such as algorithms, molecules, signs, databases, and ways of doing business—the techniques and technologies of capitalism, one might say. For a hegemonic state that is also a war-making state, successful innovation by another state is perceived as a threat to hegemony. So, putting the matter starkly, innovation success by China raises its threat to US power; at least, this is how the United States will see this success. This in turn increases the tensions between the world's two biggest economies.

Innovation success by China would not, on its own, be enough if we keep in mind the global scale of climate change. China would have to deliver a more equalizing form of innovation transformation. Based on the evidence of a faster-tipping climate, citizens everywhere have interests in the rapid diffusion of life-saving or adaptive technologies (think, for example, cheap medicines, solar panels, and water filters). If, as many scientists believe, climate change increases the risks of pandemics then states will have interests in rapid and cheap diffusion of vaccines and treatments. Under the current globalized model of US innovation, intellectual property monopolists rather than markets diffuse innovation. Monopolists are interested in monopoly rents, and thus restrict diffusion.

This model is essentially a death sentence for the hundreds of millions of extremely poor people in the world surviving on less than $2 a day. The same might be said about the half of the world's population surviving on less than $6 a day. In fact, monopoly models of knowledge asset diffusion are not

[35] Daniel Yergin, *Shattered Peace: The Origins of the Cold War and the National Security State*, Andre Deutsch, London, 1978; Gautam Sen, *The Military Origins of Industrialisation and International Trade Rivalry*, Frances Pinters Publishers Limited, London, 1984.

successful models for anybody except the super-rich. New diffusion models for life-saving technologies are required if poor people are to have any chance of surviving global temperature increases. China understands what is required to reduce poverty. It probably has more incentive to rethink the current winner-take-all pricing models for technology that US corporations have globalized. Worth keeping in mind is that China over a period of almost 40 years (1978–2017)—through public good investments in areas such as education, agricultural research, and rural infrastructure—reduced the poverty rate of its population from 97.5% to 3.1%.[36]

Finally, China has to move quickly on the innovation front if the world is to have any chance of avoiding the worst climate change scenarios. The view that later-action scenarios of carbon reduction can start after 2030 is likely wrong. We are probably already in a period of late action. Can China lead the creation of a rapid path to a very different kind of energy future than the one currently confronting us? I argue in the coming chapters that China has an opportunity to create a bio-digital innovation paradigm using the scale advantages of its cities. Innovation aimed at infrastructure and cities represents our best and perhaps last chance to avoid the worst climate scenarios now coming into view.

[36] Cai Fang, Ross Garnaut and Ligang Song, "40 Years of China's Reform and Development: How Reform Captured China's Demographic Dividend," in Ross Garnaut, Ligang Song, and Cai Fang (eds.), *China's 40 Years of Reform and Development, 1978–2018,* ANU Press, Acton, Australia, 2018, 5, 12.

7

Backing the Bio-Digital Energy Paradigm?

The Threads of a New Innovation Paradigm

China's search for models for a circular economy began in the 1990s. It signaled the realization of the limits to coal-fueled growth. A circular economy model on its own will probably not be enough to avoid warming beyond 2°C. Two other major shifts need to happen. The first is the rapid retirement of China's comparatively new coal infrastructure; the second is China's transformation into the nodal center of global innovation. Lying at the heart of this possible innovation transformation of China is the digitalization of energy, with large cities forming the practical levers of such a deep change. Cities form the focus of chapter 8. Of course, China cannot singlehandedly develop all the innovation that is needed. No nation contains all the answers to all technical problems within its borders, but China could constitute the prime hub for much of the capital organization of this innovation. Its Belt and Road (BR) network could make it the center of a global green financial system.

The speedy retirement of China's coal capital, the first required major shift, does not seem to be a realistic prospect. Many new Chinese coal-fired power plants were built in the first decade of this century, raising the prospect of locked-in emissions if those plants have an operating life of 30 or 40 years. While China's coal consumption has hit something of a plateau, it is a high plateau. An unhurried rather than radical transition to renewable energy in China seems much more likely, but this reduces the world's chances of a viable low-carbon future.

What are the incentives for China to retire its coal capital prematurely as measured by standard principles of cost recovery and depreciation? The answer lies in China viewing investment in renewable energy as something more than rooftop solar panels and smart meters for consumers. Instead the ambition behind any such move has to be the construction of an innovation paradigm for the global economy, one in which China would benefit as the most competitive diffuser of the core technologies constituting the paradigm.

In order to support the idea of renewable energy as the basis for a new global innovation system, I look at how the adoption of coal had everything to do with its role in anchoring an advanced innovation paradigm, one that featured sectors such as steel and cement, and the development of dyes and pharmaceuticals. Coal played a role in all of these. Coal's story is much more than one of a fuel for burning. The digitization of renewable energy and the application of the biological sciences to digital technologies and renewable energy have the potential to ground a bio-digital energy paradigm of great scope, one in which services to ecological systems predominate. The emphasis, I argue, has to be on services to ecosystems and not ecosystem services. The former is a value to be found in many ancient indigenous cultures. The latter is an idea to be found in the boardrooms of places like Goldman Sachs.

Solar technologies were part of the 19th century's scientific landscape. They did not usher in a new innovation system because other major scientific advances such as those in particle physics and computing science had not yet arrived. Processes of technological convergence among suites of technologies, such as the internet of things, artificial intelligence, big data, and block chain technology, can help to promote radically new markets in energy. Converging technologies of computing science and renewable energy are in turn converging with biological techniques. Just as the synthesis of scientific disciplines studying the climate problem has led to richer conceptual framings, such as the earth system, so solutions to the problem lie in innovation processes of synthesis, especially among renewable energy, biology, and computing science.

The Circular Economy in China

Chinese policy-makers devote time to trawling the world for real-world, real-time regulatory experiments that might be potentially useful for China. The polite groups of Chinese visitors arriving at various universities, technology parks, and industrial centers worldwide are on the lookout for solutions to China's many difficult problems. China's reluctance to be a first mover is perfectly understandable. Everything in China happens quickly and on a large scale, including environmental pollution. Time is short for China. Just like the *Titanic*, there are no brakes to apply to bring about an instantaneous stop if an iceberg is sighted. Setting the right course matters.

According to Jianguo Qi and others, the inspiration for the adoption of an industrial model of the circular economy concept in China came from German laws related to the management of waste and the Kalundborg Eco-Industrial Park in Denmark.[1] The concept of the circular economy, along with benchmarks, made an appearance in China's 11th Five-Year Plan (2006–2010). From 2001 to 2005, the period of the 10th Five-Year Plan, China achieved growth rates at an average of 9.4%, but it failed to meet 10 out of 13 of its goals for reducing air and water pollution.[2]

The Kalundborg Park is perhaps not everybody's idea of a pin-up for the circular economy because included in its industrial ecological network is an oil refinery, the heat from which is used by other factories. It also includes Denmark's largest coal plant. The coal plant sends the many thousands of tonnes of fly ash it produces each year to cement manufacturers and road builders, while the gypsum from its sulfur dioxide scrubber ends up with a plasterboard manufacturer located within the park. The presence of the fossil fuel industry, one guesses, was probably what attracted Chinese attention.

Kalundborg, which started building in the early 1970s, has been studied around the world in order to understand how to apply ecological principles to industry. The principles take the form of design prescription: create closed material loops; do not damage, but take advantage of, natural metabolic processes; and look for energy efficiencies.[3] The practice of industrial ecology does not rely on virtue being its own reward. There are also potential cost advantages. A study of networked water recycling among the bigger firms in Kalundborg found both cost and environmental benefits.[4]

The global economy is not a circular economy, and no state has a circular economy. One might ask why the ecological alchemy of turning polluting waste into productive inputs and profit has not spread like wildfire. The variables relevant to the success of Kalundborg also hint at the limits of its replication. These include the supportive high-trust nature of the broader Kalundborg community, the willingness of firms to share information, and a supportive regulatory framework. Ironically, one also needs plants that

---

[1] Jianguo Qi, Jingxing Zhao, Wenjun Li, Xushu Peng, Bin Wu, and Hong Wang, *Development of Circular Economy in China*, Springer, Singapore, 2016, xxvi–xxvii.

[2] World Bank and the State Environmental Protection Administration (P. R. China), *Cost of Pollution in China—Economic Estimates of Physical Damages*, World Bank, Washington, DC, 2007.

[3] John Ehrenfeld and Nicholas Gertler, "Industrial Ecology in Practice: The Evolution of Interdependence at Kalundborg," *Journal of Industrial Ecology*, 1 (1997), 67–79.

[4] N. B. Jacobsen, "Industrial Symbiosis in Kalundborg, Denmark: A Quantitative Assessment of Economic and Environmental Aspects," *Journal of Industrial Ecology*, 10 (2006), 239–255.

produce sufficiently high volumes of waste to make them reliable suppliers of input products such as heat, water, steam, organic sludge (for fertilizer), and fly ash, a waste/input product requiring little or no further treatment.[5] Geographical closeness also features. The oil refinery and coal power station are across the road from each other, making, for example, the disposal of wastewater from the oil refinery to the power station an easy matter.

Probably Chinese policy-makers have learned valuable lessons from Kalundborg, but they would also have noted its small population (around 16,000 in 2015), and the time it has taken to refine the model. Kalundborg's industrial ecology experiment, which has been running since the early 1970s, is one example of what can be done in a small town in a small developed country over a period of more than 40 years. China's population is bigger than Kalundborg's by a factor of more than 62 million. A lot would have to be done to scale this model in China.

The task of engineering a circular economy for a population of 1.3 billion has made it into official Chinese policy discourse with a fair amount of speed. The sequence in rough outline seems to be some discussion by academics in the 1990s; a speech endorsing the concept in 2002 by Jiang Zemin, the then president and general secretary of the Communist Party of China; work by the National Development and Reform Commission; policies issued by the State Council in 2005; the adoption of the concept as a key goal of the 11th Five-Year Plan; the adoption of the Circular Economy Promotion Law at the fourth session of the Standing Committee of the 11th National People's Congress on August 29, 2008; and its continuation as a goal in the 12th Five-Year Plan.[6] The Circular Economy Promotion Law defines the *circular economy* as simply "reducing, reusing and recycling activities conducted in the process of production, circulation, and consumption" (see Article 2) and assigns responsibility for its creation in the following terms: "The development of a circular economy shall be propelled by the government, led by the market, effected by enterprises and participated in by the public" (Article 3).

Five-year plans can be read as road maps in which a particular generation of leaders set agendas and targets, or they can be linked together in various ways by virtue of shared themes. China's first Five-Year Plan (1953–1957) was the first step in what was then estimated to be a 40- to 50-year process of turning China into an industrial powerhouse.[7] By the time of the 10th

---

[5] Ehrenfeld and Gertler, "Industrial Ecology in Practice.".
[6] Jianguo et al., *Development of Circular Economy in China*, 1–2.
[7] Theodore Shabad, "Communist China's Five Year Plan," *Far Eastern Survey*, 24 (1955), 189–191.

Five-Year Plan (2001–2005), the heavy industries such as iron and steel, chemicals, and fuels, which had been targeted in the first Five-Year Plan, had grown into globally dominant industries. This was also the last plan in which ecological and environmental issues received comparatively little attention. Beginning with the 11th Five-Year Plan (2006–2010), China's commitment to the principles of the circular economy now stretches across three five-year plans. China's combination of a one-party state and five-year planning cycles offers, at least potentially, the advantage of being able to project temporal policy credibility to investors when it comes to the construction of a new economy.

China's 50-year-old model of industrial development based on maximizing heavy industry production irrespective of its externalities is now being progressively changed using principles of industrial ecology. These principles form part of China's longer-term economic change strategy because they allow China to search for valuable uses for its vast volumes of industrial waste. For example, coal mining produces a solid waste known as coal gangue that contains dangerous compounds. In 2007 China produced 4.5 billion tonnes of coal gangue.[8] Using circular economy principles this waste has become an input for power plants.

The circular economy may be environmentally friendlier than the industrial economy, but as the case of coal gangue shows, it is not necessarily a long-term friend of the environment. Billions of tons of coal gangue can be burned as an input for China's power sector, but this in turn produces waste emissions. Coal gangue has low calorific content, and firing it produces sulfur, CO_2 emissions, and particulates. Dealing with these requires investment in technologies to minimize the output of these wastes. In essence, one set of negative externalities is traded for another. The circular economy may slow the rate of China's depletion externalities with the actual rate being heavily dependent on innovation. In the case of coal gangue, boiler technology needs continuous improvement to burn this low-quality and chemically toxic waste.

The circular economy does offer policy-makers some useful principles for thinking about the management of negative environmental externalities, but as I argue in the next section, much more than better management

---

[8] Jianglong Yu, Fanrui Meng, Xianchun Li, and Arash Tahmasebi, "Power Generation from Coal Gangue in China: Current Status and Development," *Advanced Materials Research*, 550–553 (2012), 443–446, 443.

of negative externalities is needed if world capitalism is to avoid the kind of crash scenarios identified in *Limits to Growth*.

Renewable Energy—The Gateway to a Postcircular Economy

Starting with the work of pioneers such as Nicholas Georgescu-Roegen and Herman Daly, ecological economics has over time reconceptualized the economy as a nested system, interacting with physical systems through a complex array of input and output flows. Within such models, the ecological world is no longer assumed to be a source of extraction for natural capital goods such as water or land, but rather is seen as a group of systems on which the stability of the economic system rests. Depending on the scale of the interaction between ecological systems and the prevailing economic system of growth and consumption, the impacts of the economy may overwhelm the existing support and regenerative functions of ecosystems. A factory polluting a river is typically thought of as producing a negative externality, but when, for example, hundreds of factories destroy a river's capacity to sustain most aquatic life or thousands of factories produce ozone-destroying chemicals, we have a depleted system. Depletion impacts or externalities can be thought of as scaled-up externalities that diminish ecosystems, often to the point of no return. Ecosystem depletion was a problem before climate change. Greenhouse gas emissions are a global accelerant of ecosystem depletion because they target the earth system, the system in which all other ecosystems are housed. Dealing with depletion impacts requires us to move well beyond fiddling with externalities by adjusting property rights. The circular economy is one attempt to move to the level of a systems rethink.

There are, of course, different views on what constitutes a circular economy.[9] For my purposes, *circular economy processes* are ones in which production and consumption are looped in some way in order to reduce the depletion impacts of production. Core ideas here include designing products for durability and repair rather than to be discarded, changing business models to consumption of services rather than the purchase of products, and implementing systems for the recovery and reuse of valuable materials.

---

[9] See Martin Charter, "Introduction," in Martin Charter (ed.), *Designing for the Circular Economy*, Routledge, London, 2019, 1–11.

Production and consumption continuously create negative externalities that modern global markets generally scale into depletion impacts. For example, the mining and refining of materials for an endless array of electronic goods creates one set of depletion impacts on ecosystems. The disposal of these goods adds to an e-waste problem that also impacts ecosystems.

In the way that I have defined a circular economy process it is possible to have a circular economy based on fossil fuel, if the principal focus of such an economy is to slow the rate of depletion externalities. One can slow depletion impacts by improving the efficiency of coal-fired power stations, recycling the waste from coal, or switching to gas. However, staying with fossil fuel continues to generate depletion externalities. Moreover, innovation aimed at slowing the rate of fossil fuel depletion externalities is innovation in the wrong direction. It creates too many opportunities for fossil fuel owners to price their assets so as to foreclose on the possibility of keeping the global temperature rise to less than 2°C.

Ultimately global capitalism will have to shift toward a postcircular economy if it is to avoid hotter equilibria. By this I mean an economy in which the primary focus moves from the management of depletion externalities to the maintenance of the regenerative function of ecosystems. The repletion of ecosystems rather than the management of depletion externalities will be the chief characteristic of the postcircular economy. I should add here that there will, of course, be different views as to where to locate the philosophical center of a postcircular economy. For transhumanists, for example, the focus might be on accelerating the meld between humans and technology in order to turn us into bionic creatures impervious to the physiological dangers of hotter worlds.

The importance of services to ecosystems is an ancient idea. It is not to be confused with ecosystem services. Duties of service owed to the land of one's ancestors is a primary value in many indigenous cultures. For indigenous cultures in Australia, duties to "country," where "country" is the land and ecology as marked out by ancestral creators, serve as fundamental organizing norms.[10] "Country" for indigenous people is the place where one can sit down, a place that sings of home. Maintaining the health of Country is an overriding duty for indigenous people in Australia.

---

[10] Peter Drahos, *Intellectual Property, Indigenous People, and Their Knowledge*, Cambridge University Press, Cambridge, 2014, ch. 2.

The postcircular economy will also need to be characterized by open data flows about the state of ecosystems. Far more of the big-data economy will have to be devoted to gathering data about the state of the world's ecosystems. The role of digital platforms in amassing data in order to lure citizens into worlds of specially tailored unsustainable consumption will have to be rethought. We will want to train algorithms for the purpose of producing public goods like clean air and water. Digitized mathematical algorithms are simply too dangerous a tool to leave in the private hands of those who have no interest in public goods. Digital platforms could do much more to provide consumers with information about the carbon and ecological costs of their purchasing behavior. Innovation itself will have to travel in the direction of a convergence between digital technologies, biological technologies, and renewable energy. Digital technologies are fundamental to the efficient generation, storage, deployment, and trade in renewable energy. Of course, the production and maintenance of these digital technologies will have to meet very different standards of production and consumption. We cannot have a situation in which the production and use of one MacBook Pro leads to 592 kilograms of greenhouse gases.[11] We cannot have a digital economy serving up carbon emissions and e-waste that is also increasing paper consumption and a polluting pulp and paper industry to feed that consumption. Biological techniques have a huge range of applications in areas such as carbon fixation, materials manufacture, and energy storage. Out of this bio-digital energy paradigm will need to come innovations aimed at producing new materials that either do not disturb or actually help our ecosystems to produce the biological wealth that sustains life.

China's cities, I argue in the next chapter, may be the places where the strands of digital, biological, and renewable techniques might be woven together into a new and practical paradigm for our climate-changing world. They are sites of experimentation and engineering for the testing and evaluation of a vast range of technologies.

In the remainder of this chapter I turn to the history of electricity and coal because it demonstrates how the properties of coal offered science a much broader set of research puzzles, leading to the formation of industrial and research networks to explore these puzzles. Coal stimulated a research paradigm. The innovation flowing from this paradigm kept coal in use, even in

---

[11] Kyle Wiens, "iFixit: A Case Study in Repair," in Martin Charter (ed.), *Designing for the Circular Economy*, Routledge, London, 2019, 307–315, 311.

the face of mounting evidence about its dangers to health and then the earth system. This research paradigm was as important to the penetration of coal into the economy as its price.

Of course, coal was not the only fossil fuel at the center of a research paradigm, as the history of the petrochemical industry shows. After World War II, oil and chemical companies both led a boom in petro-chemistry that drove the emergence of sectors such as synthetic fibers, plastics, and agrochemicals.[12] Innovating with oil was not just important to the industrial performance of states. It mattered to their military power. The US Navy in 1897 began experimenting with oil to replace coal as a fuel in their ships.[13] Oil's superior thermal qualities held the promise of giving warships a much greater range. The research paradigm in petro-chemicals mattered to military power in many different ways. Natural rubber spread into all kinds of military equipment, ranging from shoes and raincoats to uses in aircraft, submarines, artillery, and battleships. The US military turned to the petro-chemical industry for the manufacture of synthetic rubber after the Japanese captured key centers of natural rubber production in Southeast Asia. War-making states institutionalized the coal and oil research paradigm because it permeated industries important to defense, ranging from iron and steel manufacture to aircraft and space programs. The large chemical and oil firms invested in the research paradigm because it made them indispensable to the military. These industries and the military together carbonized the world's economy.

Coal is now part of a narrow and largely failing research paradigm. Stopping coal's run and displacing it from the electric power system requires a new dominant innovation paradigm. The rapid development of this paradigm is more important than a regulatory approach to coal. Of course, both are needed, but a new innovation paradigm offering new circuits of commodity accumulation in world capitalism is now vital to the abandonment of coal. Price alone did not entrench coal in the power system of the 20th century, nor will price alone remove it in the 21st, at least not in the time we have left to make the needed deep cuts to greenhouse gas emissions.

---

[12] Thomas L. Ilgen, "'Better Living through Chemistry': The Chemical Industry in the World Economy," *International Organization*, 37 (1983), 647–680, 653.

[13] John H. Maurer, "Fuel and the Battle Fleet: Coal, Oil, and American Naval Strategy, 1898–1925," *Naval War College Review*, 34 (1931), 60–77, 70.

The Coal-Electricity Paradigm: Four Lessons

The last two decades of the 19th century were decades in which energy research crackled with discovery and societal turning points. On September 4, 1882, an electrical engineer threw a switch to send electricity from Pearl Street Station in New York to lamps in the district. Pearl Street Station had been built by the Edison Electric Illuminating Company of New York. Other Edison electric companies operating as patent licensees of Edison's various electric inventions spread his system through the United States.

Edison was not the only one making discoveries. In 1883 a solar cell was made by Charles Fritts using selenium.[14] Fritts had huge hopes for his solar cell, believing it could compete with Edison's system. However, Fritts had not understood his cell's fundamental inefficiency. It was only converting into electricity 1% of the sunlight it captured. Moreover, he had not incorporated his cell into a system. Edison's great strength was as an "inventor-entrepreneur."[15] Edison did not confine himself to single product inventions but pushed on to build the systems needed to make large-scale commercial use of the product.

An incandescent lamp on its own is not of much use, especially if it is competing against a reliable system of gas lighting based on stable generation and transmission. Gas lighting systems had made their appearance in the cities of Europe in the first couple of decades of the 19th century. Companies such as the London-based Gas Light and Coke Company invested heavily in building an infrastructure of gas pipes and burners that ensured reliability of supply to their customers.[16] Gas companies had to solve many problems along the way, such as keeping the system pressurized, dealing with peak demand, and minimizing dangerous leaks in the system. These citywide distribution systems of gas lighting were Edison's competitors, not a solar cell of 1% efficiency. In particular, the laying of underground cables posed large engineering and cost challenges for Edison and others seeking to compete against gaslight.[17]

---

[14] L. M. Fraas, *Low-Cost Solar Electrical Power*, Springer International Publishing, Cham, Switzerland, 2014, 2.

[15] Thomas P. Hughes, *Networks of Power: Electrification in Western Society, 1880–1930*, Johns Hopkins University Press, Baltimore, 1983, 18.

[16] L. Tomory, "Building the First Gas Network, 1812–1820," *Technology and Culture*, 52 (2011), 85–102.

[17] Hughes, *Networks of Power*, 41.

From 1880 to 1930 the electrical power system went from invention to innovation to a maturing set of technologies.[18] These were decades of disruption as gaslight companies lost ground to electric light companies. They were also the decades in which battles over the technical standards to run the system took place. The most notable of these was between direct current and alternating current, popularly depicted as the "war of the currents" between Thomas Edison and Nicolas Tesla. Edison's entrepreneurial wizardry alone does not, of course, explain the rise of the electrical power system. Manufacturers, research and educational organizations, and scientific groups played crucial roles in the research and commercialization of electrical power. Influential actors such as Werner von Siemens in Germany and the Massachusetts Institute of Technology in the United States were creating initiatives for the greater training of electrical engineers, which in turn led to many people working on solutions to the problem of the electricity supply system.

Edison's electrical lighting system was revolutionary, dramatically increasing the amount of light available to individuals living in cities, but it was also a system reliant on fossil fuels. The large "jumbo" dynamos in Edison's Pearl Street Station in New York were directly linked to high-speed steam engines that consumed a lot of coal. What was true of Pearl Street Station became true of entire economies. As the demand for electricity in Western economies began to increase, so did the demand for coal. Coal and electricity became the closest of partners in the 20th century.

The history of coal and electricity in the 20th century is rich in experience and examples of the growth of new technologies, their supporting politics, and stories of their economic, environmental, and social effects. The beginnings of this coal-energy paradigm contain four lessons that matter to an understanding of the conditions for the rapid transformation of the energy paradigm in the 21st century. Boiled down to a sentence apiece, the lessons are as follows:

1. Changing the paradigm takes longer than you think.
2. The construction of the innovation paradigm is at least as and probably more important than price.
3. Beware networks of incremental innovation since they can kill you.
4. If you want to delay life-saving disruptive innovation, give it to the market as soon as possible.

---

[18] Hughes, *Networks of Power*.

Lesson 1: It Takes Longer Than You Think

In the 1890s the United Kingdom was at the center of the world's largest empire. It was one of the world's technology leaders. The electrification of its economy, however, took time. In 1900 electricity provided less than 1% of the economy's power needs. By 1930 this had risen to a little less than 40%, with almost complete electrification of the industry not arriving until the 1960s.[19] Coal was the fuel of choice for electricity generators, accounting for almost 100% of total generation in 1929 and over 80% in 1960.[20]

In the first part of Britain's industrial revolution, steam power did not come into rapid use, playing only a modest role.[21] From 1870 onward, however, the steam engine grew in dominance as a direct source of power in British industry. Steam power was not replaced by electric power as swiftly as one might have expected. Steam remained important in some industries, including textiles, for a long time, while in other industries such as shipbuilding steam was replaced quite quickly. In 1930 steam was still a source of direct power for 40% of UK industry.[22]

Schumpeter famously attributed one source of innovation in capitalism to the entrepreneur who would transform product or process markets like a creative gale of destruction. In the case of energy transitions, the gale seems to slow to a gentle breeze, stopping altogether at times. Energy transitions in the 20th century moved at a more pedestrian pace over a period of many decades.

When we look more closely at energy transitions, we see a complex of network components (for example, transmission networks or the standardized devices of industrial production) and subsystems (for example, different sources of power generation) that do not march rapidly to the beat of best available technology. Instead energy transitions move arrythmically, their pace affected by politicians, organizations' entrepreneurial skills, firms' differing assessments of investment risk and uncertainty, patent and lobbying battles, and investor perceptions and behavior—with these factors caught up in mutually affective relationships. In more abstract terms, there

---

[19] R. Fouquet, *Heat, Power and Light: Revolutions in Energy Services*, Edward Elgar, Cheltenham, UK, 2008, 130.

[20] R. Fouquet, *Heat, Power, and Light: Revolutions in Energy Services*, Edward Elgar, Cheltenham, UK, 2008, 132, Table 5.3.

[21] A. E. Musson, "Industrial Motive Power in the United Kingdom, 1800–70," *Economic History Review*, new series, 29 (1976), 415–439.

[22] Fouquet, *Heat, Power, and Light*, 130.

are problems of regulatory and government capture, problems of collective action, innovation financing problems, public good problems, and information problems (captured in many different ways through concepts such as bounded rationality, information asymmetry and the psychology of framing). As I explained in chapter 4, through its networks (collective action) the coal industry has institutionally embedded itself in different ways in its wider political and social systems, solving problems such as innovation financing and public good problems (for example, the vast sums devoted by government to carbon capture and storage research) on terms highly favorable to it. Similarly it has managed information problems to its advantage (for example, the framing of coal as "clean coal").

Edison seems to be the perfect example of the Schumpeterian entrepreneur wreaking productive havoc in the markets of capitalism. His innovations transformed city lighting systems and contributed to the construction of electrical power systems upon which industry after industry came to depend. But as the UK data show, electrification was a process of stops and starts, taking many decades in some industries.

The next big energy transition requires the rapid solarification of our electricity system (where solar is a proxy for renewable energies). Schumpeterian entrepreneurship on the scale of an Elon Musk has an important role to play in this transition, but the speed of this transformation in the 21st century will need to be quicker than it was in the 20th century. Coal and the other fossil fuel industries have become embedded as institutions of commodity and capital accumulation. Markets cannot quickly remove them, nor can the advocacy of civil society networks, no matter how passionate. Action by at least one strong state is needed if an energy transition is to take place at a speed greater than that of a gentle breeze. This takes us back to the list of four states discussed in chapter 1.

Lesson 2: Constructing the Energy Innovation Paradigm Matters more than price

It's All about Price

One way to think about the climate energy problem is to say it is essentially a price problem. Once the cost of renewable energy technologies comes down sufficiently, they will surge to the front of the per-kilowatt-hour cost race and become the dominant source of electricity generation. Decarbonized electricity is the first critical step to decarbonizing the global economy. Price appears to have stood in the way of decarbonized electricity for a long time. In the early 1970s Farrington Daniels, in a survey of progress of solar technology, was able to point to only one practical success for solar—batteries for use in space exploration. Photovoltaic cells based on silicon were taking the sun's free energy and converting it into electricity at the cost of $50,000 per kilowatt.[23]

From the mid-1970s laboratories around the world worked on improving cell efficiencies. In 1998, scientists in Sandia National Laboratories achieved 30% efficiency. However, this was under laboratory conditions using a complex and expensive method of stacking cells on top of each other, as well as a system for concentrating the light on the cells.[24] The solar industry faced a dilemma. Improving the efficiency of cells was costly, while making cells cheaply saw efficiency drop. Whether one went down the path of fewer expensive cells or batches of cheap cells, the cost of solar per kilowatt hour was in the order of 30 to 40 cents. This was too expensive for utilities to meter. They were looking for a price under 10 cents per kilowatt hour.

Solar was not the only renewable energy technology facing the price hurdle. In a review of alternative energy technologies including solar, wind, oceans, and geothermal published in 2000, Cassedy pointed to a history of failures of alternative technologies despite their promise of a sustainable energy future.[25] Price was the most common problem. For example, the costs of photovoltaic electricity had come down by the year 2000, but the levelized costs of photovoltaic per kilowatt hour were, when compared to utility tariffs, still three to five times higher.[26]

Over the last decade more attention has been paid to the lifetime costs of using different technologies to generate electricity. The levelized cost of electricity allows for some comparison of costs between, say, a nuclear power plant that can have a life span of 60 years but is expensive to build, and a coal-fired power plant that may go for 40 years but is much cheaper to build. Renewables, especially solar photovoltaics, are no longer outliers when it

---

[23] Farrington Daniels, "Utilization of Solar Energy—Progress Report," *Proceedings of the American Philosophical Society*, 115 (1971), 490–501, 497.

[24] Robert Pool, "Solar Cells Turn 30," *Science*, new series, 241, no. 4868 (August 19, 1988), 900–901.

[25] Edward S. Cassedy, *Prospects for Sustainable Energy: A Critical Assessment*, Cambridge University Press, Cambridge, 2000.

[26] Cassedy, *Prospects for Sustainable Energy*, 59.

comes to costs.[27] In the last decade the cost of generating electricity from renewables has fallen and is projected to keep on falling, making the future global decarbonization of the electricity sector a realistic cost possibility.[28]

Despite the increasing competitiveness of electricity generated from renewable energy technologies, the International Energy Agency (IEA), in its World Energy Outlook (WEO) 2015 study concluded that, on all of its three scenarios for sources of world energy up to 2040, fossil fuels remain dominant. Its WEO of 2018 comes to much the same conclusion. Based on plausible enough assumptions about future energy demand, sunk costs, prices, and investor behavior, the IEA's work consistently points to the likelihood of a longer rather than shorter transition out of fossil fuels with a corresponding drop in the chances of remaining within the 2°C limit.

Price and competition races, of course, will affect the market penetration of renewable energy. But in the next section, drawing on the 20th-century history of coal, I want to suggest that the speed of transition to a new energy future depends less on market-based price evolution and more on an exogenous state-led shock in the form of the construction of an innovation paradigm, one I have labeled the *bio-digital energy paradigm*. The state has to send massive pulses of research and development, along with some large-scale technology testing, through the world system to show the feasibility of the new innovation paradigm. Without the delivery of this external shock, the new paradigm cannot take hold in time. We are instead left with the kind of scenarios that the IEA has been refining over the last decade or so. Price drives the continuing penetration of renewables but does not shock the world system into a transformative trajectory.

It's Not about Price

Charles Berg develops an interesting hypothesis around transitions in sources of fuel use by US industry, which went from relying on wood, then wood and coal, then largely coal and then shifting to oil and gas.[29] Price, on

<hr>

[27] International Energy Agency / Nuclear Energy Agency / Organisation of Economic Co-operation and Development, *Projected Costs of Generating Electricity: 2015 Edition*, France, 2015, https://www.oecd-nea.org/ndd/pubs/2015/7057-proj-costs-electricity-2015.pdf.

[28] International Renewable Energy Agency, *Renewable Power Generation Costs in 2018*, IRENA, Abu Dhabi, 2019.

[29] Charles A. Berg, "Process Innovation and Changes in Industrial Energy Use," *Science*, new series, 199 (1978), 608–614.

his account, cannot fully explain these transitions. Fuel wood was not in short supply during the 1800s when coal and fuel wood were competing as industrial fuels. Coal did not have a clear price advantage during this period, and in some periods coal was the more expensive fuel. Coal ended up becoming the fuel of choice because it complemented process innovation in a variety of industries: blast furnaces for making high-quality iron, coal's use in steel making, its role in cement production, and its applicability to techniques such as the gasification of coal for extracting higher levels of heat needed for other industrial processes. These are all examples of how coal underpinned the growth of an industrial research and innovation paradigm in which the best and brightest forged careers.

In Europe, England was an early entrant into coal-based innovation processes. Its deforestation problems caused it to turn to coal sooner than other European countries. As coal became the principal source of energy in England's economy, various industries began to experiment with it so as to adapt it to their processes. It was a different matter on the Continent. The costs of experimentation and uncertainty deterred or delayed some French industrialists from switching from their wood-fuel processes to coal-based ones.[30] For example, using coal in glassmaking required new furnaces and solutions to the problem of coal smoke coloring the glass.[31] As a result, in European countries where wood fuel was obtainable it continued to play an important role in energy consumption well into the 19th century.[32]

There was, however, another cost to not using coal. British industries, through their widespread adoption of coal, were forced into continuous process innovation ranging from redesigning boilers and furnaces to having to develop new ways of working with coal's properties. The level of industrial progress in Britain was such that during the course of the 18th century it became the target of industrial espionage by other European powers, especially France and Russia.[33]

A good example of coal's broad industrial utility is in the synthetic dye industry of the 19th century. In the 1850s William Henry Perkins, who had trained in the Royal College of Chemistry, discovered a means of deriving a

[30] Berg, "Process Innovation and Changes in Industrial Energy Use," 610.

[31] Warren C. Scoville, "Technology and the French Glass Industry, 1640–1740," *Journal of Economic History*, 1 (1941), 153–167, 159.

[32] E. A. Wrigley, "Energy and the English Industrial Revolution," *Philosophical Transactions of the Royal Society*, (2013), https://royalsocietypublishing.org/doi/pdf/10.1098/rsta.2011.0568, 1–10, 5.

[33] J. R. Harris, *Industrial Espionage and Technology Transfer: Britain and France in the Eighteenth Century*, Ashgate, Aldershot, UK, 1998.

color from coal tar, which was shipped to a London silk works in 1857 under the trade name of Tyrian purple.[34] Coal tar, a byproduct of using coal to make coke and gas, became the basis of the industrial dye and pharmaceutical industries as more and more organic chemists were drawn to studying its complex mixtures of compounds.

Coal turned out to be much more than a fuel. It gave birth to the carbon-based industrial research paradigm. Thomas Kuhn referred to *paradigms* or *normal science* to describe a period in which a community of researchers, initially drawn together by major breakthroughs, work through a set of problems generated by the initial breakthroughs. Paradigms are characterized by shared assumptions and a widespread acceptance of a need to solve a layer of problems flowing from those assumptions. Science enters a phase of acceptance rather than revolution. Normal science after the Industrial Revolution became industrial-scale science. Staying with the example of Perkins, there was huge demand from the dye industry for cost-effective colors that would hold fast because of the ever-growing consumer demand for silk, cotton, and wool products in Britain and elsewhere. The silk industry, for example, in the late 1850s employed some 150,000 workers.[35]

Coal's innovation paradigm came with an opportunity cost. Fewer scientists, inventors, and entrepreneurs were interested in the development of renewable energy technologies even though there were, as we have seen, solar inventions in the 19th century. The big research drawcard was coal, to which were added oil and gas. Those in pharmaceutical research working on coal tar compounds probably did not see themselves as being coal workers, but they were certainly part of the research paradigm exploring its many uses.

Coal, oil, and gas came to be at the center of industrial processes of innovation. As the true costs of coal manifested themselves in the form of air pollution, health impacts, and mounting evidence of its contribution to global warming, a possible response in the second half of the 20th century might have been a solar energy revolution led by entrepreneurs who saw huge profit opportunities in clean energy innovation. The efficiencies of solar cells were being improved and could have been even further accelerated after the shock of the OPEC oil crisis. Nothing like this happened. In 1973 coal's share of the world's total energy primary supply was a little under 25%, rising to 28% in

---

[34] Anthony S. Travis, "Perkin's Mauve: Ancestor of the Organic Chemical Industry," *Technology and Culture*, 31 (1990), 51–82.
[35] Travis, "Perkin's Mauve."

2015.[36] Solar technologies remained bit players. The world's most used form of renewable energy was hydro, a precarious form of renewable energy in a warming world. Entrepreneurs had not generated creative gales of destruction to remove capitalism's fossil fuel energy system. What had happened?

Lesson 3: Incremental Innovation Can Kill You

States in the second half of the 20th century began to regulate more strongly coal's pollution effects. London's Great Smog of 1952 led to the UK Clean Air Act in 1956, and the United States in 1963 and 1967 passed air pollution legislation. Through incremental innovation the coal industry lessened its polluting effects and improved its efficiency as a fuel. Minimizing health impacts was not the only driver for the coal industry. After World War II, coal found itself in competition with gas, oil, and then nuclear power for the generation of electricity. It was essentially in an innovation race.

During the 1970s the UK National Coal Board worked on the fluidized combustion of coal and processes for turning coal into gas so that gas turbines could be employed to generate electricity. Spurred on by energy insecurity, the United States in the same decade injected much more money into research on coal gasification and the liquification of coal to obtain fuels and chemicals. Coal gasification had a history of incremental innovation upon which to build. Thousands of coal gasifiers had been built in the United States in the 1920s, and the technology was also widely employed in France and Germany in the early part of the 20th century.[37] Interest in developing this technology had fallen away in the United States after World War II because of the availability of cheap oil and natural gas. The 1970s and 1980s saw a renewed interest in improving these technologies and in particular the development of what came to be known as integrated coal gasification combined cycle (ICGCC) power plants.

Research into these coal technologies came at a vital time for the coal industry because the utility companies in the United States and elsewhere were facing much stricter emission and environmental laws. The investment outlook was bleaker as investors wondered about the viability of those utilities

---

[36] International Energy Agency, *Key World Energy Statistics 2017*, OECD/IEA, Paris, 2017, 6.

[37] Dwain F. Spencer, Michael J. Gluckman, and Seymour B. Alpert, "Coal Gasification for Electric Power Generation," *Science*, new series, 215 (1982), 1571–1576, 1571.

that had filled their baskets with coal. ICGCC plants seemed to be an answer. Removing sulfur compounds from gasified coal was more efficient than from the flue gas coming from a conventional coal-fired power station; there were fewer waste solids such as scrubber sludge to dispose of, and these plants used less water.[38]

The reason ICGCC plants seemed to be the answer was not because of coal's price or wide availability—which was hardly more available than sunlight, and certainly much less clean—but rather because coal was part of industrial normal science supported by old commercial networks. This paradigm had long historical roots. The manufacture of gas from coal had started at the beginning of the 19th century in both the United Kingdom and the United States.[39] A lot was already understood. The researchers and laboratories working on solving the problems of coal also knew that any breakthrough they made in their respective labs would not be treated as an unwanted Frankenstein. Instead a laboratory breakthrough had a chance of making it into industrial application because the coal industry, the utilities, and governments in developed countries were all part of a support network for the coal-electricity paradigm. Plenty of laboratories were working on solving the problems of coal precisely because their solutions had a market. This paradigm continues to draw bets from large players like General Electric, despite the fact that building ICGCC plants, like the one GE built in Knox County, Indiana, is "wildly expensive" (interview).

Incremental innovation worked for coal, as it did for gas and oil. The health problems of coal did not go away. Multicountry studies examining the relationship between electricity consumption and coal consumption continue to show the negative effects of coal-fired power stations on global public health, even today.[40] But events such as the London smogs became the subject of history, and the industry was able to increase its share of global primary energy provision. Incremental innovation within the coal-electricity paradigm more than kept the coal industry in the game. Normal science for fossil fuel, as the next section shows, eclipsed the revolutionary potential of solar and other renewables.

---

[38] Spencer, Gluckman, and Alpert, "Coal Gasification for Electric Power Generation," 1573–1574.

[39] Robert L. Hirsch, John E. Gallagher, Richard R. Lessard, and Robert D. Wesselhoft, "Catalytic Coal Gasification: An Emerging Technology," *Science*, new series, 215 (1982), 121–127.

[40] Julia M. Gohlke, Reuben Thomas, Alistair Woodward, Diarmid Campbell-Lendrum, Annette Prüss-Üstün, Simon Hales, and Christopher J. Portier, "Estimating the Global Public Health Implications of Electricity and Coal Consumption," *Environmental Health Perspectives*, 119 (2011), 821–826.

Lesson 4: Delay Disruptive Innovation by Giving It to the Market Alone

Fritts's invention of the solar cell in 1883 was not the only breakthrough for solar in the 19th century. A solar concentrator, invented by the French teacher Augustin Mouchot, became the belle of the ball at the Universal Exhibition in Paris in 1878. John Ericsson, one of the 19th century's prominent engineers and inventors, looked at solar sources for the design of his heat engine. The history of invention in solar stretches further back than one might think, leading one to ask why some of these invention moments did not become innovation processes for a much earlier transformation of the world's energy system.

The answer lies in the different constitution of the research paradigms for coal and other fossil fuels compared to solar. Early on, the coal-electricity paradigm was characterized by intermeshed networks of governmental, industrial, and research support. Solar for a long time remained a laboratory paradigm.

In 1954, two researchers at Bell Labs invented the first practical solar silicon cell, it being able to convert about 6% of the energy it received into electricity. Taking advantage of the publicity and excitement, scientists, financiers, and industrialists formed in that same year the Association for Applied Solar Energy (AASE) in Phoenix, Arizona, and, along with the Stanford Research Institute and the University of Arizona, pushed for a world symposium on applied solar energy.[41] The timing seemed right. President Harry Truman's Materials Policy Commission had recommended a much more aggressive approach toward the development of solar and atomic energy. US oil reserves were falling, creating a dependence on oil from the Middle East. President Dwight Eisenhower's administration pushed resources into atomic innovation. Continuing research to deliver atomic bombs of ever greater thermal energy was seen as the means for dealing with threats from the Soviet Union. Among the express purposes of the Atomic Energy Act of 1954 were programs of fostering research and development, along with the dissemination of scientific information. The Atomic Energy Commission was given wide powers to support research in everything from the theory of atomic energy to all conceivable industrial uses of such energy. The commission was directed to use these powers as well as to make grants to the civilian sector for

---

[41] Harvey Strum, "Eisenhower's Solar Energy Policy," *Public Historian*, 6 (1984), 37–50.

the construction of reactors. This was a law mandating the provision of vast sums of public money to an industry that would keep the United States at the front of the arms race. The development of solar, on the other hand, was left to the market.

The world symposium on solar energy went ahead, and for a while the AASE became a meeting place for solar researchers and industrialists. The problem lay in the lack of federal funding. The National Science Foundation allotted to solar research $100,000 per year (roughly $1 million in today's dollars). Various individual efforts in Congress in the 1950s and 1960s to increase federal dollars for solar failed.[42] The government pipeline for solar research was a trickle.

As one of the pioneers of solar research observed, the sun's radiation might be widespread and endless in supply, but it is of low intensity; ways of collecting it efficiently have to be found, and storage is critical in order to overcome intermittency.[43] Not only was much more basic research required, but it had to be of a highly interdisciplinary kind, involving physics, chemistry, and astronomy, as well as the engineering disciplines. Without serious federal funding, universities were not likely to take on the big problems of solar energy. For those in atomic research, especially on the weapons side, lots of federal funding was available. The scientists who chose to take the money entered a world of secrecy in which they were servants to the masters of national security.

The predictable run of events followed. Financiers began to drift away, perceiving a long road ahead for solar. The AASE fell on hard times, losing members and income, eventually reemerging in Australia in 1971 as the International Solar Energy Society. Solar energy research struggled, overshadowed by the funds devoted to nuclear and fossil fuel research. In 1975, for example, the US government allotted $678 million to fission research, $147 million to fusion research, and $253 million to fossil fuels. Only $25 million was found for solar, an improvement, nevertheless, on the $9 million budgeted in 1974.[44]

Apart from the lack of federal funding for basic solar research, the US market for energy was less a market and more a government welfare game in

[42] Harvey Strum, "The Association for Applied Solar Energy / Solar Energy Society, 1954–1970," *Technology and Culture*, 26 (1985), 571–578.

[43] Farrington Daniels, "Utilization of Solar Energy-Progress Report," *Proceedings of the American Philosophical Society*, 115 (1971), 490–501.

[44] Denis Hayes, "Solar Power in the Middle East," *Science*, new series, 188 (1975), 1261.

which various energy industries competed for massive subsidies. One 1978 study estimated that US energy production subsidies from 1918 lay somewhere between \$123 billion and \$133 billion (undiscounted), 60% of that going to the petroleum industry.[45]

One can see why renewables were providing so little of the world's energy supply in 1974 and fossil fuels so much. Coal was an institutional industry embedded not just in electricity systems, but in a large number of industrial processes ranging from pharmaceuticals to cement production. It was also a politically mature industry organized both nationally and internationally, with established lines of communication and influence into government policy networks. To solve problems of its use and improve its efficiency, coal was serviced by a large industrial research paradigm well funded by governments, especially like those, as in Australia, with strong export interests in coal. This paradigm kept coal in the innovation race, improving on coal-burning technology just enough to meet the tougher air pollution and environmental standards that developed countries were imposing on the industry. And, of course, the industry was relying on this paradigm to make credible its claims to be able to deliver the holy grail of clean coal.

Military Power, Energy Revolutions

The geo-energy trilemma has a military version (see chapter 4). War-making states need fuel for their war machines to function. Fossil fuels came to permeate national energy systems because in many different ways the military power of nations depended on fossil fuels, becoming part of what Daniel Headrick calls the "tools of empire."[46] A crucial factor in Britain's extraordinary naval domination of the 19th century was coal. Faced by competition from more cheaply built American wooden boats, Britain turned toward building ships from iron and steel. Coal was critical to the production of iron and steel. Britain's rule of the oceans was also hugely aided by a monopoly-like grip on naval coal supplies.[47] During the course of the 20th century, the capacity of modern military nations to carry on war depended on fossil

---

[45] Michael D. Yokell, "The Role of the Government in Subsidizing Solar Energy," *American Economic Review*, 69 (1979), 357–361, 359.

[46] Daniel R. Headrick, *The Tools of Empire: Technology and European Imperialism in the Nineteenth Century*, Oxford University Press, New York, 1981.

[47] Headrick, *Tools of Empire*, 175.

fuel. After World War II, US science entered the era of what is often called *Big Science*. More accurately, it was the era of Big Weapons Science. Money flowed to nuclear power research, driven by US fears of the Soviet Union. The Korean War (1950–1953) also elevated the strategic importance of nuclear weapons to the United States. Although the United States did not use nuclear weapons in that war, or in any other war since, it did signal the possibility of their use.[48]

State pursuit of military power turned fossil fuel into an indispensable strategic asset. The military's massive consumption of fossil fuel helped to grow fossil fuel's paradigm of incremental innovation. As I argued earlier in this chapter, petro-chemistry research served the equipment needs of militaries in many different ways. Nuclear power research was accelerated because the threatened use of nuclear bombs was the most potent threat a state could make. States raced to build arsenals of potency. Nations and their militaries did not perceive in renewable energy research the tools of domination. So, as we have seen, this research languished, despite repeated warnings in the second part of the 20th century about the existential crisis that the use of fossil fuels would bring. Now the crisis has arrived, and states have little time in which to build the renewable energy tools of survival.

Ironically, the military has now become interested in how renewable energies might improve the performance of their war machines. Militaries will incorporate renewable energy technologies into their war machines in preparation for the various climate-based conflict scenarios they have developed. However, they will make comparatively little difference to the global scale of energy change that is required. The US military may improve its own carbon footprint, but it will not stop the fracking revolution. It will take more than defense procurement to create the bio-digital energy innovation paradigm.

Summing Up

The transition that China and the rest of world needs this century is to a postcircular economy in which service to ecosystems becomes a primary value, much as it has been in the cultures of indigenous people. The focus on the price of photovoltaics, along with how many panels and gigawatts solar

---

[48] Roger Dingman, "Atomic Diplomacy during the Korean War," *International Security*, 13 (1988–1989), 50–91.

manufacturers are producing, obscures what is much more crucial to the survival of the world system: constructing the bio-digital energy paradigm. The lessons of the coal-electricity paradigm are, I suggest, quite clear. Energy transitions are not quick. A strong state has to catalyze a new paradigm of innovation as an exogenous shock in order to create new trajectories for world capitalism. The approach the United States took to atomic research funding is something like what is needed.

China, as the first part of this chapter showed, has taken steps toward the creation of a circular economy. Economists seem to be in agreement that services and the environment are playing a much more important role in China's economy. But we are also a long way away from anything we might call the bio-digital energy innovation paradigm. Many contradictory signals come out of China, including from President Xi's speeches. In a June 13, 2014, speech, for example, while urging the importance of renewable energy he also emphasized the need to build new, large coal-based electricity plants.[49]

Yet the possibility of China leading the development of a bio-digital paradigm of innovation should not be dismissed. An emphasis on an innovation-led economy has been a central theme of Chinese planning over at least the last decade. Its innovation goals, not surprisingly, include the key areas of information technology, biology, and renewable energy. The success of the bio-digital energy paradigm, where success will be measured by how well countries combine and adapt these technologies to the problems of climate change, depends on city markets. Cities, or rather city networks, will be the terrains where systems solutions and adaptations to climate change will be deployed. China's cities, I argue in the next chapter, can be the places where many of the inventions of the bio-digital energy paradigm make the crossing into innovation.

---

[49] Xi Jinping, "Revolutionize Energy Production and Consumption," June 13, 2014, in Xi Jinping, *The Governance of China*, vol. 1, Foreign Language Press, Beijing, 2014, 143–145.

8

City Pathways to the Bio-Digital Energy Paradigm

The Empty City

Stories about China's "ghost" cities have been circulating for a decade or more. Television journalists and photographers have been drawn to their vast emptiness that holds an eeriness associated with the end of the world.

Much of the media attention focused on Kangbashi in the Ordos province. International media in a hurry for a story would take footage of shopping malls devoid of customers. The New South China Mall in Donguan, described as the greatest shopping mall in the world because of its five million square feet of leasable space, became the "not so great mall" because of its voids.[1] Opened in 2005, television crews drifted through its cavernous halls interviewing the occasional desperate shopkeeper. But then a CNN report in 2015 reported the mall as full of shops and busy with customers.[2]

Media explanations for what is happening in China fasten onto the hypothesis of a Chinese real estate bubble about to burst. It has happened before. During the late 1990s Shanghai was said to be the center of the world's biggest property collapse. One can understand why the real estate bubble hypothesis receives so much press. An average of 5.5 million apartments per year were built in the period between 2003 and 2014, with vacancy rates in Chinese cities sitting at somewhere between 13% and 20%.[3]

Wade Shepard in his book *Ghost Cities of China* describes them as new cities, with most of them having been built in the mid-2000s or later.[4] But people eventually arrive. These cities follow a pattern in which the urban core is built quickly. This stage is followed by a trickle of people that eventually

---

[1] See "China's Ghost Cities," http://www.sbs.com.au/news/dateline/story/chinas-ghost-cities.

[2] Johan Nylander, "Chinese 'Ghost Mall' Back from the Dead?," *CNN*, June 24, 2015.

[3] Edward Glaeser, Wei Huang, Yueran Ma, and Andrei Shleifer, "A Real Estate Boom with Chinese Characteristics," *Journal of Economic Perspectives*, 31 (2017), 93–116, 93.

[4] Wade Shepard, *Ghost Cities of China*, Zed Books, London, 2015.

becomes a flood. As Shepard suggests, the real story about China is the scale of city and town building. Six hundred new cities were built in 65 years with hundreds of cities and towns still to come. In his 2008 book, *Concrete Dragon*, Thomas Campanella tells a similar tale. China at that time had 102 cities with populations in excess of one million while the United States had nine such cities.[5] This, he says, is only the beginning. Once it hits an urbanization rate of around 80%, China will have more than a billion people living in cities.

The power, steel, and cement demands of changing China into an urban colossus explains everything about China's greenhouse gas emissions over the last two decades. Cities in China and elsewhere have drawn in vast material resources and pumped out greenhouse gases. City building on this scale is climatically unsustainable.

China's urban gigantism translates into a seemingly endless consumer demand for more—more shopping malls, exclusive resorts, private clubs, theme parks, hotels, brand goods, and luxury cars. A culture of consuming less is not taking hold. Instead, consumption has taken China's ecosystems to the brink of collapse. China's rich follow the same pattern of conspicuous consumption practiced by other capitalists. Property developer Zhang Yuchen imported Chantilly stone to build his $50 million replica of the Chateau de Maisons-Laffitte, designed in 1650 by the architect of Versailles, Francois Mansart.

China's cities, it seems, will rapidly gobble up the planet's remaining sustainable carrying capacity. Just as Galbraith wrote in *The Affluent Society* (1958), wants become needs become demands. Private production is a force for persuasion, creating wants rather than responding to them. China's urbanization (along with India's) is a road to ever-faster collapse. This is one, not implausible view of where China's cities are going to take us. But there is another possibility to which we now turn.

The Opportunity of Cities

The building of new cities also offers the chance to experiment with cities, to assess whether in fact it is possible for cities to be real drivers of sustainability rather than gigantic greenhouse gas pumps. New cities or revitalized

---

[5] Thomas Campanella, *The Concrete Dragon: China's Urban Revolution and What It Means for the World*, Princeton Architectural Press, New York, 2008.

cities might be levers of change that China can pull to switch from an industrializing carbon economy at destructive odds with nature to a postcircular economy in which the sustainability and resilience of the economy rests on the management of ecological networks.

Old cities have to find ways to adapt new technologies. New cities can spread novel systems of design and distribution, ones that can integrate technologies into decarbonization solutions. The decarbonization of the power sector, beginning with the elimination of coal power, is the first necessary step toward stabilizing and then reducing emissions. But this is just a first step. The city is a crucial part of the remaining steps. Decarbonization of the power sector has to connect with three other sectors in which the city is vital: buildings (heating and cooling), transportation, and industry. In order to reduce the use of fossil fuels in transport or heating in industry, more attention is being paid to how flows of energy that begin as renewable energy in the power sector can be utilized, either directly or indirectly, as energy in the transport or industry sector.[6]

Hydrogen, for example, can be produced from water, using electricity drawn from renewable sources. This hydrogen can be used as a fuel in the transport sector, as a fuel for heating purposes, or as an alternative to gas in gas turbine plants. The ease of conversion of renewable energy into other energy forms depends on city infrastructures. Pipeline infrastructures can be designed or modified with hydrogen in mind. Hydrogen as a transport fuel requires hydrogen refueling stations. Hydrogen for use as a source of baseload power or for use by industry in heating requires storage facilities. In short, the potential of the hydrogen economy is heavily affected by what is feasible in the city. What is feasible in the city is a matter of engineering trial and error.

The advance of the hydrogen economy in China is following a well-developed pathway. It starts with a variety of foreign partners and grows through the use of pilot schemes. Then the big moment comes in which a city announces it is going to be an "X City" by year Y, where X stands for hydrogen, solar, or some other targeted technology. Before we look at this pathway to city experimentation in more detail we need a better understanding of how the city can be an opportunity for innovation.

---

[6] Azadeh Maroufmashat and Michael Fowler, "Transition of Future Energy System Infrastructure: Through Power-to-Gas Pathways," *Energies*, 10 (2017), 1089, doi:10.3390/en10081089.

Shenzhen—How Cities Contribute to Innovation

The importance of cities and urbanization to economic development is much discussed. Here I want to focus on two "master economic processes" of growth to be found in cities: innovation and import replacement. We owe the clear identification of these processes to the work of Jane Jacobs.[7] Innovation is standardly theorized within economics as a resource allocation problem in which problems of indivisibilities, appropriation, and uncertainty combine to produce market failure, necessitating government interventions of various kinds. Jacobs focuses not on the problems of innovation but on the success of cities in producing innovation.

Cities are, by virtue of their size and diversity, hotbeds of innovation in which innovation is the proximate response to problems generated by a city's many industries. Jacobs's example of innovation leading to new jobs is the invention of the brassiere that solved problems for the fashion industry related to the fitting of dresses. But as I show later, China's cities take the endogenization of types of innovation to a new scale. Smart cities, for example, are aimed at networked innovation, user innovation, and shifting the center of gravity for technological standardization.

Import replacement sees a local entrepreneur in a city develop a product to substitute for a product coming into the city economy. These two processes are master processes of growth for a city because of the multiplier effects and externalities they generate. Both bring new types of work, the demand for new services and suppliers, as well as new imports that in turn may be replaced. Of the two processes, Jacobs sees import replacement as being the more important growth process for a city. The city-based product, which replaces the imported product, draws in its own mix of imports, setting up the city for another cycle of import substitution.

After China's implementation of its open-door policy in 1979, the nation's coastal regions began to undergo a monumental transformation. A good example is the Pearl River Delta region in southern China. Created in the 1980s through a series of government directives, it is an example of how a predominantly agricultural region was turned into a region of dense urbanization with manufacturing industries in areas such as food processing, shoes,

---

[7] The contribution of Jane Jacobs is detailed in Peter Taylor, *Extraordinary Cities*, Edward Elgar, Cheltenham, UK, 2014.

textiles, and electronics.[8] Foreign investment, much of it coming from Hong Kong, poured into the region to take advantage of its low labor costs. Two of China's earliest special economic zones, Shenzhen and Zhuhai, were founded here. During the 1980s and 1990s the economic growth of cities in the Pearl River Delta region was based on a factory export model satisfying foreign markets. This factory growth produced something else along the way, a "silicon delta" capable of entrepreneurship and innovation to rival other regions of high-technology development.[9]

Shenzhen, in particular, is seen as a city capable of stirring start-up action in the information technology and communications sector. Its most well-known success story is Huawei Technologies. Founded in 1987 in Shenzhen, Huawei broke free of just being a factory for the manufacture of goods under license from a foreign intellectual property owner. By 2003 it was a manufacturer of telecommunications technologies for network operators all over the world, spending some 10% of its revenues on research and development. It also built the massive patent portfolio needed in the global telecommunications market to defend itself against other companies.[10]

Shenzhen and Huawei are examples of Jacobs's master economic processes in action. Before the Chinese Communist Party began its open-door experiments, Shenzhen was a small market town of some 30,000 people surrounded by rice fields in the county of Bao'an. For at least the first decade or so, Shenzhen's growth from a rural township to a manufacturing giant was dominated by the growth of factories making shoes, clothes, electronic goods, and other goods for export markets. In the electronics sector, for example, by 1983 the number of factories in Shenzhen had grown to over 60, but the inputs for goods such as radio–cassette recorders, calculators, and televisions were imported.[11] This expansion best fits into Jacobs's innovation process in which a city gains new jobs and the benefits of an export multiplier. The more dynamic growth process of import substitution seems to have come later for Shenzhen, as it drew into its urban networks a mix of different skills, scientific and technological knowledge, and services. From

[8] Roger C. K. Chan, "Cross-Border Regional Development in Southern China," *GeoJournal*, 44 (1998), 225–237.

[9] See http://www.economist.com/news/special-report/21720076-copycats-are-out-innovators-are-shenzhen-hothouse-innovation.

[10] Biswatosh Saha, "State Support for Industrial R and D in Developing Economies: Telecom Equipment Industry in India and China," *Economic and Political Weekly*, 39 (2004), 3915–3925, 3921.

[11] Jici Wang and John H. Bradbury, "The Changing Industrial Geography of the Chinese Special Economic Zones," *Economic Geography*, 62 (1986), 307–320, 316–317.

these networks, entrepreneurs such as Ren Zhengfei, the founder of Huawei, were able to organize the local research and development needed to make the substitute products for those being imported. Huawei's shift into research and development and its emergence as one of the world's dominant suppliers of smartphone technology and then 5G technology is an example of how cities and firms contribute to each other's growth.

Shenzhen was one of four special economic zones to be declared by the central government in 1980, the other three being Zhuhai, Shantou, and Xiamen. These zones were established to bring in foreign investment. [12] But they were also designed to bring in the seeds of innovation with which China could begin reproducing Western innovation processes. China's peasant socialist economy could never hope to compete with a network of high-technology capitalist states. The special economic zones were the first step in obtaining access to the knowledge and skills needed to create networks of innovation capability. The lures of these zones for foreign capital were favorable tax rules, a lighter regulatory touch from government, access to cheap labor, and eventually a vast consumer market. Once technology multinationals had alighted upon these zones, they would inevitably release the knowledge and technology that served to move forward China's innovation processes, which had largely come to a standstill.

Shenzhen has probably more than fulfilled the original hopes of its central planners. In a little over 30 years it has grown from a small rural town into a megacity, its high-rise apartments and factory dormitories filled by more than 10 million people. It is more than just a factory assembly point. It is also headquarters to homegrown telecommunication and internet start-ups such as Huawei, ZTE, and Tencent. No other city, points out Erza Vogel, has risen this swiftly.[13]

Shenzhen is one highly visible model of urbanization in China. It is an experiment from which much has been learned. But it is only one model of urban growth, one demonstration project, albeit one that has been running longer and on a larger scale than many other projects and pilot programs in China. Perhaps this model has also run its course. Shenzhen's success was helped by a large pool of cheap labor, the availability of low-cost land

---

[12] Wang and Bradbury, "The Changing Industrial Geography of the Chinese Special Economic Zones."

[13] Ezra F. Vogel, "Foreword," in Mary Ann O'Donnell, Winnie Wong, and Jonathan Bach (eds.), *Learning from Shenzhen: China's Post-Mao Experiment from Special Zone to Model City*, University of Chicago Press, London, 2017, vii–xiv, vii.

for industrial expansion, weak environmental regulation, and global export markets.[14] Today China's labor costs are rising. Land use reform and the environment have become major issues.

Reproducing Shenzhen's explosive but conventional growth path of carbon-based industrialization will only accelerate the speed at which China hits the wall of unsustainable growth. And so Shenzhen, like other places in China, has become a test bed for a new generation of urban experiments aimed at assessing the workability of new regulatory and technological systems such as carbon-trading schemes. China's cities are laying the foundations for a Chinese economy based on innovation.

Experimenting with Cities

Cities are the axes around which much of China's planning experimentalism revolves. The scope for experimentation is like nothing in urban history. By 2030 China's cities are projected to have added another 300 million or more residents.[15]

The phrase "pilot project" does not really capture what is happening in China's cities. China's low-carbon city experiments began in 2010, with eight cities and five provinces, expanding to 29 provinces. Its seven pilot carbon-trading schemes, which launched during 2013 and 2014, covered major business and industrial centers such as Beijing, Shanghai, Shenzhen, and Tianjin.[16]

When it comes to creating a new low-carbon economy, swift and transformative solutions are not in abundance and what has worked in one country may not work in another. The approach of the Chinese state to this multilevel institutional and natural systems uncertainty has been to comb the world looking for regulatory models and technologies to take back to China for practical evaluation. The visits to Kalundborg in Denmark were, as we saw in the previous chapter, one of many that helped Chinese planners make concrete the idea of the circular economy. China today is a hotbed of

---

[14] Organisation of Economic Co-operation and Development, *OECD Urban Policy Reviews: China 2015*, OECD Publishing, Paris, 2015, 85.

[15] United Nations Development Programme, *China Human Development Report. 2013: Sustainable and Liveable Cities: Toward Ecological Urbanisation*, UNDP, Beijing, 2013, 3.

[16] Zhong Xiang Zhang, "Carbon Emissions Trading in China: The Evolution from Pilots to Nationwide Schemes," CCEP Working Paper 1503, April 2015, https://ccep.crawford.anu.edu.au/sites/default/files/events/attachments/2015-04/paper_by_professor_zhang.pdf.

testing in agriculture, transport, clean energy technologies, and regulatory techniques.

What in the West would be thought of as "think tanks" or "policy networks" compete for attention and resources from the central government so that they can launch the flotilla of pilots and projects needed to demonstrate to party leaders that their technical plans most fit with the goals framed by party leaders. Marxism-Leninism may be the guiding thinking of the Chinese Communist Party when it comes to floating goals, but what is decisive in state interventions are successful demonstration projects.

Capturing the scale of experimentation in and with Chinese cities is difficult. In the Western media, China's failures receive more attention than China's successes. There are, of course, failures. If the outcome to an experiment is certain, there would be little point in running it.

City concepts used in China such as the sponge city, the eco-city, the circular city, or the smart city refer to trials of different technologies. Each city concept represents the ambition to make China the global center of market gravity in the continuous innovation of technologies relevant to the concept. So, for example, there are sponge cities for water technologies, eco-cities for ecosystem technologies and services, forest cities for green building technologies, and smart cities for information technology infrastructure. There are also hybrid cities such as the low-carbon eco-city.

Concepts such as the eco-city, the smart city, or the low-carbon city are precisely that: concepts. In order to turn the abstract and philosophical into a functioning system, Chinese authorities have done two things. The first is to encourage the grounding of these concepts in systems of measurable indicators. Different systems of indicators represent different interpretations of the concepts. The second is to allow cities to in effect become laboratories for testing technologies, the success of which are evaluated against various systems of indicators. The winning technologies and systems then have the potential to proliferate through the regional network of cities that China is constructing through its Belt and Road Initiative. There has never been a market opportunity like this. No high-tech multinational worth its name can stay out of China. China's city markets have the potential to create the waves of innovation needed by it and the rest of the world to survive rapidly advancing ecological crises.

Types of Experimental Cities

China's 13th Five-Year Plan (2016–2020) continues to commit it to building exemplars of different kinds of cities. Before I describe the different types of experimental cities, we need to remind ourselves of China's pressure-driving mechanism (see chapter 2). Through this mechanism the big goals of climate and energy governance such as green and sustainable cities are decomposed into precisely defined, fine-grained tasks such as targets for recycling, rules for the separation of garbage, and the building of treatment facilities to process different forms of waste. Local officials have clear promotion incentives to meet the targets set by higher-level officials, who in turn are responding to the environmental goals of the Party's leaders. But the pressure-driving mechanism is part of much larger active and intense social fields in China. Everyone is caught up in complex social webs that deliver monitoring and reporting, incentives and deterrence, praise and blame, fines and prizes. Shanghai's new garbage management laws of 2019 have fines attached to them. The pressure-driving mechanism, we can be confident, will be in full official flight to meet the objectives of these laws. However, the success of these laws also depends on many other things. It will help, for example, if the elderly, who have time on their hands, take an interest in what happens on their block, perhaps deciding they want to win a prize for the best community for the sorting of waste.

The explanation for generating these intense social fields of pressure has everything to do with trying to create new relationships between the city and the countryside. Burning or burying the garbage generated by the 24 million residents of Shanghai is not sustainable. It is not sustainable for any of China's cities, which are not only experiments in material technologies and urban design. They are also experiments in the rapid formation of the habits needed to stop the city from plundering and trashing its ecosystems. As one senior Chinese interviewee put it,

> People in new cities will have higher psychological awareness. In the old city only money drives. People in new cities will have the habit of thinking about the environment and therefore [will be] more public spirited.

One might be tempted to link this kind of thinking about cities to earlier movements of green urban planning and garden cities that rose up in reaction to the soot and smoke of the Industrial Revolution. But I would argue there is a more pragmatic impulse at work here. Climate change threatens China at the biophysical level. The Party's survival depends on successful survival governance. China's cities are experiments driven by necessity.

Forest City Projects

The Italian architect Stefano Boeri designed a forest skyscraper in Milan in which the concrete skyscraper acts as a trunk for shrubs and cascades of plant life. From Milan this design idea has traveled to Nanjing, where more forest towers are being built. A model for buildings has become a model for a new kind of city. Boeri's firm is now involved in the design of forest city pilots in China in which all the buildings are draped with plants and trees.[17] A concrete jungle is turned into a platform for holding aloft a giant forest that captures carbon, cools in summer, and reduces air pollution. So far two sites have been chosen in China as locations for forest cities—Shijiazhuang, one of the most polluted urban locations in China's north, and Luizhou, a small city in China's south.

Sponge Cities

The sponge city concept is aimed at the problem of water supply extremes—droughts or floods. The basic idea is for cities to develop networks for the absorption, collection, and reuse of excess rainwater. Water is managed by the sponge city to minimize its waste and the risk of flooding. Sixteen cities were listed in 2015 as pilot cities by the Chinese ministries responsible for rolling out the program, with another 14 added in 2016.[18] The goal is to have 80% of China's cities reusing around 70% of their rainwater by 2030.

---

[17] See https://www.stefanoboeriarchitetti.net/en/portfolios/forest-city/.

[18] Embassy of the Kingdom of the Netherlands, Factsheet Sponge City Construction in China, 2016, https://www.nederlandenu.nl/binaries/nl-netherlandsandyou/documenten/publicaties/2016/12/06/2016-factsheet-sponge-cities-pilot-project-china.pdf/2016-factsheet-sponge-cities-pilot-project-china.pdf.

Sponge cities are giant and indispensable engineering projects of risk management for China in an era of climate change. Flooding has probably been the greatest source of destruction in China in recent times, with 641 of China's 654 cities now experiencing frequent flooding.[19]

The sponge city program in China shows how the scale of China's environmental problems has turned it into the world's largest market for environmental technology solutions. With piles of money on the table, providers of those technology solutions enter China, keen for a slice of the action. In the case of sponge cities, China's central government has set aside hundreds of millions of dollars to allow cities to reengineer themselves into water sustainability through the creation of new drainage networks, permeation systems, filtration systems, the building of wetlands, and many other technologies. Foreign firms with expertise in these areas enter China, hooking up with the local partners in joint ventures. Over time they find that local firms absorb the workings of their technology, improve it, and above all manufacture it on a scale and at a cost that foreign firms simply cannot match.

Low-Carbon Cities

Another set of experiments is being run under a low-carbon cities project. China's cities are energy-hungry places. In 2009 their energy intensity was close to three times the world average, leaving much scope for improvement.[20] The technologies being targeted here fall into categories such as energy saving and efficiency technology, low-emissions technology, and renewable energy. China's National Development and Reform Commission approved a low-carbon cities project in 2010. The project involves eight existing cities (Tianjin, Chongqing, Shenzhen, Xiamen, Hangzhou, Nanchang, Guiyang, and Baoding) and the construction of low-carbon cities in five provinces (Guangdong, Liaoning, Hubei, Shanxi and Yunnan). Thirty-six cities were part of the project by 2012.[21]

---

[19] Chris Zevenbergen, Dafang Fu, and Assela Pathirana, "Transitioning to Sponge Cities: Challenges and Opportunities to Address Urban Water Problems in China," *Water,* 10 (2018) 1230.

[20] United Nations Economic and Social Commission for Asia and the Pacific (UNESCAP), *Case Study: China's Low-Carbon City Project*, Bangkok, n.d.

[21] Biliang Hu, Jia Luo, Chunlai Chen, and Bingqin Li, "Evaluating Low-Carbon City Development in China: Study of Five National Pilot Cities," in Ligang Song, Ross Garnaut, Cai Fang, and Lauren Johnston (eds.), *China's New Sources of Economic Growth*, Vol. 1, ANU Press, Acton, Australia, 2016, 315–336, 316.

One evaluation of the success of carbon cities looked at the performance of Tianjin, Shenzhen, Hangzhou, Nanchang, and Baoding across the dimensions of economic growth, energy consumption, urban construction, government support, and residential consumption.[22] Cities, the study found, showed variability in terms of low-carbon development, but importantly low-carbon development and economic growth could be complementary.

The Emissions Trading City

China's 12th Five-Year Plan (2011–2015) included the goal of developing a carbon trading market. Five cities and two provinces were chosen to develop emission trading schemes (ETS). The usual practical step-by-step process of experimentation followed, including the simulation of an ETS for the Chinese power sector.[23] Chinese authorities sent the ETS into a national phase in 2017. The initial target of the ETS is the power sector, covering around 1,700 companies responsible for three gigatonnes of CO_2 emissions.[24] As China moves to bring its national scheme into full operation, the various pilot schemes have intensified their experiments with trading, sometimes in tough ways. For example, the carbon cap in the Chongqing pilot was unexpectedly dropped in 2017 to below what companies had been reporting they would need.[25]

Our Korean interviewees (see chapter 1) emphasized how important it was to watch China. Korea's own earlier simulations with carbon trading and then moving to the creation of an ETS were probably based on careful observations of what was happening in China well before the 12th Five-Year Plan. Entry into China's market in the longer run may well come to depend on being able to work with what will be the largest carbon trading market in the world, especially if it is rolled out along the countries of the Belt and Road. Preparing Korea's companies for that day has been a long-term project.

---

[22] Biliang et al., "Evaluating Low-Carbon City Development in China," 316.

[23] Christopher Guelff and Liwayway Adkins, *Emissions Trading in the People's Republic of China: A Simulation for the Power Sector*, OECD/IEA, Paris, 2014, 5.

[24] International Carbon Action Partnership, *Emissions Trading Worldwide: Status Report 2019*, ICAP, Berlin, 73.

[25] World Bank, *State and Trends of Carbon Pricing 2019*, World Bank, Washington, DC, 35.

Hydrogen Cities

In the case of hydrogen China's long-term partner has been the United Nations Development Programme. It has helped to create pilots for hydrogen fuel cell vehicles in Beijing, Shanghai, Foshan city in Guangdong province, Zhengzhou city in Henan province, and Yancheng city in Jiangsu province.[26] City announcements have followed, with Rugao being declared the site for the Hydrogen Economy Pilot in 2016 and Wuhan announcing in 2018 its goal of becoming the Hydrogen City by 2025.[27]

Electric Vehicle Cities

As we saw in chapter 5, the shifting peak of global oil demand will be affected by what China does with its car market, especially concerning the spread of electric vehicles. As with so many technologies, city pilots in China formed the launching pad for electric vehicles. A program known as the Ten Cities, Thousand Vehicles Program commenced in 2009 with another 25 cities being added by 2011.[28] More plans and cities followed over the next few years. The aim of the pilots was to use cities and electric vehicles to help develop and test systems solutions for problems of climate change, energy security, air pollution, and market competitiveness in the auto industry. Among other things, the large-scale adoption of electric vehicles will transform value chains in the auto industry as the lifetime energy costs of running such vehicles decline, software innovation for cars becomes more important, and steel in cars is dramatically reduced to be replaced by lightweight composite materials and electronics.[29]

Today China's market accounts for almost half of the world's stock of electric cars.[30] It would be easy to think of electric cars simply as product units in a market.

[26] United Nations Development Programme, "Accelerating the Commercialization of Fuel Cell Vehicles in China," UNDP, Beijing, September 5, 2016, http://www.cn.undp.org/content/china/en/home/presscenter/articles/2016/09/05/accelerating-the-commercialization-of-fuel-cell-vehicles-in-china.html.

[27] See http://www.cn.undp.org/content/china/en/home/presscenter/speeches/2016/08/29/carsten-germer-undp-china-hydrogen-economy-pilot-project-in-rugao.html and http://www.xinhuanet.com/english/2018-01/21/c_136913339.htm.

[28] World Bank and PRTM Management Consultants, *The China New Energy Vehicles Program: Challenges and Opportunities*, World Bank, Washington, DC, 2011, siteresources.worldbank.org/EXTNEWSCHINESE/Resources/.

[29] World Bank and PRTM Management Consultants, *The China New Energy Vehicles Program*.

[30] International Energy Agency, *Global EV Outlook 2019: Scaling Up the Transition to Electric Mobility*, IEA, Paris, 2019, 9.

But this would be to miss the way in which China's cities are experimenting with electric vehicles as part of a many-systems transformation. The petrol-based motorization of China's cities was never really an option. What would a billion petrol cars have done to China's environment and quality of life in its cities? Motorization eats up land and space.[31] For China's already congested cities there is no choice but to think more holistically about the electrification of mobility. China cities are at the center of many electric mobility experiments, which include the rollout of fleets of electric buses, the creation of an infrastructure of charging points, and replacing diesel trucks with electric ones.

Circular Economy Cities

As we saw in the previous chapter, China's investigation of the circular economy concept began in the 1990s. It is now a focal point of city testing. By 2015 there was in place a national circular economy program taking in 44 cities and 57 counties.[32] Many cities in China, such as Dalian, have a long history with heavy industries in sectors such as machinery and chemicals. These cannot be closed down overnight. Circular economy models are a critical first step in minimizing the depletion externalities generated by heavy polluting industries. The indicators released by the National Development and Reform Commission for the evaluation of circular economy initiatives, such as the resource consumption rate and waste disposal pollutant emissions, speak to the cleaning up of old industries.[33] Other city experiments such as smart-city experiments or eco-city experiments are more relevant to building a postcircular economy.

Smart Cities

Smart cities in China form another distinct line of blueprint generation and piloting. The smart city is based on the pervasive use of sensory networks to

---

[31] Wei-Shiuen Ng, Lee Schipper, and Yang Chen, "China Motorization Trends New Directions for Crowded Cities," *Journal of Transport and Land Use*, 3 (2010), 5–25.

[32] Wang Ning, Lee Jason, Zhang Jian, Chen Haitao, and Li Heng, "Evaluation of Urban Circular Economy Development: An Empirical Research of 40 Cities in China," *Journal of Cleaner Production*, 180 (2018), 876–887, 877.

[33] Yuan Hu, Xuan He, and Mark Poustie, "Can Legislation Promote a Circular Economy? A Material Flow-Based Evaluation of the Circular Degree of the Chinese Economy," *Sustainability*, 10 (2018), 990–1012, 992, doi:10.3390/su10040990.

obtain and integrate real-time information about many city functions and systems such as transport, water, and energy. The concept took off in China after the consummate concept promoter IBM, went on a city tour in China in 2009, speaking with some 200 city mayors and around 2,000 officials.[34] In 2013 the Ministry of Housing and Urban Development produced a list of 90 smart-city pilot projects. By 2015 more than 285 of these pilots were in place.[35]

Many of the world's biggest information technology companies are part of China's growing smart-city market because only they have the capacity to build infrastructure at this scale. No single company has all the technology (together with the accompanying patent portfolios) and the knowhow to build a smart city. Networks of companies are needed to build smart-city networks. Smart cities in China are the sites of some the biggest projects of digital technology integration in the world. It is infrastructure for which the Chinese state is willing to pay. At the time of IBM's smart-city sales pitch in China, the Chinese government had approved the equivalent of €581 billion for infrastructure and welfare improvement. Around this time, Wall Street firms and the US government were preoccupied with subprime securities and bailouts.

For global information technology companies, the smart-city concept offers the chance to articulate visions of better city worlds. So, for example, according to IBM, through the use of video surveillance and predictive analytics, smart cities can be made safer from crime, improve healthcare outcomes through integrating patient data and health systems, introduce more dynamic systems to lower traffic congestion, reduce water shortages through managing water ecosystems and leakages in pipe systems, and improve the impact of consumer demand in energy markets through systems of price signaling. Cities always change, their concrete form being altered through cycles of building, demolition, and rebuilding. Smart-city technologies bring cities closer to being organic mainframes. There seem to be endless possibilities for rearranging the many social, cultural, and business networks of cities, as well as the way in which systems and services in cities operate.

---

[34] Yongling Li, Yanliu Lin, and Stan Geertman, "The Development of Smart Cities in China," paper for the 14th International Conference on Computers in Urban Planning and Urban Management, July 7–10, 2015, Cambridge, MA, http://web.mit.edu/cron/project/CUPUM2015/proceedings/Content/pss/291_li_h.pdf.

[35] EU SME Centre, *Smart Cities in China*, 2015, https://www.eusmecentre.org.cn/report/smart-cities-china.

Binary code has become a powerful tool through which to implement visions of civic life.

New communication technologies also provide new means for old practices of eavesdropping, interception, and surveillance. The combination of smartphones and smart surveillance turns city residents into trackable data subjects. Smartphones have turned out to be automation devices for registering uninformed consent to massive data-gathering exercises. Cities, once associated with the anonymity of the jungle, will become much closer to life in a glass bowl. Communist societies have been among the worst perpetrators of mass surveillance for the purpose of creating fear and controlling populations. In 2018 the UN Committee on the Elimination of Racial Discrimination drew attention to numerous reports of Chinese authorities using extensive surveillance techniques against Uighurs and other Muslim groups living in the Xinjiang Uighur Autonomous Region of China's northwest.[36]

The dystopian evolution of smart technologies is one very real possibility. It is also one that exists independently of climate change. Authoritarian regimes do not need climate change as a cover for such an agenda. Large technology firms do not need the climate change crisis to create surveillance capitalism.[37] Experiments in the digital capture of local urban data, such as the one run by Sidewalk Labs (a Google affiliate) on the Toronto waterfront, are taking place around the world.

Climate change, however, is likely to have impacts on the future of the digital engineering of cities. City populations living in the midst of new climate equilibria will produce demands for problem solving as city infrastructure comes under much greater stress. Cities around the world will need systems to manage lethal combinations of heat and humidity, flooding threats, and increased numbers of people seeking better conditions in cities than those they have left behind in rural areas. Cities in South Asia and in East China face, according to the modeling, the likelihood of zones in which people will in summer be regularly exposed to "wet-bulb" temperatures of more than 30°C (86°F).[38] A wet-bulb temperature measures the combination of

[36] UN Committee on the Elimination of Racial Discrimination, "Concluding Observations on the Combined Fourteenth to Seventeenth Periodic Reports of China (including Hong Kong, China and Macao, China)," August 20, 2018, CERD/c/chn/co/ 14-17.

[37] Shoshana Zuboff, *The Age of Surveillance Capitalism: The Fight for a Human Future at the New Frontier of Power*, Hachette Book Group, New York, 2019.

[38] Eun-Soon Im, Jeremy S. Pal, and Elfatih A. B. Eltahir, "Deadly Heat Waves Projected in the Densely Populated Agricultural Regions of South Asia," *Science Advances*, 3, no. 8 (August 2, 2017), e1603322, DOI: 10.1126/sciadv.1603322.

humidity and heat and is an indirect measure of the human body's ability to maintain normal body temperature. At a 35°C wet-bulb temperature the fittest humans struggle to survive for more than a few hours. In 2015, wet-bulb temperatures close to 35°C were recorded in the Iranian Persian/Arabian Gulf.

China's smart-city projects offer China a means to release rapidly the forces of endogenous innovation. Cities in China are concentrated spaces in which hundreds of millions of users can participate in feedback loops of user data generation and engineering response to improve products and services. Ken Shao, in an analysis of the innovation strategies of companies like Taobao, Tencent, and Xiaomi, shows how these companies involve their millions of users in fast-moving cycles of product improvement.[39] Xiaomi, for instance, has processes in place allowing it to make engineering responses to customer feedback within a week. User innovation is hardly new, but in China a great many users drive the speed of this innovation.

Elites, irrespective of their political dogmas, face pressures from many millions of urbanites worried about the impacts of climate change on city life and security. A failure to respond to these pressures risks elites' political tenure. Creating the smart climate city is likely to become an imperative no government will be able to ignore.

How Smart Cities Help Set Smart Standards

China's smart-city projects are also helping Chinese companies to enter standard-setting clubs. Standard-setting in the telecommunications and information technology sector requires companies to have a large patent portfolio before they can sit at the table of a standards game. Without a patent stake there is no playing. Chinese telecommunications companies well understand this, with Huawei and ZTE having become global leaders in using the Patent Cooperation Treaty to file for patents in many countries. As I mentioned earlier, China's smart-city concept functions to pull in investment and technology from foreign companies. For the foreign firm this means working with a local firm in a joint venture; in the case of the information

---

[39] Ken Shao, "Taobao, WeChat, and Xiaomi: How Innovation Flourishes in China's 'Fertile Land of Intellectual Property Piracy,'" in Gustavo Ghidini, Hanns Ullrich, and Peter Drahos (eds.), *Kritika: Essays on Intellectual Property*, Vol. 2, Edward Elgar, Cheltenham, UK, 2017, 22–43.

technology sector, this creates an opportunity for the local firm to gain access to the standard-setting process. For example, in 2014 there was a report that IBM and Sichuan Huaxun Zhongxing Technologies had entered into a smart-city project involving the establishment of a smart-cities research and development center along with a big data and cloud computing services center.[40] Sichuan Huaxun Zhongxing Technologies was also invited to join the OPENPower Foundation. This foundation, which includes IBM, Google, Red Hat, and Xilinx, has many working groups examining technical standards in areas such as machine learning, cloud computing, and big data.[41] By having a seat at the table, the Chinese members of OPENPower have a voice in the process as well as advance notice of the standards likely to take hold in the smart-city marketplace, and so can tailor their manufacturing plans accordingly.

The smart-city initiatives in China also reveal another economic process at work, one in which technology developed for the Chinese domestic market is then exported to other cities around the world. Huawei, for example, is a sophisticated player in standard-setting games, in which its rise has been remarkable. By 2011 Huawei was a member of 150 standard-setting organizations and had hundreds of experts able to attend and propose standards at meetings of those organizations.[42] Those experts had drafted over 23,000 standards by 2011. Every year they continue to draft thousands of proposals. Huawei has been piloting smart-city initiatives in Chinese cities in cooperation with other Chinese partners, announcing plans in 2017 to export the hardware and software to cities in 20 countries.[43] I address US attempts to stop this rollout in the last chapter.

This is a think-big, do-big strategy. No doubt there will be failures that the Western press will gleefully report. Failures will not stop the running of thousands of experiments so that smart-city technology can be developed and refined in China. Fail fast—learn fast—adapt fast. It is the "in China" bit that really matters. The ambition is to make the Middle Kingdom a center of technological convergence and standardization. Even if that ambition

[40] See "IBM launches Chinese Smart City R&D Base," http://usa.chinadaily.com.cn/business/2014-07/14/content_17765553.htm.

[41] See https://openpowerfoundation.org/.

[42] See Wenshan, Linhongji, Mengke, Network World, "The Power of Standards," https://e.huawei.com/en/publications/global/ict_insights/hw_124325/feature%20story/HW_198604?source=corp_comm.

[43] See "China Telecom and Huawei Co-Convene an IoT-Themed Symposium, Inspiring the Construction of the NB-IoT-Based Smart City Ecosystem," April 5, 2017, https://www.huawei.com/en/press-events/news/2017/4/nb-iot-and-smart-city-ecosystem.

only ends putting it at the center of a regional bloc, it is, so far as China is concerned, a better world than when US and EU companies dominated the world of telecommunications standard-setting. China wants to leave behind the days when it was somebody else's standard-bearer. As a low-cost manufacturer of technologies like the DVD, Chinese firms paid for standards set and owned by foreign companies.

China's city-based strategy of survival governance is also a strategy for altering its position in technology standard-setting games. Before World War II, Europe and the United States ruled the International Telecommunication Union (ITU), probably then the most important forum for standard-setting in telecommunications. After World War II the importance of the ITU progressively declined. Non-state fora such as the Institute of Electrical and Electronics Engineers or industry consortia became much more important, but the dominance of Western companies along with Japanese companies continued. Developed states have long argued among themselves about processes of standard-setting, with the United States and the European Union each accusing the other of using standards to gain economic advantages.[44] In these arguments between the United States and the European Union, the myth of the international standard is exposed for what it really is: a regional standard being pushed by a firm or group of firms that will gain global rents from the standard's globalization. EU and US complaints about China's entry into standard-setting smacks a little of two bullies complaining about having to deal with someone their own size.

A technology incorporated into a network as a standard and protected by intellectual property rights is a hugely powerful lever with which a company can maintain its dominance. The IP-protected standard allows for the extraction of royalties, bargaining around royalties (both with other companies and competition authorities), and the slowing down of access so that the owner company can be the first to improve the technology and be dominant in the next generation standard. IP-protected standards in digital network industries are not guarantees against disruption, but something of a quantum leap to achieve their disruption is required, as the example of the entrenchment of the Windows operating system for personal computers suggests.

---

[44] Krishna Jayakar, "Globalization and the Legitimacy of International Telecommunications Standard-Setting Organizations," *Indiana Journal of Global Legal Studies*, 5 (1998), 711–738, 724.

The world's big information technology companies, along with many small ones, have been invited into China to help build climate-smart cities. It is a case of "Invite them, and they will build it." Chinese cities will be among the first to face the danger of urban unlivability from climate change. There is some urgency in working out how digital machines and services can better help inhabitants when a city is in the grip of life-threatening wet-bulb temperatures. Whether the center of technological standardization will shift to China is hard to say, but Chinese companies will certainly own more standards as a result of these city projects than they did before them.

The Eco-City

Cities incorporating the beauty of nature into their design are a part of China's ancient past. Quinsai, the capital of the Southern Song Dynasty (1127–1279) was said by travelers such as Marco Polo and the Franciscan Odoric of Pordenone to be an earthly paradise floating on lagoons of water. Centuries later Communist China's program of heavy industrialization produced cities floating in pollution.

During the 1980s and 1990s some areas in China, such as Dafeng in 1986, began to incorporate the eco-city concept into their growth plans. Over the next 15 years or so, more than 80 cities were designated by Chinese environmental authorities as ecological demonstration districts, with Shenzhen hosting the eco-city world summit in 2002.[45] These eco-city summits, which began in 1990 in Berkeley, have generated sets of abstract ecological, economic, political, and cultural principles for thinking about ways to improve cities for the people who call them home. The core ecological principle is that "cities should have a deep and integrated relationship with nature."[46] Under the umbrella of these broad principles, ideas for the eco-city have blossomed. By 2009, one survey had identified some 79 practical eco-city initiatives around the world, ranging from entirely new cities to retrofitting initiatives.[47] The two regions of greatest activity were Europe (34) and Asia/Australasia (27).

---

[45] Rusong Wang and Yaping Ye, "Eco-City Development in China," *Ambio*, 33 (2004), 341–342.

[46] See https://www.ecocity2017.com/about/principles-for-better-cities/.

[47] S. Joss, "Eco-Cities—A Global Survey 2009," *WIT Transactions on Ecology and the Environment*, 129 (2010), 239–50.

The Failed Eco-City

Eco-cities might spread their benefits to many citizens or they might end up as luxury eco-bubbles for elites seeking environmental goods of increasing scarcity. Eco-cities might also fail. In 2006 the world's first eco-city was to arise from the wetlands of Dongtan on Chongming Island close to Shanghai. Descriptions of the future Dongtan city hinted at the restoration of the paradise of Quinsai seen centuries earlier by Marco Polo and Odoric. In Dongtan, residents would have abundant green space, proximity to good public transport, waste would be recycled, solar-powered water taxis would glide along its clean waterways, and renewable energy would power the city.

The Dongtan eco-city concept was a product of high politics. Tony Blair and Hu Jintao signed a deal in 2005 that gave the design responsibility to the British engineering firm Arup. Some three years later Western media were describing Dongtan as an especially bad case of greenwash. Almost nothing had been built. Corruption, China's persistent stalker of deals, had played a part. Officials connected with the project ended up with long jail sentences for bribery and fraud, including Chen Liangyu, the Communist Party chief of Shanghai at the time. Chen was part of a group of senior politicians and businessmen involved in the diversion of hundreds of millions of yuan from Shanghai's pension fund. A senior figure from Arup engineering stated that people at the Shanghai Industrial Investment Company had "gone quiet. We just don't know if anything will happen or when. The project office is shut."[48]

The Answer to Failure: More Experimentation

High-profile failures like Dongtan have not deterred China from continuing on with the eco-city model. In fact there is no model. Instead, over the last 10 years or so there have been investigations into different systems of indicators for evaluating and measuring the implementation of the concept. Examples of indicator systems include the 146-indicator sustainable development system developed by the Chinese Academy of Sciences and the 141

---

[48] Fred Pearce, "Greenwash: The Dream of the First Eco-City Was Built on Fiction," *The Guardian*, April 23, 2009, https://www.theguardian.com/environment/2009/apr/23/greenwash-dongtan-ecocity.

Caofeidan eco-city indicator system, a joint product of the Tsinghua Urban Planning Institute and Sweden's Sweco.[49]

These indicator systems are designed to help measure progress toward targets. They are often detailed systems covering areas such as energy, water, air, transport, the economy, and land use. These systems are further sliced into subcategories, each with their own sets of measurable indicators. So, for example, starting with water, subcategories such as water resources or water quality can be specified, and in turn indicators devised for these, such as an industrial water recycling rate for water resources. Once measurable indicators are formulated, the pressure-driving mechanism (see chapter 2) is set in motion, sending officials hurrying toward targets as measured by indicators. But before the mechanism can be brought into play, there must be an agreed-upon concept backed by a system of indicators.

The eco-city concept in China is no longer an abstract philosophical discussion of principles, but rather a matter of metric development. The work of developing indicator systems is technical, requiring high levels of critical contestation in order to develop a robust system. All levels of government, from major central government ministries to provincial and city governments, are involved in policies, programs, and pilots to speed up the evolution of the eco-city concept and to link it with other city concepts such as low carbon. Dontang was a failure, but to see it as the story of China's eco-cities writ large is a mistake.

Global Networks of Climate Action Cities

Cities in China are hardly the only places of green experimentation around the globe. Networks of cities to share experiences of low-carbon urban futures have been growing worldwide. A good example is the C40 initiative started by Ken Livingstone when he was mayor of London. A meeting of representatives from 18 megacities in 2005 produced a network interested in reducing climate emissions using tools such as procurement policy.[50] The mayors of megacities are in charge of lots of services and infrastructure,

---

[49] Nan Zhou, Gang He, and Christopher Williams, *China's Development of Low-Carbon Eco-Cities and Associated Indicator Systems*, Ernest Orlando Lawrence Berkeley National Laboratory, 2012, https://china.lbl.gov/sites/all/files/china_eco-cities_indicator_systems.pdf.

[50] See http://www.c40.org/history.

and so their purchasing decisions matter to the growth of markets in green technologies. Today the C40 network is made up of some 80 cities whose respective populations add up to 600 million people. Shenzhen is one of nine Chinese city members of C40 and is involved in a variety of initiatives such as new energy vehicles, low-carbon development, and an emissions trading scheme.[51]

The Belt and Road City Network

Countries continue to sign Belt and Road (BR) cooperation agreements with China, despite warnings from the United States about the BR's debt traps and predatory practices. At the beginning of 2019, BR cooperation agreements had been signed with 125 countries and 29 international organizations.[52] Many more countries are in than out. The World Bank has begun an empirical assessment of BR, pointing out that its transport projects have the potential to lift 7.6 million people out of extreme poverty.[53]

Probably almost every country will eventually join. Even some of the United States' closest partners in signals intelligence cooperation have signed onto BR. New Zealand has signed a BR cooperation deal, and the United Kingdom is sending delegations to Beijing to negotiate closer commercial ties with China.

BR's infrastructure dimensions make a lot of sense to cities and to states within federal systems. For example, Victoria within Australia has signed a BR agreement even though the Australian government has not. Perhaps many of these actors see the looming era of survival governance. Coastlines, ports, rail, and air transport links will have to be managed in very different ways as extreme weather patterns become more frequent. US financial capitalism has delivered an infrastructure of hidden intangibles, such as the derivatives deal that Goldman Sachs designed for Greece so that Greece could hide the true scale of its budget deficits from other European states. China's BR projects offer something tangible.

---

[51] C40 Cities, "Shenzhen: New Energy Vehicles (including Electric Buses)," in *C40 Good Practice Guides: Low Emission Vehicles*, London, February 2016, http://c40-production-images.s3.amazonaws. com/good_practice_briefings/images/7_C40_GPG_LEV.original.pdf?1456788962, 8–9.

[52] Office of the Leading Group for Promoting the Belt and Road Initiative, *The Belt and Road Initiative: Progress, Contributions and Prospects*, April 22, 2019, https://eng.yidaiyilu.gov.cn/zchj/ qwfb/86739.htm.

[53] See https://www.worldbank.org/en/topic/regional-integration/brief/belt-and-road-initiative.

As an exercise in connectivity through joint building projects such as railways, ports, industrial parks, and manufacturing plants between one country and the rest of the world, BR simply has no equivalent. Its membership and projects are in a constant state of alteration. It is a platform for convening a global conversation about infrastructure and its financing. In 2015 the National Development and Reform Commission of China described BR in terms of connectivity between Asia, Europe, and Africa, but since then eight Latin American countries have agreed to participate in the initiative. BR is not just about physical infrastructure projects. It includes other goals and programs, such as cooperation on metrology and the greening of trade and investment. As I argued in chapter 2, BR could, if it offered enough green projects, make exit from fossil fuel a more credible alternative for global investors. For the moment, connectivity seems to be more of a priority than policy consistency. At the same time as the official portal espouses the urgency of greening the BR initiative, one also finds how the initiative is helping PetroChina export petroleum products to Laos.[54]

To worried outsiders, BR contributes to a rising China's sphere of influence, to alleviating its surplus manufacturing capacity through the expansion of its exports to richer markets such as Europe, and to its rise as a financial power through the holding of long-term levers of infrastructure debt over other states.

BR is many things to many people. One of those is a city networking exercise. Cities, I have argued in this chapter, are the experimental backbone of China's strategy of survival governance. In its 2015 statement of vision and actions on BR, the National Development and Reform Commission identifies 18 cities and 18 provinces in which provincial capitals assume a key role. In essence a city network architecture underpins the goal of greater connectivity within and among China's regions, as well as between China and other countries on the BR. China's cities in this network architecture become "pivots" or nodes in a networked enterprise of opening up and developing China's regions. So, by way of example, Chongqing, a city in China's southwest of some eight million people, becomes a pivot for opening up China's western region, while a network of cities comprising Chengdu, Zhengzhou, Wuhan, Changsha, Nanchang, and Hefei form a core network for the opening up of China's inland regions.

---

[54] See "China Starts Exporting Petroleum to Laos," http://www.xinhuanet.com/english/2018-10/31/c_137572546.htm.

Lying behind the building of China's corridors of city connectivity—air, rail, road, port, and digital—is the assumption that they will help to lift millions of Chinese out of poverty into the moderate prosperity the Chinese Communist Party has promised. No doubt various parts of China's bureaucracy will be collecting the data needed to evaluate whether the planned-for returns on the many billions of dollars of infrastructure spend are materializing. We will certainly end up knowing much more about the economics of city infrastructure spending as a result of China's BR.

City networks, however, have to be more than just economic growth networks if we are to avoid shifts into temperatures beyond 2°C. China's infrastructure of connectivity could export high-carbon development to China's remote cities and surrounding countries. But if this is what happens, the Chinese Communist Party will have been responsible for hastening Chinese civilization to the end of history. BR has to amount to more than the quicker export of petroleum to Laos or the building in Kenya of a $2 billion "clean" coal power plant by a Chinese company.[55] In its present form BR is an indeterminate initiative with as much possibility for elevating carbon-based development as not.

The key to China's, and ultimately global capitalism's, survival is for China's BR cities to drive the development of a bio-digital energy paradigm. Partnerships between cities and university networks could contribute much more to the civic and public good dimensions of this paradigm, a claim I expand upon briefly in the next section. Many of the technologies and systems needed for this paradigm are, as we have seen in this chapter, already being tested on a city scale in China. Some of the regulatory principles to support such a paradigm are also present. China's Ministry of Environmental Protection, for example, has formulated principles of eco-environmental protection for the Belt and Road Initiative.[56]

Hundreds of indicators have been developed in China and elsewhere creating a much more detailed picture of what eco-system repletion looks like in terms of air quality, forest coverage, areas of wetlands, water quality of rivers, and underground water. There are also indicators for how we prevent

---

[55] See "Kenya Plans to Build Cleanest Coal-Fired Plant in Africa," May 17, 2018, https://eng. yidaiyilu.gov.cn/qwyw/rdxw/55531.htm.

[56] Office of the Leading Group for Promoting the Belt and Road Initiative, *The Belt and Road Ecological and Environmental Cooperation Plan*, May 2017, https://eng.yidaiyilu.gov.cn/zchj/qwfb/13392.htm.

depletion through technologies such as those for treating urban sewage, industry waste, and the discharge of pollutants.

These systems of indicators reveal something of the scale of the organized exogenous innovation shock that the state has to catalyze if world capitalism is to escape its fossil-fuels-as-usual path. China's city networks, which are being deepened and extended through BR, could function as networks of demand for innovative solutions to problems of drought, air and water pollution, wet-bulb temperatures, and transport congestion, as well as networks of rapid diffusion for the solutions that arrive. We simply do not have the time to rely on slow-moving S-curves of technology diffusion, especially ones made even slower through heavy proprietary protection of the technologies. Finding ways to obtain and diffuse technology is both a priority and problem for the Chinese state, something we see more clearly in the last section of this chapter.

University Networks and City Innovation

China's huge urban markets draw multinationals and their technologies to China, a path of technology acquisition I say more about in the next section. But what of the innovation links between China's universities and cities? To begin with, it is probably fair to say that the role of university networks in city-based systems of innovation remains less explored by innovation studies. Within innovation theory more focus has been put on the interactions between government and industry, industry and the university, and government and university. These strands have been pulled together in the highly influential triple-helix model of innovation.[57] The city-university strand should perhaps also form a part of any organic model of innovation.

Universities are institutions engaged in the search for knowledge. They are also places in cities and towns, their students helping to add urban pep to the areas in which they live. Universities can also develop contextual knowledge for the communities of which they are a part. Functioning as technology incubation sites, they can demonstrate how the future of energy could be very different. UC San Diego, for example, generates 85% of

---

[57] Henry Etzkowitz, "Innovation in Innovation: The Triple Helix of University-Industry-Government Relations," *Social Science Information*, 42 (2003), 293–337.

its energy from various sources on its campus, including a solar network and a fuel cell.[58] The energy is distributed by an advanced micro-grid that is complemented by storage options such as different battery systems and seven million gallons of thermal energy storage. This example also shows how regulatory innovation can help the financing of a different future. UC San Diego was able to draw on different sources of financing to build its clean energy campus, including the Self-Generation Incentive Program, a rebate program run by the California Public Utilities Commission for customers installing distributed energy systems or advanced energy storage technologies.

Campuses and cities, working together within a framework of clean energy regulation, could increase the scaling tempo of an energy revolution. More importantly, I would argue, universities, at least potentially, have much to contribute to deliberation about the design of climate systems solutions for cities and their citizens. Whether Chinese universities can fulfill this role remains an open question.

China remains in search of a balanced model for its universities.[59] For the moment, city innovation approaches in China such as the smart-city concept appear to be dominated by the government-business strand of innovation. Digital service platforms for cities in China are either being developed by government or Chinese firms such as Tencent. An example of the former is Shanghai's "Cloud Citizen" platform. The "City Services Platform" being provided through Tencent's WeChat platform is an example of the latter.[60] Both these platforms have produced a proliferation of services, including apps for finding out about flooded streets after a typhoon and online booking systems for hospital appointments and improving communication between patient and doctor.

In typical fashion China has built a fleet of universities at an astonishing rate—the equivalent of one per week.[61] OECD data shows this has and will continue to bring dramatic changes to the global talent pool. In 2013 China had more 25- to 34-year-olds with a tertiary degree (17%) than any other

[58] See "Clean Energy," https://sustain.ucsd.edu/focus/energy.html.

[59] Gerard A. Postiglione, "Research Universities for National Rejuvenation and Global Influence: China's Search for a Balanced Model," *Higher Education*, 70 (2015), 235–250.

[60] Jiang Yu, Yating Wen, Jing Jin, and Yue Zhang, "Towards a Service-Dominant Platform for Public Value Co-Creation in a Smart City: Evidence from Two Metropolitan Cities in China," *Technological Forecasting & Social Change*, 142 (2019), 168–182.

[61] Andreas Schleicher, "China Opens a New University Every Week," *BBC News*, March 16, 2016, https://www.bbc.com/news/business-35776555.

country belonging to the OECD/G20 grouping.[62] The United States and India each had 14%. China and India both did much better when it came to graduates in science, technology, engineering, and mathematics. In OECD projections, by 2030, 60% of those graduating from these fields will come from China and India. A scientific labor force of this size provides the brute power needed to create the infrastructure for a bio-digital energy paradigm. BR will help China build links with universities in partner countries. The transport corridors of BR will help to build a giant research network among partner countries.

Multinationals and Bright City Lights

One standard complaint about China is that it "forces" companies, according to the European Chamber of Commerce, into technology transfer.[63] Why, if they risk being coerced into giving up their core technologies, do multinationals enter the Chinese market? The answer lies in China's network of city markets. If China is successful, this network will ripple with investment and innovation opportunities, generating demand on a vast scale.

Lying behind the contracts, licensing, and confidentiality agreements to which multinationals and Chinese authorities are parties is a grander informal bargaining process, the ground rules of which both sides well understand. Much of the science and technology vital to China's goal of innovation-based development flows through the private research networks of multinationals. China's best bet for acquiring the knowledge it needs from these networks is to allow multinationals into its city markets and in exchange strike the most favorable terms it can for access to the research and knowledge locked up in those networks.

Multinationals know all about the risks of losing control of a technology they bring to the Chinese market. They manage this risk through secrecy, being careful about who they send to research and development labs in China, and about what they import into or make in China. They are also

---

[62] Organisation of Economic Co-operation and Development, *Education Indicators in Focus*, 31, April 2015, http://www.oecd.org/education/skills-beyond-school/EDIF%2031%20(2015)--ENG--Final.pdf.

[63] European Chamber of Commerce in China, *China Manufacturing 2025: Putting Industrial Policy Ahead of Market Forces*, Beijing, 2017, www.europeanchamber.com.cn.

careful about the technical specifications they reveal to their Chinese partners. The lawyers we interviewed spoke about foreign companies "having to black-box technology" from their Chinese partners. Patents, because they require public disclosure of the invention, are of limited use. The art of secrecy is much more important.

China, in turn, counts upon at least some of these black boxes of multinational secrecy to leak over time. Both sides know the rules of this informal game. China cannot afford to have multinationals stay out of its market. Multinationals cannot afford to stay out of China's market.

An example of this Kabuki-style game can been seen with high-voltage direct current (HVDC) transmission systems. HVDC transmission technology allows for power transmission over distances of many hundreds of kilometers with much lower losses of power than the alternating current alternatives. By upping the voltage, there is a dramatic reduction in the percentage of megawatts lost as heat in the transmission process. HVDC systems have been around for decades, with, for example, the Swiss-Swedish firm ABB creating an HVDC link between the Swedish mainland and Gotland Island in the 1950s.[64] The capacity to bring in high voltages over long distances provides for all sorts of flexibilities in grid planning, including importing power to cities from distant wind farms or solar farms. For this reason HVDC is talked about as the foundation for national or regional supergrids.

Siemens, which has had a remarkably long association with China going back to the late 19th century, had by 2014 completed some 50 HVDC transmission projects around the world, of which about 25% were located in China.[65] The first 800,000-volt transmission link was completed in China in 2009. ABB was contracted to build thousands of kilometers of HVDC power lines to connect the Three Gorges power plant on the Yangtze River to Shanghai and Shenzhen.

A familiar pattern of technology diffusion appears to have occurred with HVDC. The Chinese state made sure the contracts for these massive infrastructure projects contained technology transfer obligations such as co-design between company and Chinese experts, training obligations, and the

---

[64] See ABB, "Introducing HVDC," n.d., http://www04.abb.com/global/seitp/seitp202.nsf/c71c66 c1f02e6575c125711f004660e6/d8e7ec7508118cf7c1257c670040069e/$FILE/Introducing+HVDC. pdf.

[65] See Siemens, "High-Voltage Direct Current Transmission (HVDC)," fact sheet, May 2014, https://www.siemens.com/press/pool/de/feature/2013/energy/2013-08-x-win/factsheet-hvdc-e.pdf.

transfer of knowhow.[66] Chinese companies with strong capabilities in HVDC technology projects such as China XD Group, C-EPRI, and NR Electrics have grown. This in turn has meant less Chinese dependence on foreign technology. It has also produced more competition in both the Chinese and global markets, especially in developing countries where Chinese companies have price advantages.[67] Today China leads in the development of ultrahigh-voltage AC and DC transmission.[68]

China has acted with urgency because, as I argued in the opening chapter, it is in survival governance mode. HVDC is not just a matter of energy security. Electricity will increasingly underpin multilevel security in a world of climate extremes. For example, as water supply from rivers becomes less reliable in particular areas of agricultural importance, electricity to drive irrigation systems drawing water from wells will become important.

Why have high-tech firms like ABB and Siemens entered into arrangements with Chinese state-owned enterprises in which the ultimate goal of the Chinese state is technological self-reliance? There are two answers.

China's power generation and transmission projects are simply too big for multinational firms to ignore. In 2009 the Obama administration set aside $6.5 billion to kick-start the building of power line infrastructure, something desperately needed in the United States to avoid the frequency of blackouts and to take advantage of the potential of the renewable energy revolution.[69] But this sum of money is small compared to the $250 billion plan that the State Grid Corporation of China had developed in 2013 for the upgrade and extension of the transmission network in China.[70] Today China is the global center of ultrahigh-voltage DC projects. This technology is fundamental to the greening of China's electricity supply. In 2017, the 11 ultrahigh-voltage projects already operating in China delivered 64 gigawatts of extra power to East and Central China, as well as "reducing annual coal transportation by

---

[66] See the description of ABB's contract in Leif Englund, Mats Lagerkvist, and Rebati Dass, "HVDC Superhighways for China," *ABB Review*, 4/2003, https://library.e.abb.com/public/9542415dad586f0f c1256fda004aeae5/HVDC%20superhighways%20for%20China.pdf.

[67] See "China Takes HVDC to New Level," June 20, 2013, https://www.powerengineeringint.com/ articles/print/volume-21/issue-6/special-focus-hvdc/china-takes-hvdc-to-new-level.html.

[68] International Electrotechnical Commission, *Grid Integration of Large-Capacity Renewable Energy Sources and Use of Large-Capacity Electrical Energy Storage*, white paper, Geneva, 2012, https://www.iec.ch/whitepaper/pdf/iecWP-gridintegrationlargecapacity-LR-en.pdf, 59–60.

[69] Matthew L. Wald, "How to Build the Supergrid," *Scientific American*, 303 (2010), 56–61.

[70] See "China Takes HVDC to New Level."

120 million tons, CO_2 emission by 340 million tons, SO_2 emission by 577,000 tons, NOx emission by 577,000 tons and smoke dust by 89,000 tons."[71]

By participating in China's technology infrastructure projects, foreign multinationals also have a chance to maintain their technology leadership. This may seem a paradoxical claim, but the opportunity to participate in building thousands of kilometers of transmission offers a multinational firm many opportunities for learning and incremental innovation. It can refine its own systems solutions and packages and continue to compete in the global market of new transmission grids. Staying away from these projects limits its opportunities to solve technical problems and to innovate.

A presence in China also allows a multinational to be part of what may be the most important conversations when it comes to the future of standard-setting. Beginning in the last decade, national standard-setting bodies in the power-sector field such as the US National Institute of Standards and Technology; Japan's Ministry of Economy, Trade and Industry; and regional bodies like the European Committee for Electro-Technical Standardization started the standardization process for smart grids, with the State Grid Corporation of China (fifth in the Global Fortune 500 list for 2019) entering this standard-setting process in 2010.[72]

With over a billion customers the State Grid is now a serious voice in the International Electrotechnical Commission (IEC). No one knows the future of electricity, but the world's largest experiments as to what that future might look like are taking place on a grid with almost a million kilometers of transmission line. One possible future is a globally interconnected power system that draws renewable energy from the most optimal sources and sends it via high-voltage technologies to where it is needed.

This sounds fanciful. But in a 2016 white paper a project team from the IEC led by China's State Grid explored the standard-setting implications of a globally interconnected system.[73] China's construction of a supergrid may be the prelude to something much bigger. US and EU multinationals need to be in the Chinese market because China's power technology revolution may end up not being confined to China. The most important standard-setting

---

[71] State Grid Corporation of China, *State Grid Corporate Social Responsibility Report*, Beijing, 2016, 40.

[72] John A. Mathews and Hao Tan, "The Transformation of the Electric Power Sector in China," *Energy Policy*, 52 (2013), 170–180.

[73] International Electrotechnical Commission, *Global Energy Interconnection*, white paper, Geneva, 2016, https://www.iec.ch/whitepaper/pdf/iecWP-globalenergyinterconnection.pdf.

conversations of which to be a part may be the ones taking place in China about the possibility of a global supergrid. In something of an understatement, one of our interviewees in China working for a US multinational pointed out, "You can't just sell US products to the Chinese market directly. You need to understand Chinese standards."

And, of course, the future of standard-setting for cities having to survive in extreme climate equilibria will be about much more than products. It will be about systems solutions that cross regions and borders, such as high-voltage grids for transporting energy to where it is needed, outsized and cheap systems of renewable energy storage, and global platforms for the trading of energy. This systems level will be the most important level of standard-setting. For some insight into what is needed for cities and climate, running a multitude of experiments on a million miles of transmission line connecting about a sixth of the world's population is a good place to start. This is why multinationals cannot stay out of the Chinese market.

9

India, the Janus Energy Sovereign

A Choice

India faces a profound choice. With the help of its mining and steel companies, India can make coal an "Indo-Pacific" story. Drawing another arbitrary circle on the world map to create a regional identity that enthrones India may be good for Indian political egos. Stroking egos in this way is a low-cost means for the United States to find allies to help its China containment policy. It may also help Donald Trump keep his promises to the US coal industry of a return to the good times. In 2017 India and South Korea were the two biggest importers of US coal in Asia.[1] But treading this path may also tip India into the dynamics of decline, causing it to miss out on the inclusive development growth it has been seeking for its many poor since independence.

To construe the choice facing India as being between sources of fuel to provide the energy it needs for economic development misses the argument being put forward in this book. Choices about energy alternatives are now developmental choices based on the embrace of innovation. Innovation in energy opens the door to a much larger and radical paradigm of innovation in which renewable energy, digital technologies, and bio-technologies converge and integrate, creating possibilities for the support of ecosystems.

Climate change has taken India to an innovation crossroads. It can continue on its well-worn path of a cost-reducing and incremental imitation of mature technologies developed elsewhere or it can choose to leap into the global postcircular economy as an innovator. India's strategy of low-cost imitative innovation has been hugely important, both for it and the world. The most obvious example is in the pharmaceutical sector, where India's generic industry was the key to reducing the price of antiviral treatments for HIV-AIDS, making this treatment affordable for people in developing countries.

---

[1] United States Energy Information Administration, *Quarterly Coal Report*, Washington, DC, April–June 2017, https://www.eia.gov/ccal/production/quarterly/pdf/qcr.pdf. In 2016 India was ranked the third-biggest export destination for the US coal industry, but was very likely second since the Netherlands, which was ranked first, was a destination port for distribution to European countries.

But as I argued in chapter 7, in the context of climate change, step-by-step innovation can kill you. The innovation system will have to deliver much sharper changes in direction if we are to have even a reasonable chance of staying within the 2°C limit. If China does through its cities pull the world into a postcircular economy, then the costs to India of following a carbon-based development model will come in the form of lost opportunities to share in the leadership of technologies to underpin sustainable equilibria between cities and ecosystems. Innovation that reaches poor people through radical price reduction has been a strength of the Indian innovation system. The invention of the iBreastExam, a handheld breast scanner, has made high-quality breast screening affordable for millions of women in India. Screening costs somewhere between $1 and $4 compared to a cost of $20 or more for a mammogram.[2] Indians enjoy some of the lowest prices in the world for telecommunications services. Like China, India has a huge role to play in making innovation accessible to the world's poor.

Up until the last few years one might have been inclined to bet on India staying on its well-worn path, but as we will see, the incentives for India have altered to the point where an innovation path centered on climate sustainability may end up being its choice. India has few countries to which it can compare itself. For India, no country other than China has a comparable population; no country other than China faces a similar scale of urbanization; and no country other than China needs to manage the environmental and health consequences of climate change for such a large population while maintaining economic growth targets. Together China and India have within their borders about 36% of the world's people, many of whom will be disproportionately affected by climate change. But this also heightens the incentives of both countries to move away from an emissions-as-usual approach to economic growth. Whether they recognize it or not, both countries are partners in survival governance.

The Speechmaker

India has always been an eloquent global leader on issues facing developing countries. In the decades of Western dominance of the International Monetary Fund (IMF), the World Bank, and the General Agreement on

---

[2] Sophie Cousins, "A New Way to Detect Breast Cancer," *New York Times*, August 28, 2018, https://www.nytimes.com/2018/08/28/opinion/detect-breast-cancer-developing-countries-asia.html.

Tariffs and Trade (GATT), much rested on India's shoulders as it spoke on behalf of many developing countries about problems of trade and development, access to capital and investment flows, technology transfer, and the use of intellectual property monopolies by developed countries to maintain their power in global capitalism. India took this developmental attitude into the climate change negotiations. There it helped to enshrine recognition of the historical responsibility that developed countries bore for the bulk of greenhouse gas emissions.[3] India's position was clear. Its primary duty was to address the degradations of poverty for hundreds of millions of its citizens.

India's climate negotiators, we learned from our interviews, also saw dissembling in the position of developed-country negotiators. The push for India to adopt climate change technologies was seen as part of an old game in which the West would make more profit from poor countries by selling them patented technologies. Solar technologies were expensive. How would they help hundreds of thousands of villages in India to gain access to affordable energy? Where were the multilateral mechanisms to diffuse climate technologies at a reasonable cost? Calls for the Global South to follow low-carbon growth were hardly credible when developed states continued with offshore drilling for gas and oil in high-risk but ecologically fragile regions such as the Arctic. The occasional whisper of the possibility of exploring Antarctica for oil and gas simply added to the credibility problem of Western negotiators. "Don't come and lecture me on a low carbon growth rate" (former Indian negotiator). In any case, there was no low-carbon development model for India to follow, as no state had ever developed in this way.

From the vantage point of the late 1990s and early 2000s one might have predicted that India would, like China, make use of its very large domestic coal reserves (about 12% of the world total), leaving developed countries to confront the problem of greenhouse gas emissions. Between 1990 and 2012 India more than doubled its per capita emissions, but this doubling came off a low base, and its share of global emissions was roughly one-fifth that of China's.[4] Had India moved at the speed of China to develop its coal resources, the world today would have even less chance of keeping within a 2°C limit.

Over the last decade renewable energy has featured more than one might have anticipated in India's approach to energy security. It has

<hr>

[3] H. Gupta, R. K. Kohli, and A. S. Ahluwalia, "Mapping 'Consistency' in India's Climate Change Position: Dynamics and Dilemmas of Science Diplomacy," *Ambio*, 44 (2015), 592–599, doi:10.1007/s13280-014-0609-5.

[4] International Energy Agency, *Redrawing the Energy-Climate Map*, OECD/IEA, Paris, 2013, 31.

continued to increase its renewable energy targets and is now aiming for 175 gigawatts of renewable energy by 2022.[5] It would be surprising if this target did not increase. As the next section shows, the mounting evidence of what climate change processes are doing to South Asia is providing India with regional incentives for putting its shoulder to the wheel of emissions reduction.

The Geo-Energy Trilemma for India

Innovation as means to economic growth and influence is a major policy theme for the Modi government. Energy security is a pillar on which rest policies of competitiveness through innovation. For the time being, India's energy security depends on fossil fuel. Around 75% of India's energy demand is met by fossil fuels, with coal being the single most important source (44%).[6] This reliance on fossil fuel makes India a major emitter. In 2016 India (7%) was the fourth-largest emitter of CO_2, with China (29%), the United States (14%), and the then 28 members of the EU (9.6%) occupying first, second, and third positions, respectively.[7] However, while the United States had decreased its emissions and China and the EU28 had held theirs constant, India had increased its emissions by some 5%.

Using International Energy Agency (IEA) projections India will be responsible for some 30% of the growth in world energy demand between now and 2040. If India were to meet this demand using its coal resources, it would likely move to becoming the world's largest emitter of CO_2. The decision India makes about the use of its coal resources affects the global risk of going past the 2°C boundary and, as I show shortly, creates risks particular to India. The consequences of global average increases in temperature are not equally distributed around the world.

Modeling the geographically regionalized effects of climate change remains subject to uncertainty, but two things seem clear. First, the adverse effects on ecosystems will be unevenly distributed. Second, it seems increasingly likely that India and the South Asian region will be one of the

---

[5] Ministry of New and Renewable Energy, *Annual Report 2016–2017*, New Delhi, 2017, http://mnre.gov.in/file-manager/annual-report/2016-2017/EN/pdf/1.pdf, 6.

[6] International Energy Agency, *India Energy Outlook*, OECD/IEA, Paris, 2015, 22–23.

[7] G. Janssens-Maenhout, M. Crippa, D. Guizzardi, M. Muntean, E. Schaaf, J. G. J. Olivier, J. A. H. W. Peters, and K. M. Schure, *Fossil CO_2 and GHG Emissions of All World Countries*, Publications Office of the European Union, Luxembourg, 2017, doi:10.2760/709792, JRC107877, 5.

worst-affected regions.[8] The models for this region suggest increased warming and a pattern of declining monsoonal rain with more extreme rain events. Existing rain-fed agricultural systems will likely face the double blows of more droughts and more floods.

There is less reason to argue in New Delhi over the "right" discount rate to apply to present climate policy than there is in Washington, because of the evidence of the regional consequences of climate change. The Indian planning commission, before its abolition in 2015, pointed out in its 12th Five-Year Plan that the climate challenge for Indian agriculture, upon which the rural population depended for its livelihood, had well and truly arrived in the form of declining annual rainfall and increasing temperature variability.[9] Increased temperatures in the region have been linked to declining rice yields and stagnating wheat harvests. This climate future is not just hurrying toward India. It also threatens Bangladesh and Pakistan.

Flooding in the low-lying coastal areas of Bangladesh is a regular event. The number of people forced to move is hard to comprehend. In 2007 the monsoonal floods in Bangladesh displaced around eight million people. The capital, Dhaka, provides an example of why the technologies being tested in China's experimental city programs are needed in South Asia and needed quickly. The city is constantly affected by flooding, yet paradoxically urbanization is causing water shortages. China's sponge-city concept in which the smart city stores water matters to Dhaka's future. One-third of the city does not have piped water, most of its wastewater goes untreated, and 40% of its garbage is not collected.[10] It is one of the most unlivable cities in the world, but more than 18 million people live in the city and its surrounding areas. More people are moving there, not wanting to stay in Bangladesh's coastal areas.

The Sunny Side of India's Energy Security

India's engagement with renewable energy goes back to a 1981 initiative in the form of the Commission for Additional Sources of Energy.[11] A department

---

[8] The likely effects are discussed in Intergovernmental Panel on Climate Change, *Climate Change 2014: Synthesis Report. Contribution of Working Groups I, II and III to the Fifth Assessment Report of the Intergovernmental Panel on Climate Change*, IPCC, Geneva, 2014.

[9] Planning Commission, Government of India, *Twelfth Five-Year Plan (2012–2017), Economic Sectors*, Volume II, Sage Publications India, New Delhi, 2013, 3.

[10] See World Bank, "Toward a Livable Dhaka," https://blogs.worldbank.org/endpovertyinsouthasia/toward-livable-dhaka.

[11] Rhythm Singh, "Energy Sufficiency Aspirations of India and the Role of Renewable Resources: Scenarios for the Future," *Renewable and Sustainable Energy Reviews*, 81 (2018), 2783–2795, 2783.

devoted to renewable energy policy has existed since that time. During the decade of the 2000s, India began to assess climate change from a developmental perspective, realizing that its ambitions for inclusive and sustainable growth were now increasingly hostage to changing climate patterns. The India that had gone into the climate change negotiations of the early 1990s with an agenda based on developed-country responsibility for the global injustice of climate change was, by the end of the next decade, committing to voluntary targets. At Copenhagen in 2009 India pledged a target of a 20% to 25% reduction in emissions intensity of its GDP by 2020, based on a 2005 baseline. By the time of the adoption of the Paris Agreement in December 2015 India was doing more on emission reduction targets. Its nationally determined contribution under the Paris Agreement included targets of a 33% to 35% reduction in its GDP emissions intensity by 2030, a 40% increase in installation capacity for electric power generation from non–fossil fuel sources, and a carbon sink of some 2.5 to 3 billion tonnes. Climate Tracker, which evaluates the climate and energy policies of countries over time, described India's Paris commitments as 2°C compatible, suggesting India could also be in a realistic position to implement the safer 1.5°C target [12]

The foundations for India's escalating mitigation commitment can be found in its National Action Plan on Climate Change of 2008. This plan launched eight different national missions in areas such as the Himalayan ecosystem, water, sustainable agriculture, energy efficiency, and solar energy. Another four missions on health, waste energy generation, wind generation, and coastal areas were added to the list in 2014. As the various committees, expert groups, and government departments began their work under the various missions, a bleak probability began to emerge from the evidence. Even though India had in historical terms been only a minor contributor to climate change, it would as a country suffer the most from the direction of change in the climate system. The risk of deaths from heat and tropical diseases such as malaria, yellow fever, and dengue would be much greater in a climate-changing India than they would be in developed countries.

India's national missions, including the rapid intensification of its efforts on the renewable energy front, reflect a basic realization on the part of the Indian government. Unilateral action by India to reduce its own emissions is, by virtue of the potential scale of those emissions and their reflexive bite, a rational mission to undertake.

---

[12] See http://climateactiontracker.org/countries/india.html.

India's size; its abundance of sunlight; the off-grid uses of solar technology; the lower environmental impact of solar compared to the mining, transportation, and burning of coal; the declining cost curves of solar technologies; and the potential of solar to reduce India's import dependence on fossil fuel all make for a compelling case for solar. Solar India, the national solar mission, was launched in 2010. It outlines an energy policy and an industrialization policy aimed at making India a hub for innovation and manufacturing of solar technologies. The target of 20,000 megawatts of installed solar capacity by 2022 was upgraded in 2015 to a target of 100,000 megawatts.[13]

Solar energy has also become part of India's international coalition and institution-building agenda. At the Paris Conference in 2015 India, together with France, led the formation of the International Solar Alliance (ISA). With its secretariat headquarters in India, the aim of the ISA is to draw together sun-rich countries between the Tropic of Cancer and the Tropic of Capricorn into an alliance dedicated to turning this solar wealth into affordable and secure energy systems.[14]

One can see this kind of effort as a small time exercise compared to the existing organizational depth and wealth of fossil fuel industries like oil and coal. What, one might ask, can an international secretariat in the city of Gurugram, India—a city most people outside India have not heard of—expect to achieve, given the nation's small initial investment of $30 million?[15] Another way to see this is as a networking exercise in which the network effects, much like the bulk of an iceberg, are not that visible. Each new renewable energy coalition, player, or network can connect to existing networks that in turn produce more information about investment opportunities in solar energy and therefore generate more uncertainty for potential investors in fossil fuel. Investors, like cattle before a coming electrical storm, grow ever more restless. The ISA has signed joint financial partnership declarations with the World Bank, European Bank for Reconstruction and Development, and the European Investment Bank.[16]

---

[13] See http://www.mnre.gov.in/solar-mission/jnnsm/introduction-2/.

[14] See http://isolaralliance.org/Index.aspx.

[15] Arthur Neslen, "India Unveils Global Solar Alliance of 120 Countries at Paris Climate Summit," *The Guardian*, November 30, 2015, https://www.theguardian.com/environment/2015/nov/30/india-set-to-unveil-global-solar-alliance-of-120-countries-at-paris-climate-summit.

[16] See "ISA-EBRD Joint Declaration of Financial Partnership," November 2, 2017, http://isolaralliance.org/docs/EBRD-ISA%20Press%20Release.pdf.

The Dark Side of the Sun

India's solar ambitions today are well beyond what one might have expected at the beginning of the 21st century. But energy bean counters might argue that India's efforts on solar are part of the additional energy it needs because of the projected growth in its demand. While the growth in solar might lessen some deployment of coal and gas, India will remain reliant on large-scale utilization of fossil fuel, including coal. Aside from the growth in demand, two other potential limitations exist on the extent to which solar power can replace fossil fuel.

For starters, whatever the theoretical maximum of a solar photovoltaic power plant over a year, the actual performance is something less (known as the *capacity utilization factor*). Where one ends up in projections about the contribution of solar to India's energy demands depends on assumptions about solar's capacity utilization factors. Cautious assumptions produce scenarios in which India has little choice but to look to fossil fuels for energy security, or alternatively it has to do much more on the innovation front in order to increase the supply of energy from renewables.[17] Very different scenarios emerge for India when models of its renewable energy generation incorporate storage technologies, especially battery storage for solar photovoltaics. Under some scenarios, India's power generation could be driven entirely by renewables.[18]

Another constraint on the emergence of a Solar India lies in India's regulatory capability. The possibility of switching to mainly renewable energy depends on regulatory design, intervention, compliance management, and ultimately a constant political will to drive the change. In democracies a constancy of will requires a high degree of bipartisanship.

The original 2010 plan for the national solar mission introduced regulatory ideas for making India a global solar leader, including mandatory renewable purchase obligations for India's utilities (distribution utilities would be obliged to purchase a minimum amount of renewable energy) and renewable energy certificates that allowed trading among India's states.

Aiming to be a global leader in solar would be a hugely ambitious goal for any country. Technologies, no matter how great their promise, are born

---

[17] Singh, "Energy Sufficiency Aspirations of India and the Role of Renewable Resources."

[18] Ashish Gulagi, Dmitrii Bogdanov, and Christian Breyer, "The Demand for Storage Technologies in Energy Transition Pathways toward 100% Renewable Energy for India," *Energy Procedia*, 135 (2017), 7–50.

into the real world of imperfect institutions, scarce resources, and vested interests. In 2007 the IEA reported that some 40% of India's population were without access to electricity, adding that India's Five-Year Plans had failed to meet their targets for more power generation capacity.[19] India's state utility companies are cash strapped, failing to meet the existing energy needs of their customers. The utilities are mainly interested in purchasing cheap electricity from coal generators. The renewable purchase obligations being set by India's state electricity regulatory commissions are simply another source of financial stress for utilities. One could turn a blind eye to the failure of utility companies to meet their obligations to purchase renewable energy. But this would send the wrong signal to banks in India when it comes to project financing for renewables. Indian banks, which are especially conservative on project financing, have little reason to fund solar power projects if the developers of those projects are unlikely to be paid by debt-ridden state utilities. Other solar policy measures, such as renewable energy certificates— which have been introduced in countries such as the United Kingdom and Australia—depend on a high degree of regulatory oversight.

Some progress is apparent on the regulation of these problems. A payment security mechanism has been established to ensure that solar developers are paid if state utilities cannot pay. Electricity from coal and solar is being bundled together to increase solar's cost competitiveness.[20] For the purpose of finding capital to back renewable energy innovation, the government in 2010 passed rules imposing a clean energy cess (a special tax) on coal, the amount raised to be put into a clean energy fund. The rate started at around 70 cents per tonne. By 2016 it was over $6 per tonne, accelerating the creation of a pool of public money with which to fund a renewable energy revolution. Money to fund clean energy projects was being granted, albeit at a slow pace. But then in 2017 the hands of politics found other uses for the fund. The Modi government diverted the revenue from the fund (close to $9 billion) to compensate various states within India for losses they had suffered as a result of reforms to goods and services taxes. The government also committed future cess revenues of some $15 billion to the compensation package.[21]

---

[19] International Energy Agency, *World Energy Outlook 2007*, OECD/IEA, Paris, 2007 (hereinafter WEO 2007), 522.

[20] Ministry of New and Renewable Energy, *Annual Report 2016–2017*, 53, http://mnre.gov.in/file-manager/annual-report/2016-2017/EN/pdf/1.pdf.

[21] Megan Darby, "India Diverts $25 Million Away from Clean Energy Fund," *Climate Home News*, July 24, 2017, http://www.climatechangenews.com/2017/07/24/india-diverts-25-billion-away-clean-energy-fund/.

Where this leaves India's ambition to be a global solar power is hard to say. If the goal is simply to hit a gigawatt target for solar, India can look to investors such as pension funds and investment banks to provide capital for solar projects. In 2017 there were reports of significant levels of investment activity in India's solar energy market, with Dutch fund manager APG, and the private equity arms of Goldman Sachs, JPMorgan, and Morgan Stanley all mentioned as having entered the market.[22] Other sources of finance in the Indian market include solar bonds.

Investors will include solar power development projects in India as part of their portfolios if those projects offer an acceptable return. However, investors will not fund risky research and development. Looking to investors to fund solar projects is a strategy of energy diversification rather than innovation-led transformation. The search for new knowledge is uncertain and difficult to appropriate even if found. Markets generally do not allocate sufficient resources to discovery processes.

If the opportunity cost of the Modi government's decision to divert money from the clean energy fund is a loss of strong support for R&D funding for solar and other renewable technologies, this is likely to set back the goals envisaged by a Solar India. The government is the biggest funder of R&D in India, with the central government responsible for around 45% of expenditure.[23] An important part of the original national solar mission was developing a low-cost but high-quality Indian solar manufacturing industry, one no longer highly dependent on imports and access to foreign intellectual property. Without a serious R&D program, India would simply not develop the capacity to improve on the innovations of others in the solar field, let alone make significant leaps in the technology. India's ability to embrace and reduce the price of disruptive renewable technologies would also be compromised by a failure to invest sufficiently in R&D.

The most important actor in India's plans to build solar generation capacity is China. India is weak in module manufacturing. It imports close to 90% of its needs, most of it from China. China has about 60% of annual world production of solar modules.[24]

[22] Devidutta Tripathy, "Global Pension Funds Warm to India's Solar Power Ambitions," *Reuters*, April 30, 2017 https://www.reuters.com/article/us-india-solar-analysis/global-pension-funds-warm-to-indias-solar-power-ambitions-idUSKBN17W051.

[23] Department of Science and Technology, Government of India, *Research and Development Statistics at a Glance, 2017–2018*, New Delhi, December 2017, http://www.nstmis-dst.org/statistics-Glance-2017-18-2.pdf.

[24] International Energy Agency, *Renewables 2017: Analysis and Forecasts to 2022*, OECD/IEA, Paris, 2017, 3.

Coal remains a part of India's insurance planning for energy. The 12th Five-Year Plan (2012–2017) called for ultra-super-critical or super-critical plants to replace sub-critical coal-based power plants. One could, it was argued, more quickly reduce emissions through efficient coal plants than one could reduce emissions by replacing them with renewable energy plants.[25]

For the time being, India appears to be on a path of coal reform that the IEA suggested back in 2007 when it pointed out that Coal India Limited should be broken up to avoid the risks flowing from its position of monopoly dominance.[26] Coal India Limited emerged as a state-owned enterprise in 1975 as a result of a national takeover of private coal companies. The coal-producing subsidiaries operating as part of Coal India produce around 84% of India's coal.[27] India has, much as the IEA has been urging, turned its national coal industry into a private commercial operation.[28] Coal India Limited lost its marketing monopoly in 2015, with private companies being allowed to bid for mines and sell into the free market. The Indian government approved an auction method in 2018 and opened coal mining to foreign investment in 2019.

India, by targeting the efficiency of its domestic coal mining operations, is focusing on the energy security point of its energy trilemma, since making extensive use of its domestic coal supplies reduces its need to import. Energy import dependency continues to loom large as a problem in the minds of policy-makers.

But these same policy-makers harbor worries about coal as renewables race on to new cost-reduction frontiers—worries that "the over $1 billion annual investment being made by [Coal India Limited], in raising its production capability, is not left stranded."[29] India went slow on solar because it delivered expensive electricity. It worried about the import implications of solar. Its manufacturers, went the thinking, could not compete on quality with overseas players like Germany and certainly not on price with China. But when photovoltaic auction prices fall from $250 per megawatt hour to $40, ministers pay attention.[30] An energy security based on renewables would solve many of India's problems. A rapid transition to renewables would allow India's

---

[25] Planning Commission, Government of India, *Twelfth Five-Year Plan (2012–2017): Faster, More Inclusive and Sustainable Growth*, Volume I, Sage Publications India, New Delhi, 2013, 119.

[26] WEO 2007, 521.

[27] See https://www.coalindia.in/en-us/company/aboutus.aspx.

[28] International Energy Agency, *India 2020 Energy Policy Review*, IEA, France, 2020, 237–238.

[29] National Institution for Transforming India (NITI Aayog), *Draft National Energy Policy*, New Delhi, 2017, 35, http://niti.gov.in/writereaddata/files/new_initiatives/NEP-ID_27.06.2017.pdf.

[30] International Energy Agency, *World Energy Outlook 2017*, OECD/IEA, Paris, 2017, 222.

indigenous groups to peacefully occupy and develop land according to their traditional knowledge systems rather than engaging in deadly conflicts to defend it from mining companies. The Indian government would not have to worry about what the Washington police think of its oil imports from Iran.

The City Innovation Pathway in India: Is It Available?

India, I suggested at the beginning of this chapter, has a choice to make about the development paradigm it wants to support. The consequences of its choice will reverberate globally. Climate change will disproportionately impact the huge populations of South Asia, providing India with strong incentives to participate in developing a bio-digital energy paradigm. The security benefits of this paradigm will last much longer than anything fossil fuel can deliver. India, like China, is also undergoing a monumental urban transformation. Its growth potential in terms of urbanization is, by one estimate, the largest in the world. Between 2014 and 2050 India is projected to increase its urban population by 404 million while China will add 292 million.[31]

Like China, India could use cities to steer technological development down the pathways of a bio-digital energy paradigm and ultimately into the construction of a global postcircular economy. The world's two most populous nations could harness the endogeneity of cities in this way and dislodge world capitalism from a path that is taking it past the 2°C mark. In the final two sections of this chapter, I want to offer some reasons why this admittedly optimistic scenario has more chance to unfold than one might first think. There is also a probability linkage at work here. The more successful China is with its city projects and experiments, the more likely it is that India will study and adapt those city models to its own context.

The links between science, technology, and development have always been a focus in India. After independence, India's parliament recognized the importance of science to the country's developmental aspirations. In 1958 the parliament passed a resolution that spoke of the need to invest in science if India was to close the widening gap between "advanced and backward" countries.[32] By the 1980s India had massively increased its scientific labor force,

---

[31] United Nations, Department of Economic and Social Affairs, Population Division, *World Urbanization Prospects: The 2014 Revision, Highlights*, New York, 2014, 1.

[32] Pushpa M. Bhargava and Chandana Chakrabarti, "Of India, Indians, and Science," *Daedalus*, 118 (1989), 353–368, 361.

with only the United States and the Soviet Union ahead of it. However, India's goal of increasing its technological self-reliance was a mixed and debated achievement, with some emphasizing India's continued dependence on the insecure channels of foreign technology transfer.[33] Fears about the increasing difficulty for developing countries of obtaining technology from abroad saw India and Brazil lead the opposition in the 1980s against the US–EU agenda of globalizing the intellectual property rights regime. Today, global intellectual property regimes are a fact of life with which India has to work.

A focus on growing strong indigenous technology capabilities has been a constant in India's national aspirations. Writing many years ago on India's future, Jawaharlal Nehru identified two reasons for India's embrace of deep industrialization. It was indispensable to "liquidating" poverty in India. Just as importantly, no country could do without technology and industrialization, for without technological development it would succumb to domination from outside forces, existing as a "colonial appendage."[34]

Governments have come and gone in India, but their policy frameworks have consistently echoed Nehru's observations about the necessity of technological development in order to reduce poverty and avoid rule by others. Elected in 2014 the Modi government has articulated an agenda of risky, entrepreneur-led innovation. The National Institution for Transforming India (NITI Aayog), which functions as the Modi government's high-level policy think tank, has produced various big-picture policy documents outlining ambitious innovation goals for India. These include advances in electric vehicles, battery storage manufacturing, the deployment of artificial intelligence, and clean fuel. Under Modi, India's innovation ambitions stretch well and truly beyond the success of Bangalore's information technology industry.

One of Modi's campaign promises in the 2014 election was the building of 100 new smart cities. The Smart Cities Mission, as it is now known, has focused to date on retrofitting and redeveloping existing cities rather than building new ones. Twenty cities were selected under the first phase of the program in 2016. India's growth in cities offers opportunities for new directions in innovation. A good example is India's proposal to make itself a global center of battery manufacturing for electric vehicle demand. If India were to stick to city transport networks based on fossil fuels, it would simply increase its oil import bill; the nation imports around 80% of its oil needs. Outside of an

---

[33] Aqueil Ahmad, "Science and Technology in Development: Policy Options for India and China," *Economic and Political Weekly*, 13 (December 23–30, 1978), 2079–2090.
[34] Jawaharlal Nehru, *The Discovery of India*, Oxford University Press, Delhi, 1985, 407.

innovation framework, the needs of India's rising urban population simply intensify its reliance on oil imports. Within an innovation framework, this rising urban population becomes an innovation opportunity—a chance to design a transport system to satisfy people's demands for clean air, less noisy cities, and cheap transport prices, and not to require a circus balancing act on a two-wheeled scooter with other family members.

The sheer size of India's city populations creates scaling opportunities for Indian innovation, just as China's city populations do for that country, with one important difference. At $2,000, India's GDP per capita is about a quarter of China's. The emphasis in India has to be on people's access to innovation or what is sometimes referred to as *frugal innovation*. Frugal innovation can be thought of as innovation that meets poor people's needs and budgets. Back in 2010 *The Economist* identified a number of frugal innovation successes in India, such as the hand-held electrocardiogram that had reduced the cost of an ECG to $1, and a $24 water filter made from rice husks.[35] Since then, frugal innovation has gained more recognition in the innovation literature. It is often seen as a way for corporations to rethink their approach to innovation by targeting populations characterized by need, high volume, and resource constraints.[36]

India, with its successful high-tech experience in sectors such as pharmaceuticals, aerospace, and information technology—along with its large population of poor people—could combine high technology with the value of frugality. Innovation in the bio-digital energy paradigm must help the many millions of people in India who are suffering ill health because, for example, they live in small, closed spaces and use cow dung cakes or wood as fuel. Clean air and clean energy are more urgent than speedy electric sports cars. If priority is to be given to the former rather than the latter, India will have to champion frugal innovation for the poverty-stricken.

Planning Innovation in India—Some Success Stories

For India, the challenge of the city innovation pathway lies in the nature of its planning processes. China, as we saw in the last chapter, is running

---

[35] Brett Ryder, "First Break All the Rules: The Charms of Frugal Innovation," *The Economist*, April 15, 2010, https://www.economist.com/special-report/2010/04/15/first-break-all-the-rules.

[36] Navi Radjou and Jaideep Prahbu, "What Frugal Innovators Do," *Harvard Business Review*, December 10, 2014, https://hbr.org/2014/12/what-frugal-innovators-do.

experiments at the city level and with large numbers of cities. The importance of a nexus between cities and innovation is recognized in India. Moreover, India's cities cannot continue along their present pollution paths. India has 22 out of the 30 cities with the world's worst air pollution.[37]

Perhaps the real question is whether Indian planning processes can deliver the kind of coordination and scale needed for the city innovation pathway to work. The bio-digital energy paradigm needs steering and funding from the state. Paradigms of innovation, especially since the second half of the 20th century, require government to play a role in research and development.

As I argued in chapter 2, China deploys a pressure-driving mechanism to unite, for the purposes of goal implementation, the many parts and fragments of its central and provincial bureaucracies. India's bureaucratic system has no obvious equivalent to the pressure-driving mechanism. The Indian state has also moved away from five-year plans, the Planning Commission having been replaced in 2015 by the NITI Aayog.

But even if India today does not have China's overt processes of central planning and intervention, the Indian state retains a development pragmatism based on a long experience of negotiating with multinational capital. In the pharmaceutical sector, the Indian state has been heavily involved in adjusting the rules of the patent system. Prior to the creation of the World Trade Organization (WTO) in 1995, India kept pharmaceutical products out of patentability so as to ensure that its generic industry had access to pharmaceutical molecules invented by multinationals. After the establishment of the WTO, India had to comply with its rules on intellectual property. India is often characterized as having adopted a more neoliberal orientation in the early 1990s, but this ideological switch did not quite express itself in the Indian state's approach to patent law. It took full advantage of the WTO rules to delay patent protection for pharmaceuticals and then introduced a rule in its patent system that made evergreening of pharmaceutical patents by multinationals a much more difficult trick to pull. Evergreening refers to gaming behavior in which the patent owner continues to tweak a known molecule in order to obtain a succession of patents around it, thereby stifling market competition. Developmental pragmatism, as well as long experience with foreign multinationals, led India into a rule-setting approach that recognized the interests of its generic industry.

[37] See "World Most Polluted Cities," https://www.airvisual.com/world-most-polluted-cities.

The Indian software industry is another example of government interventions over the decades producing a clear sectoral success. As Saraswati explains, the pitifully low penetration of computers in India in the 1960s produced in the 1970s policies aimed at national self-sufficiency.[38] Computing was simply too important in military and civilian terms for any other goal. The government established the Department of Electronics in 1970 and began negotiations with IBM to obtain a majority equity holding in its Indian subsidiary. While this failed in the case of IBM, causing the company to leave India in 1977, the negotiation for an equity holding was successful with International Computers Limited. Other policies, including the creation of public-sector computer companies and a software export scheme, were put in place in the 1970s. These were followed in the next decade with supporting policies, such as the provision of key telecommunications infrastructure to allow Indian software firms to export software via satellite back to US firms like Texas Instruments. Some policies of intervention—for instance, software technology parks that gave firms access to subsidies in areas such as energy—not only continued but expanded in India's neoliberal era. As Saraswati suggests, neoliberalism and the developmental state are conceptual distractions in understanding the Indian state's actions in the software sector. It is better to look at what the state did: it clearly intervened and kept on intervening, adjusting the manner of its interventions as globalization delivered new contexts within which to reach its goal of a globally capable industry. The same can be said of India's approach to its pharmaceutical industry.

Other sectoral innovation successes in India have received less attention but also show the importance of the Indian state. One example is the rise of the Tata Steel group to become one of the largest steel producers in the world. Our interviews with Tata Steel revealed the positive impact of energy efficiency schemes such as Perform, Achieve, Trade (PAT) that the Bureau of Energy Efficiency has developed under India's Mission for Enhanced Energy Efficiency for energy-intensive industries. There is a PAT scheme for the Indian steel industry. India's National Metallurgical Laboratory, which Nehru inaugurated in 1950, formed a decades-long research partnership with Tata Steel. These and other partnerships have helped Tata modernize

---

[38] J. Saraswati, "The Indian IT Industry and Neo-Liberalism: The Irony of a Mythology," *Third World Quarterly*, 29 (2008), 1139–1152.

its plants and adopt more efficient processes for making coke, as well as capturing and reusing the thermal energy from these processes (known as *coke dry quenching*).

An Indian City-Innovation Pathway: Is It Doable?

The city-innovation pathway that leads to a global bio-digital energy paradigm requires the coordination of converging technologies to produce integrated systems solutions for cities. China's smart cities, sponge cities, eco-cities, and other experimental cities are all large-scale test-beds for the feasibility and workability of systems solutions for cities moving into new climate equilibria. China's city markets have proved irresistible for high-tech multinationals. They have entered these markets, with the Chinese state playing the role of monopsony negotiator against the monopoly power of multinationals, in order to maximize the chances of the Chinese state acquiring the technology.

In a world of smart grids, artificial intelligence–driven trading of surplus energy produced by consumers, and emission trading schemes likely to be a prerequisite for entry into trade, does it make sense for India to cling to simple linear projections in which coal leads and renewable energy remains a bit actor? India has to decide whether it will be the stranded incremental innovator, fiddling with minor improvements to fossil fuel technologies it has absorbed from elsewhere or whether it will take the opportunity of its city networks to place itself in the middle of a bio-digital energy paradigm.

India would have to bargain with the high-tech multinationals that could build systems solutions for India's cities. India is no stranger to hard bargaining when it comes to its economy. It has a longer history than China of negotiating with multinational capital; it ran very tough lines in the Uruguay Round of trade negotiations; and it can, as we have seen, point to sectoral successes in pharmaceuticals and software. These are also the sectors in which India has recorded an improvement in innovation since the early 1990s.[39]

---

[39] S. Mani, "Is India Becoming More Innovative since 1991? Some Disquieting Features," *Economic and Political Weekly*, 44, no. 46 (November 14, 2009), 41–51.

However, sectoral or niche thinking will not be enough for India to be a strong innovation leader in a new bio-digital energy paradigm. The construction of a city innovation pathway requires government coordination and planning of a different order compared to a sector-by-sector innovation strategy. As China has shown, constructing a city innovation pathway requires an extensive but managed conditional openness to high-tech multinational investment in which the state maximizes the chances of its local enterprises acquiring and scaling the technology. India, like China, has to use the opportunities of its cities to draw in more of the technologies that it needs, and then use its experience as a price innovator to make those technologies affordable for its citizens.

India is unlikely to be able to move at China's pace, at least in the early phases of constructing a city innovation pathway. Before that approach can work in India, much more will have to be done to create more representative and accountable local governments. Bribes for the delivery of basic services have to be eliminated. India's democracy has not prevented it from growing its own version of systemic corruption, one in which its many levels of local government and bureaucracy provide officials with chances to extract money for their services.[40] Clean local councils are needed to create clean livable cities.

India's democracy offers it advantages in debates about how cities should shape the future. More narratives about the appropriate course of India's development compete for attention in India's democracy. Spotlights on corporate behavior shine more brightly in India than they do in China because India is a place rich in civil society networks. Even powerful companies can lose when drawn into the "activist lair" in India (interview). These networks can win battles, as they did in 2017 when the South Korean steelmaker Posco withdrew, after more than a decade of resistance by farmers over land confiscation, from its proposed $12 billion steel plant to be located in the east of India in Odisha.

India's civil society networks of resistance have the potential to become constructive forces of cooperation if India chooses to move in the direction of a bio-digital energy paradigm. They offer the possibility of local dialogue and knowledge about how the technologies of the paradigm might best be

---

[40] Yan Sun and Michael Johnston, "Does Democracy Check Corruption? Insights from China and India," *Comparative Politics*, 42 (2009), 1–19.

adapted to India's local contexts. India is also a country steeped in indigenous people's traditional knowledge of ecosystems. There is much more to this culture than knowing about the medicinal value of plant species. Civil society and indigenous groups could be partners in creating a deliberative system around the transition to a bio-digital energy paradigm.

10

Survival Governance

The Argument

Survival governance, we need to remind ourselves, is governance motivated by the desire to save the ecosystems upon which life depends. Climate change, because it targets the earth system in which all ecosystems are housed, has turned survival governance into a global project. Chances to manage this project successfully continue to be lost. The main hope now lies in opening up technology frontiers belonging to a bio-digital energy paradigm. Cities can bring this paradigm to life. China's experimental cities offer a means by which to increase our chances of positive survival governance. In turn, China's chances of success with its cities depend heavily on managing two relationships: one with multinational capital and the other with the United States. In more abstract terms, China has to become much more directive about commodity accumulation in world capitalism. It has to overcome the innovation agnosticism that I described in chapter 1 as characterizing the United States' leadership of capitalism. This means closing down innovative circuits of capital in the form of the fossil fuel industry, as well as opening new ones with the promise of better returns. We begin with some of Karl Marx's observations about commodity accumulation.

The Blindness of Commodity Accumulation

For Marx the wealth of capitalist societies presents itself as the "immense accumulation of commodities."[1] Starting with this fundamental characteristic of capitalism, Marx begins a long analytical probe into the qualities of the commodity. Central to his analysis is a distinction between the use value of a

---

[1] Karl Marx, *Capital*, Volume 1 (tr. Samuel Moore and Edward Aveling, ed. Friedrich Engels), Modern Library, New York, 1906, republished Dover Publications, New York, 2011, 41. Hereinafter Marx, *Capital*, volume 1.

commodity and its exchange value. The wealth of capitalism lies in the endless accumulation of commodities with exchange value. Things can have a use value without exchange value, as in the case of air or the making of something for one's own consumption. The capitalist, Marx drives home again and again, is not interested in use values, but in the "passionate chase after exchange value."[2] By placing into circulation more and more commodities with exchange value, capitalism creates the basis for the expansion of capital.

From Marx's analysis, capitalism emerges as a system that is indifferent to sources of commodity accumulation, as well as being blind to the directions in which processes of commodity accumulation are taking it. The expansion of the system is based on individual capitalists constantly creating new circuits of capital. Each capitalist is part of a system of ferocious competition in which the search for new exchange value opportunities is a matter of survival. Even though the system is programmed to pursue exchange value above all, some restraints do emerge for commodity circulation. Restrictions are put in place, for example, on manufacturers' use of child labor in factories. More generally, legislation is enacted to improve the safety and health of workers. The capitalist responds to the cost of improving laboring conditions through innovation. Marx, better than any other theorist of the 19th century, captures the crucial importance of innovation to capitalism's long-term development and adaptability. Through the machine, capitalism starts the process of radical improvements in labor productivity. Knowledge and technology continually reform technical processes of production, changing the way in which labor operates in the production process. The machine age, and by extrapolation the age of machine intelligence, enables the capitalist to launch new cycles of commodity accumulation.

On the face of it, a system driven by the never-ending pursuit of commodities and innovation toward that end might be able to deal with the threat of climate change. The system looks to all potential sources of commodity expansion. It is also a system of innovation revolutions. Existing systems of technical production are never seen as final, and individual capitalists are constantly looking for new and more profitable forms of commodity circulation. Out of this search for new exchange values emerges the possibility of a greening of capitalism, a capitalism in which it is better to commodify nature than to use it as a free input to underpin older commodity cycles of industrial capitalism. Marx himself, it is worth noting, sounded a skeptical note about

[2] Marx, *Capital*, volume 1, 171.

the sustainability of a "capitalistic agriculture" employing science and industrial techniques. This kind of agriculture, he claimed, would ruin the "lasting sources" of soil fertility.[3]

There is, however, a third attribute of capitalism that pushes against the rapid transition out of fossil fuels and into a bio-digital energy economy. In capitalism, individual capitalists and industry pursue cycles of capital and commodity reproduction for as long as it is profitable to do so, with innovation playing a major role in determining profitability. Innovation not only opens the door to new industries, it also creates new technology frontiers for existing industries. The oil and gas industry has, through a steady process of innovation in fracking technologies from the mid-19th century onward, expanded fossil fuel reserves. Companies like Shell continue to invest heavily in automation with the aim of reducing their pool of labor to a small but highly skilled labor force serving a fleet of well-drilling automatons. Innovation in the fossil fuel industries keeps opening up technology frontiers, which remain in play as long as they offer the possibility of capital expansion. Individual capitalist states, which depend upon these circuits of capital, do not have incentives to manage out of existence these innovative circuits of commodity accumulation. Capitalism's response to date to the exponential functions of climate change has not been an innovation revolution in energy. Instead there has been a long, drawn-out transformation in which old circuits of fossil fuel capital have reorganized, continued innovating, and delayed the revolution in renewables. Capitalism's gravedigger arrives clad as a fossil fuel miner.

States and Survival Governance

In 2018 the Intergovernmental Panel on Climate Change (IPCC) released its Special Report on Global Warming of 1.5°C. The report's clear message is that every fraction of warming matters. Governments and industry together have triggered giant cascades of earth system change and continue knowingly to accelerate this change. Looming before today's governments are choices about how much irreversibility and runaway climate change they are prepared to risk. Their choices will define the ecological endowment of the present younger generation and their children. Actors, whether state or

---

[3] Marx, *Capital*, volume 1, 555.

non-state, that understand the arriving scale of change—and that are pulling what levers of governance they have available in order to mitigate or adapt to this change—are engaged in survival governance. All over the world, many thousands of non-state actors are drawing together or are being drawn into networks to produce a living and global circuitry of action on climate change. An example of an increasingly influential non-state transnational network is the fossil fuel divestment movement.[4] Made up of mainly climate non-governmental organizations (NGOs), its message of divestment from fossil fuels targets large institutional investors. According to 350.org, the insurance sector now has fossil fuel divestment commitments amounting to over $3 trillion.[5] Overall, almost a thousand investors with over $6 trillion in assets have made divestment pledges.

Survival governance in the context of climate change is a matter of responding with techniques of intervention to interlinked processes in which we are inescapably enclosed. *Survival governance* is the right label because, as the IPCC and others make clear, the survival of large populations, human and nonhuman, is at stake. A state can be said to be in *full survival governance mode* if it has prioritized the climate change part of the trilemma, mobilized its fiscal and financial regulatory power for the purpose of creating the infrastructure of survival governance, and is rapidly moving to abandon the sunk costs of an energy security future built on fossil fuels.

No state is currently fully in survival governance mode. Despite the massive destruction by fire of its landscape, wildlife, and ecology over the summer of 2019–2020, the Australian government clings to coal as a source of export income. India continues to behave as if the seismic activity that renders carbon storage a dangerous option within its borders should make no difference to its planning for the commercial exploitation of coal.[6] Eventually this will change. Climate extremes will continue to arrive. The project of survival governance will become a necessity.

Non-state networks such as the fossil fuel divestment movement matter to survival governance, but ultimately the process of moving to a bio-digital energy paradigm depends on the first-mover leadership of a strong state. One reason for this lies in the capacity of the state to create and supply money on

[4] J. Ayling and N. Gunningham, "Non-State Governance and Climate Policy: The Fossil Fuel Divestment Movement," *Climate Policy*, 17 (2017), 131–149.

[5] Arabella Advisors, *The Global Fossil Fuel Divestment and Clean Energy Investment Movement*, Washington, DC, 2018, https://www.arabellaadvisors.com/wp-content/uploads/2018/09/Global-Divestment-Report-2018.pdf.

[6] International Energy Agency, *India 2020: Energy Policy Review*, IEA, France, 2020, 243.

a vast scale to manage a crisis. For example, the US Federal Reserve during the global financial crisis credited to the banks in its system around $1.2 trillion in reserves.[7] The fiscal powers and monetary tools of the state are fundamental to organizing the external shock needed to set world capitalism on a faster path to a bio-digital energy paradigm. Socially organized, bottom-up movements can induce trillions of dollars of fossil fuel divestment commitments. But what is required is to cut off the flow of investment and government subsidies that keeps the industry alive in capital terms. Shutting down the fossil fuel industry and creating the bio-digital energy paradigm requires the state's powers of money creation and regulation. This kind of money-creating power has to be tied to a set of infrastructure priorities for the bio-digital energy paradigm. Global capital will completely exit the institution of fossil fuel when the green economy can offer the kind of long-term investment opportunities that have been offered by fossil fuel energy projects. Something on the global scale of a green Belt and Road (BR) could cause this exit. Otherwise the funds might well flow into speculative bubbles of the kind to be found in housing markets or the processes of securitization that brought about the global financial crisis of 2007–2008.

State power is crucial in other ways. For better or worse, states have evolved as entities vested with sovereign power. The state has—through military, financial, and legal mechanisms—multiple ways to coerce. It can nationalize industries and declare national emergencies. It can send long-term signals to investors about its commitment to renewable energy. Of course, such signaling has to be clear. Closing down coal-fired power stations is an unambiguous signal. A poorly designed emissions trading scheme in which the price of carbon is low, allowing fossil fuel emitters to more or less carry on as before, is dissembling, not signaling. Dissembling by a state simply encourages the oil and gas industries to stay the course. Even worse, innovative companies like General Electric continue to include fossil fuel technologies in their development strategy because they see a world that is not taking climate policy seriously. Such companies focus on what states do, not what they say they will do. States can also negotiate with private global capital to achieve terms and conditions for access to technologies that matter to the welfare of their citizens.

---

[7] Donald L. Kohn, "The Federal Reserve's Policy Actions during the Financial Crisis and Lessons for the Future," Board of Governors of the Federal Reserve System, May 13, 2010, https://www.federalreserve.gov/newsevents/speech/kohn20100513a.htm

States can also create the regulatory conditions for the erosion of monopoly rents. If the project of survival governance is to include billions of poor people, it cannot be based on regulatory models of innovation designed to fill appetites of avarice, such as those we find in use by Big Pharma. Big Pharma's monopoly privileges have led us into an era of super-pricing of pharmaceutical products for comparatively little benefit. Kymriah, a cancer treatment marketed by Novartis involving gene-modified cells, comes with a $475,000 price tag. Big Pharma routinely makes a mockery of health equity. Frugal innovation has to be both a practice and value in the project of survival governance. In practical terms, this means states being prepared to pull the powerful regulatory levers at their disposal, such as the threat of compulsory licensing of intellectual property rights, using competition law to target excessive pricing practices by firms, or creating price regulation schemes for essential products and services. There is, to put it in Hobbesian terms, little point in citizens signing onto a social contract promising them security if the Leviathan does not use its powers to guard their security.

Choosing among Improbabilities

The scenario in which China creates a pathway to an earth system equilibrium in which the probability of many known risks of climate change is lowered rests on China recognizing its situation of climate survival governance. From this recognition the Chinese government must move to guiding the development of a paradigm of innovation in bio-digital and renewable energies. The beginnings of this paradigm come as an organized exogenous shock aimed at the fast extinction of the fossil fuel industry and the rapid uptake of renewable energy. As capital abandons fossil fuel, the endogeneity of China's city networks—those networks having been dramatically extended through its BR Initiative—takes over. Citizens living in eco-cities, smart cities, and forest cities generate demands on a scale that creates entirely new circuits of capital, ones that give the world a realistic chance of avoiding the worst climate change scenarios.

In chapter 2 I discussed some objections to my scenario. An authoritarian state with a poor track record of tackling environmental protection does not seem a good bet as the leader of a global transition to a bio-digital energy paradigm. But as I have argued, other powerful states are even more improbable candidates for organizing the required scale of exogenous shock. China represents the least improbable catalyst of hope. The United States has embraced fossil fuel innovation over the last several decades—improving fracking technologies and continually pushing down the costs of extraction—thereby turning the United States into a superpower of fossil fuel export. US manufacturers see in this innovation success story a chance to lower their own costs. US politicians perceive the promise of the export of gas to other countries as another lever of geo-political influence, another incentive for trading partners in need of gas to sign onto US free trade agreements aimed at globalizing the rules of US commodity accumulation for the world.

Climate policy is an issue in the United States—but only an issue. It is not *the issue*, just another one to be addressed when some triggering event rolls around, such as the renewal of tax credit legislation. Climate change is simply not a priority for the many lobbying networks running through Capitol Hill like some massive fibrous root system that feeds on dollar nutrients from large corporations, industries, industry associations, business interest groups, and wealthy individuals. Renewable energy industries like geothermal, wind, and solar are all players in this system, but then so are the fossil fuel industries, along with US manufacturers wanting the security of cheap energy. At the level of electoral politics, climate change policies in the United States gain some support in states like California, but then in other states such as Kentucky, West Virginia, and Wyoming, which both produce and burn coal, the politics work in favor of coal. This is especially true since the Trump administration put an end to Obama's Clean Power Plan. Fossil fuel is a major institution of accumulation. Oil companies dominate the world's top 10 companies. This institution can, through the legislatures, courts, and regulatory agencies, run enough interference to prevent the United States from leading the rapid transition to a bio-digital energy paradigm.

The thousands of rules being implemented by the European Union as part of its Energy Union package show how seriously the European Union takes climate change. However, the European Union remains a union of energy sovereigns rather than a true energy union. At a deeper level, Europe's political networks have now entered a long tunnel of internal discussion about the future of the EU project, restricting the European Union's capacity for leadership on the bio-digital energy paradigm. Just as importantly, the European Union cannot match China's capacity to scale innovation. The rapid cost reduction and diffusion of climate-related technologies is fundamental to the welfare of citizens everywhere.

I have also argued that India has, through the scale of its coming urbanization and city growth, the same kind of opportunity as China to lead in the development of a bio-digital energy paradigm. India has a long history of negotiating with multinational capital over access to technology. It has had sectoral successes in software and pharmaceuticals. Leading the development of a global bio-digital energy paradigm would require India to transcend its sector-targeted approach to innovation. Like China, it would have to use its cities to run many large-scale pilot programs to test new technologies. The planning mechanisms that have produced India's sectoral successes would have to shift into a higher gear for India to lead a new paradigm. India could be a partner in the global project of survival governance, but its capacity to take charge of such a project is questionable. China, as we saw in chapter 8, is further advanced down the track of carrying out the kind of city experiments needed to construct a city-innovation pathway. Its BR initiative is producing infrastructure linkages among countries and cities that India is simply not in a position to emulate.

Innovation under Authoritarianism

To conclude, as this book does, that our best chance of avoiding a climate catastrophe depends on China's capacity to forge a new paradigm of bio-digital energy innovation is not comforting. It is even less so if one is skeptical about China's innovation capacity. Innovation, it could be argued, depends on various freedoms. Communist surveillance "corrects" ideas with ideology, creating a world of self-checking and whispers, destroying the freedoms upon which a flourishing culture of innovation depends.

Abrami, Kirby, and McFarlan suggest this when they ask whether China can move beyond its present track record of successful incremental innovation to lead innovation, much like the United States did from the 1940s onward.[8] The authors end on a pessimistic note. The problems, they argue, do not lie in a lack of entrepreneurs, creative talent, universities, or capital, but rather in a one-party political structure that has shadows everywhere to vet and check on processes of innovation. Small firms are obliged to have a Communist Party representative and large firms a party cell. The higher

---

[8] R. M. Abrami, W. C. Kirby, and F. W. McFarlan, "Why China Can't Innovate," *Harvard Business Review*, 92 (2014), 107–111, https://hbr.org/2014/03/why-china-cant-innovate.

echelons of university governance structures are filled by Party members whose primary loyalties are to their careers and the Party. As long as the Party insists on governing innovation by means of its networks of surveillance it will very likely slow or even prevent the breakthrough innovation it wants.

For a Western audience this argument has huge resonance. Freedom, innovation, and progress all neatly fit together. Innovation cannot thrive under relentless surveillance. The implication is overwhelming. The one-party state must get out of the way and let freedom of inquiry ring and reign so that innovation may follow.

It would be nice if democratic freedoms and innovation lined up in this neat way, because, among other things, fascist states would not obtain scientific breakthroughs to drive innovation in weaponry. The evidence, however, suggests that innovation occurs under a variety of political structures. Nazi Germany continued to make progress in the development of rockets and aircraft before and during the war. The scientists who worked in these fields became the targets of recruitment by both Russia and the United States in the immediate postwar years. The Manhattan Project is an example of how breakthrough innovation can be developed under conditions of military secrecy and hierarchy.

Kojevnikov's study of the achievements of Russian scientists during Stalin's reign addresses head on the argument for the linkage between freedom and innovation.[9] As Kojevnikov points out, Karl Popper's conjecture that scientific progress depends on a broader environment of political freedoms is not borne out by the case of the Soviet Union under Stalin's tyranny. To the contrary, Stalin's rule saw "arguably the greatest progress achieved by science and technology on Russian soil since the time of Peter the Great."[10] There was more to Russian science during this period than the debacle of biologist Trofim Lysenko's rejection of genetic theory and the state-sponsored suppression, and in some cases elimination, of Lysenko's scientific critics. Lysenko cast Soviet biology into a dark age from which it took a long time to recover. Other branches of science did much better. In the early 1920s physicist Aleksandr Friedmann demonstrated a mathematics of foundational importance for later theories of an expanding universe. Research institutes were created in areas including optics, aviation, radio, and X-rays. These institutes

---

[9] Alexei B. Kojevnikov, *Stalin's Great Science: The Times and Adventures of Soviet Physicists*, Imperial College Press, London, 2004.
[10] Kojevnikov, *Stalin's Great Science*, xii.

had production arms, allowing for the possibility of turning theory and invention into innovation. One of the great successes was the Optical Institute, which made contributions to atomic theory, as well as creating designs for various optical products, such as cameras, microscopes, and telescopes, helping to turn the Soviet Union into an exporter of optical products.

The relationships between authoritarianism, capitalism, and innovation are obviously complex. Kojevnikov's study suggests that one aspect of this relationship is contingency. This opens up the possibility that an authoritarian state working with capitalist institutions of the market might be able to improve, perhaps dramatically so, its innovation system.

Pivoting to China, what we see over the last few decades is a story of the state striving for and obtaining continuous improvement in science, technology, and innovation. In a 2011 study by the Royal Society, the United States continued to lead the world in publication of research papers, but China came in second, ahead of the United Kingdom, Japan, and Germany. Through its Five-Year Plans China has committed to spend more on research and development. By 2013 its commitment had risen to over 2% of GDP. However, more fine-grained comparisons with countries in the Organisation of Economic Co-operation and Development have suggested a China lagging behind on a number of indicators, including investment in basic research, a weakness in the number of top universities, and an overreliance on state-owned enterprises for research initiatives.[11]

China's weaknesses in science, technology, and innovation have been a major concern for China's leaders. In a 2014 speech Xi Jinping suggested that China's foundations in innovation were "not solid enough," it lacked strength in "original creativity," and there was too great a dependence on others for core technologies.[12] The speech delivers the same message communicated by Nehru years before when considering India's development. Scientific knowledge autonomously gathered and socially applied by a country to its development goals is fundamental to its meaningful agency in a world of sovereign powers.

It is a mistake to think of the innovation challenge in a world of climate survival governance as forming a series of independent technology races. Rather, the challenge is to bring about the convergence of technological

---

[11] Organisation of Economic Co-operation and Development, *China in A Changing Global Environment*, OECD, Paris, 2015, 33–34.

[12] Xi Jinping, "Transition to Innovation-Driven Growth," June 9, 2014, in Xi Jinping, *The Governance of China*, Vol. 1, Foreign Language Press, Beijing, 2014, 131-142, 135.

frontiers—especially those in computing, biology, and renewables—into a new paradigm of innovation. World capitalism has proved adept at shaping, manipulating, and automating the expression of consumer preference and consumption. The Big Data sisters of Facebook, Amazon, Apple, and Google can in milliseconds deliver tailored temptation to consumers making use of their free services. The clunky physical world of getting to know your customer, working out an advertising strategy, devising ads, figuring out where to place them, finding agents to help, and deciding prices has all been automated.

If the private technocracy of digital automation can drive us deeper into unsustainable consumption of resources, then perhaps it can help us reverse direction as well. The world of algorithmic automation allows us to manage complexity, creating options for both centralized and decentralized architectures of energy supply. Digital technology when applied to grids can help deal with the complexity of supply, storage, and demands from the internet of things (where *things* range from sensors in an orchard to the electric vehicle parked in a garage) and from many customers of renewable energy, as well as creating new trading opportunities in electricity markets.[13]

The critical question for the world is whether a strong state can organize this convergence. Innovation within capitalism in the context of survival governance, whether with or without Chinese characteristics, can no longer just be about the "immense accumulation of commodities," as Marx put it in his opening page of the first volume of *Capital*. A capitalism blind to the consequences of commodity accumulation for the planetary boundaries of the earth system will likely crash.[14] That is the clear conclusion of the world system modeling in the *Limits to Growth* (see chapter 6). The work of the Intergovernmental Panel on Climate Change (IPCC) reinforces this conclusion. The state of China's ecosystems shows just how quickly processes of commodity accumulation in a large population can cross boundaries of sustainable accumulation.

China, as we saw in chapters 7 and 8, is trying to bring its processes of production into line with circular-economy principles. This represents an important beginning of what has to be a much greater transformation. China is constructing eco-cities, smart cities, forest cities, sponge cities, hydrogen

---

[13] International Energy Agency, *Digitalization and Energy*, OECD/IEA, Paris, 2017.

[14] W. Steffen, J. Rockstrom and R. Costanza, "How Defining Planetary Boundaries Can Transform Our Approach to Growth," *Solutions*, 2 (2011), 59–65.

cities, and other kinds of cities as sites of technology testing, piloting, and evaluation. What is happening in China in terms of scaling innovation for cities dwarfs anything underway in other parts of the world. China has the most power to alter the future of the oil industry from the one that the US government has opened up for that industry through its support of fracking. If China succeeds in accelerating the growth of its new energy vehicles market, already the largest in the world, it will cause investors to reconsider the oil industry's future in transport markets. The transport sector accounted for 55% of the growth in China's demand for oil from 2000 to 2016.[15]

My claim here is not that China is working toward a bio-digital energy paradigm, but rather that, more than any other state, it could through its cities accelerate the convergence of technologies for this paradigm. Of course, its capacity to scale innovation cuts both ways. A Chinese capitalism dedicated to the mass accumulation of commodities will simply hasten the entry of world capitalism into new, more dangerous climate equilibria. In such a context, survival governance would perhaps take on darker forms, as many states would, in a world of collapsing resources, eventually lose effective authority over their populations. Feudalism, reinvented in some high-tech form, might emerge from a climate-induced collapse.

When the Ground Is Slipping Away—China and Multinational Capital

More of the knowledge China needs for its innovation planning exists outside of its borders than within it. In its early days, Communist China sought for and obtained heavy industrial technologies from the former Soviet Union. In 1975 Deng Xiaoping realized that China's modernization of its agriculture, industry, science, technology, and defense depended on the knowledge assets of multinationals outside of China.[16] China's journey to acquire these assets as knowledge spillovers began in 1980 with the creation of the special economic zones of Shenzhen, Zhuhai, Xiamen, and Shantou. Steps were also taken in this decade to liberalize foreign direct investment.

[15] International Energy Agency, *World Energy Outlook 2007*, OECD/IEA, Paris, 2007 (hereafter WEO 2017), 523.

[16] Chunlai Chen, "The Liberalisation of FDI Policies and the Impacts of FDI on China's Economic Development," in Ross Garnaut, Ligang Song, and Cai Fang (eds.), *China's 40 Years of Reform and Development: 1978–2018*, ANU Press, Canberra, 2018, 595–617, 597.

As one of our Chinese interviewees remarked, Chinese ministers will often ask multinationals operating in China, "When will China get this technology?" They are always greeted with the same answer: "One day." "One day" is indeterminate, so China does what it can to hasten the technology's arrival.

As I argued in chapter 8, both sides understand the informal rules of this bargaining game. It takes place within a formal regime of intellectual property protection. China has learned to play by this set of rules. It has adapted its domestic intellectual property systems such as patents and trademarks to comply with global rules such as those contained in the World Trade Organization's Agreement on Trade-Related Aspects of Intellectual Property Rights (TRIPS). Informally, a game of mutual deception ensues in which neither side is deceived. China provides multinationals with lots of assurances about the safety of their knowledge monopolies, building the world's biggest patent office as part of the assurance game. Multinationals, in turn, assure Chinese authorities that one day they will transfer their technologies. Both sides know the polite assurances of the other are also polite deceptions. Each side takes steps to fulfill its real objective.

US multinationals fear China's stance on intellectual property and continue to partner with the US government in pressuring China to do more to protect foreign intellectual property monopolies. Schumpeter's depiction of the forces of annihilation in capitalism helps to explain the depth of this fear. Firms have to survive, to use his famous metaphor, in a perennial gale of creative destruction. The emphasis in his theory is on the perennial; there is no lull in capitalism. Patents and other forms of output restriction, along with predatory pricing, are all best understood as a way for firms "to keep on their feet, on ground that is slipping away from them."[17] Anticompetitive behavior actually expands capitalism's processes of innovation and accumulation. Schumpeter's now somewhat dated argument does not work as an economic justification for intellectual property, but his concept of the perennial gale of destruction does help capture the way in which multinational capital perceives China.

China's planners were never going to wait for the arrival of "one day" when a foreign multinational might gift China technology it no longer needed or cared about. China's Party is the final monopsony enforcer of the goals that

---

[17] Joseph A. Schumpeter, *Capitalism, Socialism and Democracy*, Routledge, 5th ed., London, 1976, 84.

have made it through its planning labyrinth. Holders of intellectual property monopolies have found themselves in hard bargaining contests over access to China's market. China has been powerless to change the rules of the global intellectual property regime, but it could and has bargained over the use and effects of that regime within its borders. No state that cares about regulatory sovereignty over its market would give up bargaining on the use of monopolies in that market.

Multinational firms have now come to realize that Schumpeter's perennial gale is blowing from China much more strongly than anything they have previously encountered. As I described in chapter 8, the technology of high-voltage direct current transmission systems was dominated by European companies such as Siemens and ABB. They introduced this technology into China through various projects, and in a couple of decades Chinese companies emerged as highly competitive providers of a technology of foundational importance to renewable energy grids.

For a world in desperate need of transmitting renewable energy, China's capability of rolling out high-voltage direct current transmission systems has arrived just in time. China's dramatic lowering of the world price of photovoltaics by 80% is well known, as is the rise of Huawei to become one of the biggest providers of equipment in the global telecommunications sector. ZTE and Huawei became the two top applicants under the Patent Cooperation Treaty in 2016 in the field of digital technology. The World Intellectual Property Organization described this result as extraordinary, given that both companies had only begun using the system about a decade earlier.[18] Patents are an imperfect proxy for innovation, but the capacity to assemble a patent portfolio of many thousands in which players like Qualcomm are competing says something about the capabilities of these Chinese firms.

In dealing with multinational capital, China has to manage inconsistent goals. It must project an image of the country as a place where the knowledge monopolies of foreign capitalists are safe and secure while it assiduously works to strip those capitalists of the very assets that lie at the basis of their capital accumulation strategies. Where China is successful in this game, it can use its scale advantages to produce at market-capturing prices, as many US and EU manufacturers have discovered. But the Chinese market also dangles the prospect of global rewards. For example, GE's joint venture in

---

[18] World Intellectual Property Organization, *Patent Cooperation Treaty Review 2017*, WIPO, Geneva, 2017, 19.

2009 with the Aviation Industry Corporation of China promised the possibility of GE's electronic operating systems becoming standard in Chinese civilian planes, with the Chinese aviation market set to become the biggest market in the world. A strong position in China would help GE move into other markets. The logic of entering the Chinese market for other holders of proprietary avionic technology, such as Honeywell and Rockwell Collins, is precisely the same, as are the risks.

One of the surprises for foreign multinationals operating in China, which became apparent through our interviews, has been the speed at which China has acquired technology and become an innovator. The surprise has occurred because the innovation processes of multinationals depend heavily on uncodified knowledge assets, including such things as the skills of manipulating laboratory equipment, producing pleasing designs, detecting errors, and working with complex materials. The nature of these skills helps to explain why it has been hard to wrest the leadership of jet engine technology from firms like General Electric, Pratt & Whitney, Rolls-Royce, and Safran. Taking a jet engine apart still leaves unanswered questions, such as how to combine the molten metals to produce alloys that do not fail under the stresses that jet engines experience. The same is true of semiconductor chip design and manufacture. One can resort to reverse engineering of complex chip circuitry, but this activity will not answer questions about formulae or how to implement processes to arrive at a certain quality.

High levels of uncodified knowledge and especially tacit knowledge should, in theory at least, make imitation more difficult.[19] Theories of innovation that emphasize the complexity of knowledge learning imply that innovation will be concentrated in particular places and organizations.[20] On this account, innovation leadership is much more closely tied to a territorial center. It is also less mobile than one might first think. But then, as the innovation successes I have described show, China may be able to shift territorial leadership of innovation much more quickly than innovation theories based on uncodified and tacit knowledge suggest. China's market share of 5G technology, which could form the infrastructure for the delivery and trade in services within the bio-digital energy paradigm, has US officials worried:

---

[19] Richard R. Nelson and Sidney G. Winter, *An Evolutionary Theory of Economic Change*, The Belknap Press of Harvard University Press, Cambridge, MA, 1982, 155.

[20] Simona Iammarino and Philip McCann, *Multinationals and Economic Geography: Location, Technology and Innovation*, Edward Elgar, Cheltenham, UK, 2013, 148.

China has built up a lead in 5G, capturing 40 percent of the global 5G infrastructure market. For the first time in history, the United States is not leading the next technology era.[21]

Innovation in reverse engineering itself is also occurring, which may help China close the gap in the catch-up game it has to play.[22] The diffusion effects of high-tech capital that is globally footloose hold potential threats for the US national security state, as the next section shows.

When National Security Is Slipping Away—China and the US National Security State

The origins of the US national security state, argues Daniel Yergin, are to be found in the breakup of the grand alliance forged by Roosevelt, Stalin, and Churchill in 1945 at Yalta.[23] Two months after the Yalta meeting, Roosevelt was dead. A little more than two months after his death, Churchill lost the general election to the Labor Party. The US-Soviet relations began to chill, quickly entering that dangerous long period known as the Cold War.

The phrase *national security*, which had not been much in use before 1940, was by the late 1940s on the lips of many in US defense policy circles. Much more important than the incantation of the phrase was the organizational outlook it engendered. It became a highly flexible concept capable of absorbing and reframing almost any issue as one of "national security." Through the binoculars of national security, existing threats were magnified and many new ones seen, in continents such as Africa, once thought too remote by those who had perceived virtue in US isolationism. A deep organizational response accompanied the national security mentality. The United States began to take steps to put itself in a state of constant readiness for war. The national security state would be the militarily prepared state.

---

[21] US attorney general William P. Barr, Keynote Address at the Department of Justice's China Initiative Conference, Washington, DC, February 6, 2020, https://www.justice.gov/opa/speech/attorney-general-william-p-barr-delivers-keynote-address-department-justices-china.

[22] In the case of semiconductors see Mirko Holler, Manuel Guizar-Sicairos, Esther H. R. Tsai, Roberto Dinapoli, Elisabeth Muller, Oliver Bunk, Jorg Raabe, and Babriel Aeppli, "High-Resolution Non-Destructive Three-Dimensional Imaging of Integrated Circuits," *Nature*, 543 (2017), 402–406.

[23] Daniel Yergin, *Shattered Peace: The Origins of the Cold War and the National Security State*, Andre Deutsch, London, 1978.

One clear lesson from World War II was that the probability of victory would be heavily affected by discovery, invention, and innovation in weaponry. The Manhattan Project was a demonstration of what was possible if a state brought together academic science, the corporate sector, and government resources. For defense planners there was a clear message. If the United States was to stay ahead in weapons innovation races, its military, industrial, and academic organizational structures would have to become much more integrated and networked.

It is easy to forget the scale and speed at which this military-industrial reorganization took place in the United States in the second half of the 1940s. Investing in R&D was put front and center of US security planning. The various arms of the US military—the army, navy, and air force—developed boards and committees to oversee R&D spending.[24] Research and development became one the central functions of the armed forces, a function which saw scientists from the private sector sitting on key advisory boards located in the highest levels of the security establishment, such as the White House and the Office of the Secretary of Defense, helping to plan weapons projects.[25] Pipelines carrying hundreds of millions of dollars found their way into civilian laboratories. The US aviation industry, which had gone into a slump after the end of the war, became a huge priority of US military R&D expenditures. As an example, the US government in 1948 funded 99% of all aeronautical research.[26] Successive US governments committed to financing national R&D, especially military R&D.[27] The US government, its military, its universities, and its corporations in the 1940s began a long journey of networked interdependence that continues to this day.

The US national security state delivered technology. Robert MacNeil puts on a short list of US military innovation achievements "the Internet, the modern computer, cellular telephones, global positioning systems, semiconductors, jet engines, radar, sonar, satellites, weather forecasting technology, lithium ion batteries, nuclear technology, a range of synthetic materials, artificial intelligence, and the foundational development of the modern robotics, chemical, and aviation industries."[28] US defense budgets

[24] Yergin, *Shattered Peace*, 267.

[25] Elliot V. Converse III, *Rearming For The Cold War 1945–1960*, Historical Office, Office of the Secretary of Defense, Washington, DC, 2012, 12.

[26] Yergin, *Shattered Peace*, 361.

[27] David C. Mowery and Nathan Rosenberg, *Paths of Innovation: Technological Change in 20th-Century America*, Cambridge University Press, Cambridge, 1998, 32.

[28] Robert MacNeil, "Between Innovation and Industrial Policy: How Washington Succeeds and Fails at Renewable Energy," *Prometheus*, 34 (2016), 173–189, 183.

have enabled many an infant company and industry to grow to power in global markets, including IBM, Boeing, GE, Texas Instruments, and Motorola. The hard nucleus of large defense contractors of the 1940s that was close to government has become, as Linda Weiss has shown, part of a much wider networked innovation system serving the high-tech demands of US military institutions.[29]

This track record has not been the product of some invisible self-organizing market force. Rather, it has come about because US state capitalism has made full use of its regulatory powers. Those powers include technology procurement programs such as the Very High Speed Integrated Circuit and the Very Large Scale Integrated Circuit programs of the 1970s and the Small Business Innovation Research program that over a 30-year period starting in 1982 saw a variety of US defense agencies invest more than $30 billion in procurement activities.[30]

Through the changes to US innovation strategies over the decades there has been one inviolable axiom: the US government, in the interests of national security, must have access to the best technological innovation. As one US report put it,

> Access to and application of the latest technologies is a vital component of being victorious on the battlefield and competitive economically. The technologies resident in U.S. cleared industry represent the latest and greatest advances.[31]

The capacity to shock and awe an adversary depends, as the first Iraq War showed, on the US military being at least a generation ahead of its opponents in terms of technology.

Innovation in today's global capitalist system is not what it was in the 1940s. During that time the US government could set up a subsidy and procurement game with its dependent national firms that no other state could come close to matching. In today's world, innovation flows through complex nodes and networks that straddle the globe, constantly interacting, assembling, disassembling, and reforming—with each of those nodes and networks

---

[29] Linda Weiss, *America Inc.?: Innovation and Enterprise in the National Security State*, Cornell University Press, Ithaca, NY, 2014.

[30] Weiss, *America Inc.?*, 63, 91–92.

[31] Defense Security Service, *Targeting U.S. Technologies: A Trend Analysis of Reporting from Defense Industry 2012*, Defense Security Service, 2012, 67.

drawing on philosophies and norms of proprietary exclusivity, openness, the public domain, and the intellectual commons to create guiding charters of innovation for themselves. The world of nodal and networked innovation is chaotically diverse, having shifted from single military technologies to dual-use technologies to a world of many-use technologies. Today it is harder for the US military to stay one generation of technology ahead of any potential adversary.

The response of the US national security state to this networked complexity of innovation has, broadly speaking, been twofold. The first has been to support the globalization of US intellectual property rights. Dominium has become a tool of imperium. The second has been to create regulatory mechanisms for the purpose of controlling the diffusion of technological knowledge.

Global protection and aggressive enforcement of US intellectual property is a bipartisan policy project in the United States and has always been so. The globalization of intellectual property took a historic turning point when the United States reformed its trade laws in the 1980s, linking intellectual property to its trade enforcement tools. Among other things, the United States created a Special 301 procedure for imposing trade sanctions against countries that were not doing enough to protect US intellectual property monopolies. If one looks at the history of Special 301 reviews carried out by the United States Trade Representative (USTR), China has been the principal enforcement priority. These reviews go back to the 1980s.[32]

Through trade agreements or specific bilateral arrangements, the US government has pushed for intellectual property exclusivities that favor the accumulation strategies of US multinationals. One of the advantages for the US state in framing intellectual property as a national security issue is that the rules of intellectual property have pervasive and deep effects on data, information, research, and technology systems in the civilian economies of states. Globalized intellectual property rights form, as Hanns Ullrich puts it, a "systemic conditioning" of a state's domestic market, affecting how it manages knowledge, information, and data as private and public goods.[33] By linking

---

[32] The reports can be accessed at https://ustr.gov/issue-areas/intellectual-property/special-301/previous-special-301-reports.

[33] Hanns Ullrich, "The Political Foundations of TRIPS Revisited," in Hanns Ullrich, Reto M. Hilty, Matthias Lamping, and Josef Drexl (eds.), *TRIPS plus 20: From Trade Rules to Market Principles*, Springer, Heidelberg, 2016, 85–129. 99.

intellectual property and national security, the United States gains, at least in its own eyes, a double legitimacy. Any regulatory action taken by a state that implicates knowledge and innovation can through intellectual property be recast as a potential theft, as well as an issue of US national security. Deep and coercive intrusion into the economies of other states obtains the cover of legal and moral legitimacy.

Donald Trump, like all US presidents before him, is simply the latest spear carrier in this agenda of intellectual property globalization. In August 2017 the Trump administration launched an investigation under its Trade Act of 1974 into China's treatment of US companies and their intellectual property. By August 2018 the USTR had imposed duties on Chinese imports with a $50 billion trade value, and by September of that year additional duties were levied on imports with a value of $200 billion. In January 2020 a temporary bilateral truce was struck. The only clear result from this particular trade brawl was that it was costly for both sides.

The second response of the US government that I mentioned was that of creating regulatory mechanisms to slow down the diffusion of technological knowledge. These have a long history. For example, at the international level, the United States has created informal regimes to help coordinate export control policies among its allies. After World War II and with the help of the United Kingdom and France, the United States established in 1949 the Coordinating Committee for Multilateral Export Controls (CoCom) for the purpose of blocking the export of strategically important military and dual-use industrial technologies to communist countries. The disintegration of the Soviet bloc saw the termination of CoCom in 1993. This was followed in 1996 by the establishment of another informal regime in the shape of the Wassenaar Arrangement for Export Controls for Conventional Arms and Dual Use Goods and Technologies.[34] The Wassenaar Arrangement, which has 42 members, promotes itself as a multilateral arrangement for export control that is not aimed at any state or group of states. The United States has also entered into bilateral arrangements to regulate the diffusion of sensitive technologies. For example, in 1986 it negotiated the Supercomputer Safeguard Plan with Japan over the export of supercomputers to third parties, an arrangement that remained in place through the 1990s.[35]

[34] See https://www.wassenaar.org/about-us/.
[35] R. Johnston, "U.S. Export Control Policy in the High-Performance Computer Sector," *The Nonproliferation Review* (Winter 1998), 44–59, 46.

The US national security state is highly interventionist, using an array of hard and soft regulatory tools to adapt to changing global security contexts. In the next section I consider whether the US security state will jeopardize the project of survival governance. China's capacity to organize in time the external shock needed to send world capitalism down the path of the bio-digital energy paradigm would obviously be affected by US global regulatory strategies aimed at hindering China's acquisition of the technologies needed for the paradigm in the first place.

The Fork in the Road Ahead: Survival Governance or Hegemony

The project of survival governance requires the leadership of a strong state, and as I have argued, China is the least improbable leader. Its city experiments represent the best chance we have for the creation of a bio-digital energy paradigm. Multinational capital is crucial to China's success in this project. China needs companies like IBM, GE, Honeywell, and others to help build its smart cities, eco-cities, forest cities, and the other types of cities I discussed in chapter 8. There are also, despite the risks to their intellectual property, strong incentives for high-tech multinationals to stay engaged with China. These multinationals know that the global high-carbon economy is running out of time. Capitalist states have entered the era of survival governance, even if states like Australia and the United States dissemble to their respective publics about this. China through its cities could, as I have argued, offer those multinational companies that stay engaged with it entirely new circuits of commodity accumulation, ones based on giant urban agglomerations of bio-digital energy production and new kinds of services and trading possibilities.

Successful partnerships between multinational capital and China are problematic from the point of view of the US security state. For the United States it is much more preferable for China to be at least a generation behind it in core technologies. Certainly, it cannot be a generation ahead. Everywhere within the US security state, alarm bells are being rung about China's capacities to acquire US technologies and what this means for US military power:

China is playing the long game, finding our weak points, using any means possible—legal and illegal—to steal our data, plans, and technologies. Without action, what's in research and development now, what's stolen now . . . is what our service members will inevitably face on the battlefield.[36]

The very technologies that are central to a bio-digital energy paradigm are also the ones that the US government sees as key to its national security. Technologies of neurobiology, neurotech, neural networks, evolutionary and genetic computation, AI cloud technologies, microprocessor technology, advanced computing technology, and quantum information and sensing technology are all emerging or foundational technologies that are coming into focus for US export control.[37]

The United States can still pull levers of control that will slow down China's acquisition of some technologies. The case of semiconductor chips is a good illustration of China's continued dependence on core technologies and how the US government can restrict an export of a technology in the name of national security concerns. US companies lead the world when it comes to the production of semiconductors (50% of the global market) and equipment for the manufacture of semiconductors (47% of the global market).[38] US industry is also highly export dependent, with 80% of its semiconductor sales and 84% of its equipment sales occurring outside the domestic market.[39] China imports over 90% of its semiconductors, with US companies supplying some 56% of China's needs.[40] Major Chinese purchasers include Lenovo, Huawei (in the top 10 of purchasers), ZTE, Datang Telecom, Xiaomi, and Haier.

As chapter 8 showed, the scale of China's many "smart" projects—such as smart cities, smart grids, and smart manufacturing—should mean it remains the most important market for US industry. Not surprisingly, this import dependence is seen by China as a "major national security concern."[41] China's plans to free itself of this import reliance through industrial policies such as Made in China 2025 have seen it criticized for practicing old-fashioned import substitution. China is hardly on its own when it comes to industrial policy.

---

[36] Kari Bingen, Deputy Under Secretary of Defense for Intelligence, quoted in *Access* (Official Magazine of the Defense Counterintelligence and Security Agency), 9, no. 1 (2020), 6.

[37] See the notice of the United States Bureau of Industry and Security, Department of Commerce, "Review of Controls for Certain Technologies," *Federal Register*, vol. 83, no. 223, November 19, 2018, 58201. See also Export Control Reform Act 2018.

[38] United States International Trade Administration, *2016 Top Markets Report: Semiconductors and Related Equipment*, Department of Commerce, Washington, DC, 2016, 5.

[39] United States International Trade Administration, *2016 Top Markets Report*, 5.

[40] United States International Trade Administration, *2016 Top Markets Report*, 26.

[41] United States International Trade Administration, *2016 Top Markets Report*, 26.

As the United Nations Conference on Trade and Development (UNCTAD) *World Investment Report 2018* points out, there was a rush to industrial policy by more than 80 countries during the 2013–2018 period.[42] For example, industrial policy packages composed of many elements have popped up in Germany (Industrie 4.0—Smart Manufacturing for the Future), Japan (the Industrial Competitiveness Enhancement Act), and the United States (the National Strategic Plan for Advanced Manufacturing).[43] The theme uniting these and other policies is "Make It Here."

The worry within the West about Chinese innovation plans like Made in China 2025 is not about their status as industrial policy, which everyone practices, but rather that China may meet its planning targets.

The US state has always been careful to ensure that semiconductors were "Made in the USA." Comparative advantage in this sector has not been left hostage to market competition. During the 1980s the Japanese semiconductor chip industry was making serious inroads into the US domestic market, with the Japanese equipment industry raising its share of the US market from 18% to 39%.[44] The United States, backed by its semiconductor chip industry, responded by using its trade law to issue trade threats. In their shadow, it negotiated with Japan the 1986 Semiconductor Trade Agreement. Tariffs were imposed on Japanese goods in 1987 because in the eyes of the United States, Japan had failed to respect the agreement. In the same year the US Defense Department formed a research consortium with US semiconductor companies. US state capitalism, as this and many other cases demonstrate, flies under various flags of ideological convenience. When its industries enjoy dominance, it is an advocate of free and open markets; when its markets are threatened, the national security, economic security, and fair trade flags are all hoisted to justify aggressive unilateralism.

Semiconductors function for the United States a little like a reserve currency in technology development. Much like access to the US dollar market, threatening access to its semiconductors provides the US government with a potential tool with which to prosecute its agendas. For example, in 2018 the US Department of Commerce, using the Export Administration Regulations, in effect banned the Chinese firm ZTE from access to US semiconductors

---

[42] United Nations Conference on Trade and Development, *World Investment Report 2018*, UNCTAD, New York, 2018, 128.

[43] United Nations Conference on Trade and Development, *World Investment Report 2018*, 136.

[44] Committee on Japan Framework Statement and Report of the Competitiveness Task Force, *Maximizing U.S. Interests in Science and Technology Relations with Japan*, National Academy Press, Washington, DC, 1997, 95.

(with Qualcomm being a big provider to ZTE). ZTE had, in the commerce department's view, breached the terms of an earlier settlement relating to ZTE's violation of the US trade embargo on Iran.[45]

There is, of course, a danger in export bans in the context of a global market where, despite current US dominance, there are other semiconductor producers. Faced by an export ban on chips from the United States, ZTE began discussions with Samsung.[46] In globally dynamic markets, the US government risks its own innovation future if it turns US companies into unreliable suppliers. The export market and its rewards are what matter to the US semiconductor chip industry.

Moreover, while the United States can impose some regulatory filters over items of technology, it does not control science. Science is now a deeply global and networked institution, with its many networks configuring and reconfiguring in ways to make the antiproliferation game for sensitive technologies rich with unforeseen consequences. Areas of science have resisted privatization through the intellectual property regime. The free software movement changed the potentially deep commodification history of software by using licensing strategies to create the option of a positive commons for source code. As a result, the values of openness and freedom of programming have created software and access rights that would not otherwise have existed. The best-known examples are the operating systems based on the Linux kernel. These matter hugely in sectors such as telecommunications. The Linux kernel has become the basis of other open-source initiatives, such as the Android operating system for a range of mobile devices.[47] Commodification has seen the Android universe split into proprietary and nonproprietary dimensions, with a positive commons remaining. This positive commons includes the Linux kernel, as well as the free algorithmic knowledge that has been developed through the free software culture.

This environment gives companies much more autonomy in markets where states intervene for the purposes of maintaining strategic technology leadership. For example, in May 2019 the US Department of Commerce added Huawei and all its non-US affiliates to the "Entity List" it keeps under

---

[45] See US Department of Commerce press release, April 16, 2018, https://www.commerce.gov/news/press-releases/2018/04/secretary-ross-announces-activation-zte-denial-order-response-repeated.

[46] Joyce Lee and Ju-min Park, "Samsung in Talks with ZTE, Others to Supply Mobile Processor Chips: Executive," *Reuters*, May 15, 2018, https://www.reuters.com/article/us-samsung-elec-chips-interview/samsung-in-talks-with-zte-others-to-supply-mobile-processor-chips-executive-idUSKCN1IG1HB.

[47] See https://source.android.com/.

the Export Administration Regulations.[48] The effect of the listing is that US companies like Google, Intel, and Qualcomm can no longer provide technology to Huawei unless they are given a license to do so. In effect, Huawei was frozen out of business dealings with US tech companies. But Huawei, it turned out, had planned for such a possibility, having, according to some reports, prepared its own operating system.[49] Huawei can do this because over 80,000 of its employees work in research and development.[50] Obviously Huawei would have preferred not to have to do this, but the point is that in a world of global networked innovation, other options are available when confronted by US regulatory boycotts. Huawei's thousands of software engineers can draw upon the open universe of software knowledge created by pioneers of the free software movement such as Richard Stallman.

The only certainty from all this export control maneuvering by the United States is that China will hasten ever faster to remove its technological dependencies in critical areas such as semiconductors and software. The United States has massively increased China's incentives to accelerate the growth of a technology ecosystem that is not compromised by the sovereign commands and cooperation of other states.

The US government is also taking risks with the ecosystem over which companies like Google, Intel, and Qualcomm preside. The bigger question is whether this ecosystem will continue to grow or whether, in creating the global fork that it has, the United States has set the stage both for its own diminishment as well as that of the ecosystem that has served its innovation needs. The US security state and global capital have overlapping but not necessarily matching interests. The US government through a highly restrictive nonproliferation strategy could do much to interfere with the creation of new circuits of capital for a world of survival governance. A US failure to create the technical architectures or institutions of commodity accumulation for a world of survival governance might in the end threaten the reproduction and expansion of capital, creating incentives for capital to bypass such a state. Ultimately it is question of whether global high-tech capital itself will respect the boundaries of this present fork.

<hr>

[48] Federal Register, v. 84, no. 98, May 21, 2019, 22961.

[49] Kieren McCarthy, "Can't Do It the US Way? Then We'll Do It Huawei—and Roll Our Own Mobile Operating System," *The Register*, March 14, 2019, https://www.theregister.co.uk/2019/03/14/huawei_own_os/.

[50] See Huawei's 2018 Annual Report, https://www.huawei.com/en/press-events/annual-report/2018

Conclusion

The climate crisis can be understood in the abstract as an exponentially scaling process with negative feedback loops. The rapid construction of a bio-digital energy paradigm is now fundamentally dependent upon pathways of technology diffusion. We know in broad outline what needs to happen in the time remaining if there is to be any chance of keeping warming below 2°C.

Beginning with coal as an urgent priority, all fossil fuels have to be stripped out of the energy system—more or less at a gallop, in the next two to three decades—and replaced by renewable energy technologies. Arguments for the climate benefits of gas should be treated with the deepest skepticism. Even the International Energy Agency has pointed to a worryingly large gap between its estimates of oil and gas methane emissions and the levels reported by industry.[51] The true level of methane emissions makes large differences to projected global temperature rises and therefore the role that the use of gas plays in those rises. We are dangerously ignorant about the quantity of methane emissions. In a world where our chances of staying below a 2°C rise continues to tumble, we need to work toward the rapid elimination of all fossil fuels. We need to take fossil fuel bullets out of the climate roulette game, not continue to play with them.

For the full potential of renewable energy grids to be realized for consumers, the digitization of energy will have to take place. Semiconductors and software will open up grids to all sorts of storage, transmission, and trading possibilities. Unlike the proven technologies of solar and wind, the software and semiconductor possibilities of a new energy world are yet to be demonstrated on a sufficiently large scale. China's cities hold the key to such large-scale demonstration.

US capitalism will not manage the fossil fuel industry out of existence in anything like the time that is needed. In fact, as I have argued, the United States supports incremental innovation in this sector. Within the factional politics of the United States, some elites continue to support fossil fuels. As a result, the United States will probably not be at the global political center of a rapid transition out of fossil fuels and into renewables. Renewables will increase their market share in the United States as part of a diversification strategy for investors and power generators, but this type of incremental change makes climate worlds of 2°C or more a probability. Whether China

[51] WEO 2017, 415.

will take the necessary steps to close down the fossil fuel industry is an open question, but at least the question is open.

Whether a bio-digital energy paradigm can be drawn together in time from the invention and innovation going on in many specific areas of biotechnology, computing and energy development is dependent on the pace of technology piloting and experimentation going on in China's cities. No other country is deploying cities on the scale that China is to assess whether technologies in renewable energy, power transmission, electrification of transport and industrial processes, and energy storage can be synthesized into proven systems solutions for cities.

Cities will be the adaptive units for the new climate equilibria we have already locked in, as well as those we fail to lock out in the coming decades. They will also form the agglomeration nodes of innovation in a postcircular economy. China needs access to many technologies held outside of its borders if its city projects are to deliver workable systems solutions in the time remaining. The United States can affect the rate at which China acquires these technologies. As we have seen in this chapter, there are signs that the United States is moving ever harder to restrict China's access to critical technologies. A US-led confrontation with China may fit with the prescriptions of offensive realism. From the point of view of helping to steer world capitalism away from dangerous climate equilibria, it represents a catastrophic error of judgment. Climate change, I claimed in chapter 1, will turn all coming hegemonic contests into Pyrrhic victories.

World capitalism under US leadership has led national economies into extraordinary levels of commodity accumulation. We now know in a reasonable amount of detail the climate and ecological consequences of this accumulation. The economics profession in the United States has failed over many decades to contextualize its production and growth models within ecological limits, failing to build on the intuitions and insights of pioneers such as Schumacher and Daly. Ecological economics has arrived too late in the day. In any case, the true insights into the nature of the climate crisis come not from economics but from science. Mainstream economics has largely chosen to ignore the data and the science of earth system boundaries and the exponential functions triggered when those boundaries are crossed. The idea captured in Kuznet's environmental curve that states could repurchase their environment once they were rich assumes the reversibility of environmental damage. It completely ignores the exponential nature of the feedback effects once particular boundaries of sustainability are crossed.

Worse has been the way in which the tragedy of the commons has been grotesquely overplayed, when the real tragedy has been that of commodification. US state capitalism and US multinationals have together globalized as a value, as ideology, and as instrumental law a paradigm of knowledge commodification. This has allowed world capitalism to create new commodification frontiers from the discoveries of science, the human pursuit of art in its many forms, and the many digital data traces left by human behavior and action. This commodity expansion through use of property rules has created opportunities for monopoly pricing, erecting barriers to market entry, and collusion through cross-licensing. This paradigm will affect the rate at which China can acquire technologies with which to build and trial the systems solutions it needs for its cities. It is a paradigm at odds with the survival of world capitalism, which now depends on technology pathways of rapid diffusion, beginning, as I have said, with proven renewable energy systems.

The diffusion of renewable energy systems solutions is only the first of many steps. Climate change will alter global disease burdens, with pathogens no longer confined by climate to their traditional territories of evolution. Pandemics will become more frequent. Issues of access to medicine will become ever more urgent. The mass of innovation demand for medicines, as in so many areas, will be for fast-diffusing and frugal innovation rather than slow-diffusing and monopoly-based innovation. The health of citizens and the health of capitalism will rest on fast and frugal innovation. China can dramatically accelerate technologies down the cost curve.

But will it? This question also remains open, although not in the case of the United States. We know the United States will continue to drive world capitalism ever deeper into a knowledge monopoly paradigm of protection because this paradigm has served it well in terms of maintaining a military and economic lead over its competitors. But by propagating the paradigm at this point in history, the United States risks capitalism being able to adapt to its greatest challenge.

China and the United States have to find the deeper cooperation they need to escape the narrow logic of "inevitable" superpower conflict. But even if they do, they will, as capitalist states depend on the circulation of commodities. As Marx points out, this is the beginning of capital. The science we have of ecological systems and climate systems points us to the primary importance of the use values of these systems for our survival. To use the language of standard economics, climate and ecological systems function as a mosaic of public goods, providing us with use values such as biodiversity, reliable rainfall, or clean air at both regional and global levels. Capital, however, depends for its existence and expansion on the exchange values of commodities. It cannot expand on the basis of use values alone, and so, as a restless evolving method of economic growth, it hunts for new commodities and exchange relations, selecting for those and not for use values alone. All the evidence we have to date about the increasing rate of collapse of major ecosystems, the inability of states to deal with the loss of biodiversity, and the climate crisis itself shows how difficult it is to shift capitalism away from commodification processes. We have little evidence that a market in ecosystem services or biodiversity will work. We have something to learn from indigenous cultures in which service to ecosystems is the fundamental value rather than the Goldman Sachs version of markets in ecosystem services.

Whether this kind of shift in outlook is possible within the world capitalism of the 21st century is simply a guess. What is a little clearer is that if the system of world capitalism is to move in a direction where the greatest number of citizens have the greatest chance of survival, more—at this moment in history—rests on the planning and decisions of China than of any other capitalist state.

Bibliography

Abrami, Regina M., William C. Kirby, and F. Warren McFarlan, "Why China Can't Innovate," *Harvard Business Review*, 92 (2014), 107–111.

Adesina, Oluwakemi, Isao A. Anzai, Jose L. Avalos, and Buz Barstow, "Embracing Biological Solutions to the Sustainable Energy Challenge," *Chem*, 2 (2017), 20–51.

Agrawala, Shardul, "Early Science—Policy Interactions in Climate Change: Lessons from the Advisory Group on Greenhouse Gases," *Global Environmental Change*, 9 (1999), 157–169.

Ahmad, Aqueil, "Science and Technology in Development: Policy Options for India and China," *Economic and Political Weekly*, 13 (December 23–30, 1978), 2079–2090.

Andersson, David Emanuel, Ake E. Andersson, and Charlotte Mellander, *Handbook of Creative Cities*, Edward Elgar, Cheltenham, UK, 2011.

Ansar, Atif, Bent Flyvbjerg, Alexander Budzier, and Daniel Lunn, "Does Infrastructure Investment Lead to Economic Growth or Economic Fragility? Evidence from China," *Oxford Review of Economic Policy*, 32 (2016), 360–390.

Arabella Advisors, *The Global Fossil Fuel Divestment and Clean Energy Investment Movement*, Washington, DC, 2018.

Arrhenius, Svante, "On the Influence of Carbonic Acid in the Air upon the Temperature of the Ground," *Philosophical Magazine and Journal of Science*, 41 (1896), 237–276.

Arrow, Kenneth J., "Economic Welfare and the Allocation of Resources for Invention," in National Bureau of Economic Research, *The Rate and Direction of Inventive Activity: Economic and Social Factors*, Princeton University Press, Princeton, NJ, 1962, 609–626.

Australian Energy Market Operator, *Initial Operation of the Hornsdale Power Reserve Energy Storage System*, Melbourne, April 2018.

Ayling, Julie, "A Contest for Legitimacy: The Divestment Movement and the Fossil Fuel Industry," *Law & Policy*, 39 (2017), 349–371.

Ayling, Julie, and Neil Gunningham, "Non-State Governance and Climate Policy: The Fossil Fuel Divestment Movement," *Climate Policy*, 17 (2017), 131–149.

Baldwin, Richard, *The Great Convergence: Information Technology and the New Globalization*, The Belknap Press of Harvard University Press, Cambridge, MA, 2016.

Banister, Judith, "Manufacturing Employment in China," *Monthly Labor Review*, 11 (2005), 11.

Barbier, E. B., *Rethinking the Economic Recovery: A Global Green New Deal*, Report prepared for the Economics and Trade Branch, Division of Technology, Industry and Economics, United Nations Environment Programme, April 2009.

Barbose, Galen L., *U.S. Renewable Portfolio Standards: 2018 Annual Status Report*, Lawrence Berkeley National Laboratory, November 2018.

Basel Committee on Banking Supervision, *Basel III: Finalising Post-Crisis Reforms*, Basel, December 2017.

Bates, D. V., "The Effects of Air Pollution on Children," *Environmental Health Perspectives*, 103 (supplement 6) (1995), 49–53.

Bell, Daniel, *The China Model*, Princeton University Press, Princeton, NJ, 2015.

Belt and Road, "Twenty-seven global institutions sign up to green investment principles for Belt & Road", 3 May 2019, https://beltandroad.hktdc.com/en/insights/twenty-seven-global-institutions-sign-green-investment-principles-belt-road.

Ben-Atar, Doron S., *Trade Secrets: Intellectual Piracy and the Origins of American Industrial Power*, Yale University Press, New Haven, CT, 2004.

Berg, Charles A., "Process Innovation and Changes in Industrial Energy Use," *Science*, new series, 199 (1978), 608–614.

Bernauer, Thomas, and Vally Koubi, "Are Bigger Governments Better Providers of Public Goods? Evidence from Air Pollution," *Public Choice*, 156 (2013), 593–609.

Bhargava, Pushpa M., and Chandana Chakrabarti, "Of India, Indians, and Science," *Daedalus*, 118 (1989), 353–368.

Biliang Hu, Jia Luo, Chunlai Chen, and Bingqin Li, "Evaluating Low-Carbon City Development in China: Study of Five National Pilot Cities," in Ligang Song, Ross Garnaut, Cai Fang, and Lauren Johnston (eds.), *China's New Sources of Economic Growth*, Vol. 1, ANU Press, Acton, Australia, 2016, 315–336.

Block-Lieb, Susan, and Terence C. Halliday, *Global Lawmakers: International Organizations in the Crafting of World Markets*, Cambridge University Press, Cambridge, 2017.

BP, *BP Statistical Review of World Energy 2016*, London, 2016.

Braithwaite, John, Hilary Charlesworth, and Adérito Soares, *Networked Governance of Freedom and Tyranny: Peace in Timor-Leste*, ANU E Press, Canberra, 2012.

Braithwaite, John, and Peter Drahos, *Global Business Regulation*, Cambridge University Press, Cambridge, 2000.

C40 Cities, "Shenzhen—New Energy Vehicles (including Electric Buses)," in *C40 Good Practice Guides: Low Emission Vehicles*, London, February, 2016, 8–9.

Campanella, Thomas, *The Concrete Dragon: China's Urban Revolution and What It Means for the world*, Princeton Architectural Press, New York, 2008.

Cassedy, Edward S, *Prospects for Sustainable Energy: A Critical Assessment*, Cambridge University Press, Cambridge, 2000.

Cavusoglu, Ahmet-Hamdi, Xi Chen, Pierre Gentine, and Ozgur Sahin, "Potential for Natural Evaporation as a Reliable Renewable Energy Resource," *Nature Communications* 8, no. 617 (2017).

Chan, Hon S. "Cadre Personnel Management in China: The Nomenklatura System, 1990–1998," *The China Quarterly*, 179 (2004), 703–734.

Chan, Roger C. K., "Cross-Border Regional Development in Southern China," *GeoJournal*, 44 (1998), 225–237.

Charter, Martin, "Introduction," in Martin Charter (ed.), *Designing for the Circular Economy*, Routledge, London, 2019, 1–11.

Cheng Li, *China's Leaders: The New Generation*, Rowman & Littlefield, Lanham, MD, 2001.

Cheng, Wenting, and Peter Drahos, "How China Built the World's Biggest Patent Office: The Pressure-Driving Mechanism," *International Review of Intellectual Property and Competition Law*, 49 (2018), 5–40.

Chunlai Chen, "The Liberalisation of FDI Policies and the Impacts of FDI on China's Economic Development," in Ross Garnaut, Ligang Song, and Cai Fang (eds.), *China's 40 Years of Reform and Development: 1978–2018*, ANU Press, Canberra, 2018, 595–617.

Commission on the Theft of American Intellectual Property, *The Report of the Commission on the Theft of American Intellectual Property*, The National Bureau of Asian Research, 2013.

Committee on the Elimination of Racial Discrimination, "Concluding Observations on the Combined Fourteenth to Seventeenth Periodic Reports of China (including Hong Kong, China and Macao, China)," August 20, 2018, CERD/c/chn/co/14-17.

Committee on Japan Framework Statement and Report of the Competitiveness Task Force, *Maximizing U.S. Interests in Science and Technology Relations with Japan*, National Academy Press, Washington, DC, 1997.

Communication from the Commission to the European Parliament, the European Council, the Council, the European Economic and Social Committee, and the Committee of the Regions, *The European Green Deal*, COM/2019/640 final.

Converse III, Elliot V., *Rearming For The Cold War 1945–1960*, Historical Office, Office of the Secretary of Defense, Washington, DC, 2012, 12.

Cousins, Sophie, "A New Way to Detect Breast Cancer," *New York Times*, August 28, 2018.

Daniels, Farrington, "Utilization of Solar Energy—Progress Report," *Proceedings of the American Philosophical Society*, 115 (1971), 490–501.

Darby, Megan, "India Diverts $25 Million Away from Clean Energy Fund," *Climate Home News*, July 24, 2017.

Dedrick, Jason, Kenneth L. Kraemer, and Greg Linden, "Who Profits from Innovation in Global Value Chains? A Study of the iPod and Notebook PCs," *Industrial and Corporate Change* 19 (2010), 81–116.

Defense Security Service, *Targeting U.S. Technologies: A Trend Analysis of Reporting from Defense Industry 2012*, Defense Security Service, 2012.

Department of Science and Technology, Government of India, *Research and Development Statistics at a Glance, 2017–2018*, New Delhi, December 2017.

Dianwu Zhao and Bozen Sun, "Air Pollution and Acid Rain in China," *Ambio*, 15 (1986), 2–5.

Dingman, Roger, "Atomic Diplomacy during the Korean War," *International Security*, 13 (1988–1989), 50–91.

Downie, Christian, *The Politics of Climate Change Negotiations: Strategies and Variables in Prolonged International Negotiations*, Edward Elgar, Cheltenham, UK, 2014.

Drahos, Peter, *Intellectual Property, Indigenous People and Their Knowledge*, Cambridge University Press, Cambridge, 2014.

Drahos, Peter, and John Braithwaite, *Information Feudalism*, Earthscan, London, 2002.

Ebenstein, Avraham, "The Consequences of Industrialization: Evidence from Water Pollution and Digestive Cancers in China," *Review of Economics and Statistics*, 94 (2012), 186–201.

Eckhouse, Brian, "Wall Street Sours on $9 Billion Mechanism for Green Projects," *Bloomberg News*, July 10, 2017.

Ehrenfeld, John, and Nicholas Gertler, "Industrial Ecology in Practice: The Evolution of Interdependence at Kalundborg," *Journal of Industrial Ecology*, 1 (1997), 67–79.

Ellul, Jacques, *The Technological Society* (tr. John Wilkinson), Vintage Books, New York, 1964.

Embassy of the Kingdom of the Netherlands, "Factsheet: Sponge City Construction in China," 2016, https://www.google.com/url?sa=t&rct=j&q=&esrc=s&source=web&cd=&ved=2ahUKEwi03NfXnOTsAhUNilwKHYysD1kQFjAAegQIBRAC&url=https%3A%2F%2Fwww.nederlandenu.nl%2Fbinaries%2Fnl-netherlandsandyou%2Fdocum

enten%2Fpublicaties%2F2016%2F12%2F06%2F2016-factsheet-sponge-cities-pilot-project-china.pdf%2F2016-factsheet-sponge-cities-pilot-project-china.pdf&usg=AO vVaw3GMERlQSv0E07w43OpMRFb

Engen, Ole Andreas H., "The Development of the Norwegian Petroleum Innovation System: A Historical Overview," Centre for Technology, Innovation and Culture (TIK), Working Paper on Innovation Studies, No. 20070605, University of Oslo, 2007.

Englund, Leif, Mats Lagerkvist, and Rebati Dass, "HVDC Superhighways for China," *ABB Review*, 4/2003.

Etzkowitz, Henry, "Innovation in Innovation: The Triple Helix of University-Industry-Government Relations," *Social Science Information*, 42 (2003), 293–337.

Eun-Soon Im, Jeremy S. Pal, and Elfatih A. B. Eltahir, "Deadly Heat Waves Projected in the Densely Populated Agricultural regions of South Asia," *Science Advances*, 3, no. 8 (August 2, 2017), e1603322.

European Chamber of Commerce in China, *China Manufacturing 2025: Putting Industrial Policy Ahead of Market Forces*, Beijing, 2017.

European Commission, *Closing the Loop—An EU Action Plan for the Circular Economy*, Brussels, COM (2015) 614 final.

European Commission, "Financing the Green Transition: The European Green Deal Investment Plan and Just Transition Mechanism," press release, January 14, 2020, https://ec.europa.eu/commission/presscorner/detail/en/ip_20_17.

European Commission, *A Framework Strategy for a Resilient Energy Union with a Forward-Looking Climate Change Policy*, Brussels, 25.2.2015 COM (2015) 80 final.

European Commission, *Monitoring the Application of European Union Law, 2016 Annual Report*, Brussels, 6.7.2017 COM (2017) 370 final.

EU SME Centre, *Smart Cities in China*, Beijing, 2015.

Fang, Cai, Ross Garnaut, and Ligang Song, "40 Years of China's Reform and Development: How Reform Captured China's Demographic Dividend," in Ross Garnaut, Ligang Song, and Cai Fang (eds.), *China's 40 Years of Reform and Development, 1978–2018*, ANU Press, Acton, Australia, 2018, 512.

Federal Ministry of Economics and Technology and Federal Ministry of Environment, Nature Conservation, and Nuclear Safety, *Energy Concept for an Environmentally Sound, Reliable, and Affordable Energy Supply*, Berlin, 2010.

Fegley, Randall, "The Human Rights Commission: The Equatorial Guinea Case," *Human Rights Quarterly*, 3 (1981), 34–47.

Fialka, John, "Why China Is Dominating the Solar Industry," *Scientific American E & E News*, December 19, 2016.

Fligstein, Neal, and Adam Goldstein, *The Transformation of Mortgage Finance and the Industrial Roots of the Mortgage Meltdown*, Institute for Research on Labor and Employment, Working Paper #133-12, Berkeley, CA, October 2012.

Florida, Richard, "Cities and the Creative Class," *City & Community*, 2 (2003), 3–19.

Florida, Richard, *Cities and the Creative Class*, Routledge, New York, 2005.

Fouquet, Roger, *Heat, Power and Light: Revolutions in Energy Services*, Edward Elgar, Cheltenham, UK, 2008.

Frynas, Jędrzej George, "The Oil Boom in Equatorial Guinea," *African Affairs*, 103 (2004), 527–546.

Fraas, L. M., *Low-Cost Solar Electrical Power*, Springer, Cham, Switzerland, 2014.

Frank, Lawrence P., "The First Oil Regime," *World Politics*, 37 (1985), 586–598.

Fraunhofer Institute for Solar Energy Systems ISE, *Levelized Cost of Electricity— Renewable Energy Technologies*, Fraunhofer Institute for Solar Energy Systems ISE, Freiburg, Germany, November 2013.

Garnaut, Ross, Cai Fang, and Ligang Song (eds.), *China: A New Model for Growth and Development*, ANU E Press, Canberra, Australia, 2013.

Giffard, Hermione, "Engines of Desperation: Jet Engines, Production and New Weapons in the Third Reich," *Journal of Contemporary History*, 48 (2013), 821–844.

Glaeser, Edward, Wei Huang, Yueran Ma, and Andrei Shleifer, "A Real Estate Boom with Chinese Characteristics," *Journal of Economic Perspectives*, 31 (2017), 93–116.

Gohlke, Julia M., Reuben Thomas, Alistair Woodward, Diarmid Campbell-Lendrum, Annette Prüss-Üstün, Simon Hales, and Christopher J. Portier, "Estimating the Global Public Health Implications of Electricity and Coal Consumption," *Environmental Health Perspectives*, 119 (2011), 821–826.

Grafton, R. Quentin, Tom Kompas, and Ngo Van Long, "Biofuels Subsidies and the Green Paradox," CESifo Working Paper No. 2960, 2010.

Graham, John, *Obama on the Home Front: Domestic Policy Triumphs and Setbacks*, Indiana University Press, Bloomington, 2016.

Green Finance Task Force, *Establishing China's Green Financial System (Final Report)*, People's Bank of China and United Nations Environment Programme, Beijing and Geneva, 2015.

Grigas, Agnia, *The Politics of Energy and Memory between the Baltic States and Russia*, Ashgate, Aldershot, UK, 2013.

Guelff, Christopher, and Liwayway Adkins, *Emissions Trading in the People's Republic of China: A Simulation for the Power Sector*, OECD/IEA, Paris, 2014.

Gueorguiev, Dimitar, and Jonathan Stromseth, "New China Agency Could Undercut Other Anti-Corruption Efforts," *Brookings Blog*, March 6, 2018.

Gulagi, Ashish, Dmitrii Bogdanov, and Christian Breyer, "The Demand for Storage Technologies in Energy Transition Pathways towards 100% Renewable Energy for India," *Energy Procedia*, 135 (2017), 7–50.

Guoguang Wu, "China in 2010 Dilemmas of 'Scientific Development,'" *Asian Survey*, 51 (2011), 18–32.

Gupta, Himangana, Ravinder Kohli, and Amrik S. Ahluwalia, "Mapping 'Consistency' in India's Climate Change Position: Dynamics and Dilemmas of Science Diplomacy," *Ambio*, 44 (2015), 592–599.

Haines, Fiona, *The Paradox of Regulation: What Regulation Can Achieve and What It Cannot*, Edward Elgar, Cheltenham, UK, 2011.

Harris, John R., *Industrial Espionage and Technology Transfer: Britain and France in the Eighteenth Century*, Ashgate, Aldershot, UK, 1998.

Hayes, Denis, "Solar Power in the Middle East," *Science*, new series, 188 (1975), 1261.

Hayward, Joel, "Too Little, Too Late: An Analysis of Hitler's Failure in August 1942 to Damage Soviet Oil Production," *Journal of Military History*, 64 (2000), 769–794.

He Zengke, "Building a Modern National Integrity System: Anticorruption and Checks and Balance of Power in China," in Kenneth Lieberthal, Cheng Li, and Yu Keping (eds.), *China's Political Development: Chinese and American Perspectives*, Brookings Institution Press, Washington, D. C., 2014, 366–395.

Headrick, Daniel R., *The Tools of Empire: Technology and European Imperialism in the Nineteenth Century*, Oxford University Press, New York, 1981.

Hinton, Diana D., "The Seventeen-Year Overnight Wonder: George Mitchell and Unlocking the Barnett Shale," *Journal of American History*, 99 (2012), 229–235.

Hirsch, Robert L., John E. Gallagher, Richard R. Lessard, and Robert D. Wesselhoft, "Catalytic Coal Gasification: An Emerging Technology," *Science*, new series, 215 (1982), 121–127.

Holler, Mirko, Manuel Guizar-Sicairos, Esther H. R. Tsai, Roberto Dinapoli, Elisabeth Muller, Oliver Bunk, Jorg Raabe, and Babriel Aeppli, "High-Resolution Non-Destructive Three-Dimensional Imaging of Integrated Circuits," *Nature*, 543 (2017), 402–406.

Houghton, J. T., G. J. Jenkins, and J. J. Ephraums (eds.), *Climate Change: The IPCC Scientific Assessment*, Cambridge University Press, Cambridge, 1990.

Howard, E., *Tomorrow: A Peaceful Path to Real Reform*, Swan Sonnenschein & Co., Ltd., London, 1898.

Hughes, Thomas P, *Networks of Power: Electrification in Western Society, 1880–1930*, Johns Hopkins University Press, Baltimore, 1983.

Hurtig, Anna-Karin, and Miguel San Sebastian, "Geographical Differences in Cancer Incidence in the Amazon Basin of Ecuador in Relation to Residence near Oil Fields," *International Journal of Epidemiology*, 31 (2002), 1021–1027.

Hutchens, Anna, *Changing Big Business: The Globalisation of the Fair Trade Movement*, Edward Elgar, Cheltenham, UK, 2009.

Iakovleva, Tatiana, "Open Innovation at the Root of Entrepreneurial Strategy: A Case from the Norwegian Oil Industry," *Technology Innovation Management Review*, 17 (2013), 17–22.

Iammarino, Simona, and Philip McCann, *Multinationals and Economic Geography: Location, Technology and Innovation*, Edward Elgar, Cheltenham, UK, 2013.

Ilgen, Thomas L, "'Better Living through Chemistry': The Chemical Industry in the World Economy," *International Organization*, 37 (1983), 647–680.

Intergovernmental Panel on Climate Change, *Climate Change: The IPCC Scientific Assessment*, Cambridge University Press, Cambridge, 1990.

Intergovernmental Panel on Climate Change, *Climate Change 2013: The Physical Science Basis, Contribution of Working Group I to the Fifth Assessment Report of the Intergovernmental Panel on Climate Change*, Cambridge University Press, Cambridge, 2013.

Intergovernmental Panel on Climate Change, *Climate Change 2014: Synthesis Report. Contribution of Working Groups I, II and III to the Fifth Assessment Report of the Intergovernmental Panel on Climate Change*, IPCC, Geneva, 2014.

Intergovernmental Panel on Climate Change, *Global Warming of 1.5°C: An IPCC Special Report*, World Meteorological Organization, Geneva, 2018.

Intergovernmental Panel on Climate Change, *Summary for Policymakers in Climate Change 2014: Mitigation of Climate Change, Contribution of Working Group III to the Fifth Assessment Report of the Intergovernmental Panel on Climate Change*, Cambridge University Press, Cambridge, 2014.

Intergovernmental Panel on Climate Change, "Vulnerability to Climate Change and Reasons for Concern: A Synthesis" in *Climate Change 2001: Impacts, Adaptation, and Vulnerability*, Cambridge University Press, New York, 2001, 915-967.

Intergovernmental Science-Policy Platform on Biodiversity and Ecosystem Services, *Summary for Policymakers of the Global Assessment Report on Biodiversity and Ecosystem Services*, Bonn, 2019.

International Carbon Action Partnership, *Emissions Trading Worldwide: Status Report 2019*, ICAP, Berlin, 2019.

International Electrotechnical Commission, *Global Energy Interconnection*, white paper, Geneva, 2016.

International Electrotechnical Commission, *Grid Integration of Large-Capacity Renewable Energy Sources and Use of Large-Capacity Electrical Energy Storage*, white paper, Geneva, 2012.

International Energy Agency, *Cleaner Coal in China*, OECD/IEA, Paris, 2009.

International Energy Agency, *CO_2 Emissions from Fuel Combustion (2018 edition)*, OECD/IEA, Paris, 2018.

International Energy Agency, *Digitalization and Energy*, OECD/IEA, Paris, 2017.

International Energy Agency, *Gas 2018: Analysis and Forecasts to 2023*, OECD/IEA, Paris, 2018.

International Energy Agency, *Global Energy and CO_2 Status Report*, OECD/IEA, Paris, March 2019.

International Energy Agency, *India Energy Outlook*, OECD/IEA, Paris, 2015.

International Energy Agency, *India 2020: Energy Policy Review*, IEA, France, 2020.

International Energy Agency, *Key World Energy Statistics 2017*, OECD/IEA, Paris, 2017.

International Energy Agency, *Key World Energy Statistics 2018*, OECD/IEA, Paris, 2018.

International Energy Agency, *Nuclear Power in a Clean Energy System*, IEA, Paris, 2019.

International Energy Agency, *Prospects for CO_2 Capture and Storage*, OECD/IEA, Paris, 2004.

International Energy Agency, *Redrawing the Energy-Climate Map*, OECD/IEA, Paris, 2013.

International Energy Agency, *Renewables 2017: Analysis and Forecasts to 2022*, OECD/IEA, Paris, 2017.

International Energy Agency, *World Energy Investment 2016*, OECD/IEA, Paris, 2016.

International Energy Agency, *World Energy Investment 2018*, OECD/IEA, Paris, 2018.

International Energy Agency, *World Energy Outlook 2007*, OECD/IEA, Paris, 2007.

International Energy Agency, *World Energy Outlook 2012*, OECD/IEA, Paris, 2012.

International Energy Agency, *World Energy Outlook 2013*, OECD/IEA, Paris, 2013.

International Energy Agency, *World Energy Outlook 2015*, OECD/IEA, Paris, 2015.

International Energy Agency, *World Energy Outlook 2017*, OECD/IEA. Paris, 2017.

International Energy Agency, *World Energy Outlook 2018*, OECD/IEA, Paris, 2018.

International Energy Agency, *World Energy Outlook: Looking at Energy Subsidies: Getting the Prices Right*, IEA, Paris, 1999.

International Energy Agency / Nuclear Energy Agency / Organisation of Economic Co-operation and Development, *Projected Costs of Generating Electricity: 2015 Edition*, France, 2015.

International Renewable Energy Agency, *Renewable Power Generation Costs in 2018*, IRENA, Abu Dhabi, 2019.

International Renewable Energy Agency and Climate Policy Initiative, *Global Landscape of Renewable Energy Finance 2018*, IRENA, Abu Dhabi, 2018.

Jacobsen, Noel B, "Industrial Symbiosis in Kalundborg, Denmark: A Quantitative Assessment of Economic and Environmental Aspects," *Journal of Industrial Ecology*, 10 (2006), 239–255.

Janssens-Maenhout, G. M. Crippa, D. Guizzardi, M. Muntean, E. Schaaf, J. G. J. Olivier, J. A. H. W. Peters, and K. M. Schure, *Fossil CO_2 and GHG Emissions of All World Countries*, EUR 28766 EN, Publications Office of the European Union, Luxembourg, 2017.

Jayakar, Krishna, "Globalization and the Legitimacy of International Telecommunications Standard-Setting Organizations," *Indiana Journal of Global Legal Studies*, 5 (1998), 711–738.

Jian Xie with Andres Liebenthal, Jeremy J. Warford, John A. Dixon, Manchuan Wang, Shiji Gao, Shuilin Wang, Yong Jiang, and Zhong Ma, *Addressing China's Water Scarcity: Recommendations for Selected Water Resource Management Issues*, International Bank for Reconstruction and Development / The World Bank, Washington, DC, 2009.

Jiang Yu, Yating Wen, Jing Jin, and Yue Zhang "Towards a Service-Dominant Platform for Public Value Co-Creation in a Smartcity: Evidence from Two Metropolitan Cities in China," *Technological Forecasting & Social Change*, 142 (2019), 168–182.

Jianglong Yu, Fanrui Meng, Xianchun Li, and Arash Tahmasebi, "Power Generation from Coal Gangue in China: Current Status and Development," *Advanced Materials Research*, 550–553 (2012), 443–446.

Jianguo Qi, Jingxing Zhao, Wenjun Li, Xushu Peng, Bin Wu, and Hong Wang, *Development of Circular Economy in China*, Springer, Singapore, 2016.

Jici Wang and John H. Bradbury, "The Changing Industrial Geography of the Chinese Special Economic Zones," *Economic Geography*, 62 (1986), 307–320.

Jixi Gao, "How China Will Protect One-Quarter of Its Land," *Nature*, 569 (May 23, 2019), 475.

Johnston, Robert, "U.S. Export Control Policy in the High-Performance Computer Sector," *The Nonproliferation Review* (Winter 1998), 44–59.

Joss, Simon, "Eco-Cities—A Global Survey 2009," *WIT Transactions on Ecology and the Environment*, 129 (2010), 239–250.

Kander, Astrid, Paolo Malanima, and Paul Warde, *Power to the People: Energy in Europe over the Last Five Centuries*, Princeton University Press, Princeton, NJ, 2013.

Kang Chao, "The Production and Application of Chemical Fertilizers in China," *China Quarterly*, 64 (1975), 712–729.

Karasov, Corliss, "Water Pollution. Reviving China's Ruined Rivers," *Environmental Health Perspectives*, 110 (2002), A510–A511.

Kojevnikov, Alexei B., *Stalin's Great Science: The Times and Adventures of Soviet Physicists*, Imperial College Press, London, 2004.

Knight, Richard, "Expanding Petroleum Products in Africa," *Review of African Political Economy*, 30 (2003), 335–339.

Kuramochi, Takeshi, Niklas Höhne, Sebastian Sterl, Katharina Lütkehermöller, and Jean-Charles Seghers, *States, Cities and Businesses Leading the Way: A First Look at Decentralized Climate Commitments in the US*, New Climate Institute, Cologne, 2017.

Kynge, James, Arthur Beesley, and Andrew Byrne, "EU Sets Collision Course with China over 'Silk Road' Rail Project," *Financial Times*, February 20, 2017.

Large, Daniel, "China and the Contradictions of 'Non-Interference' in Sudan," *Review of African Political Economy*, 35 (2008), 93–106.

Larsson, Jörgen, Anna Elofsson, Thomas Sterner, and Jonas Åkerman, "International and National Climate Policies for Aviation: A Review," *Climate Policy*, 19 (2019), 787–799.

Larsson, Robert L., *Tackling Dependency: The EU and Its Energy Challenges*, Swedish Defence Research Agency, Stockholm, 2007.

Lee, Joyce, and Ju-min Park, "Samsung in Talks with ZTE, Others to Supply Mobile Processor Chips: Executive," *Reuters*, May 15, 2018.

Levine, Steve, "The Era of Oil Abundance," *Foreign Policy*, July 17, 2012.

Lokuge, Buddhima, Peter Drahos, and Warwick Neville, "Pandemics, Antiviral Stockpiles and Biosecurity in Australia: What About the Generic Option?," *Medical Journal of Australia*, 184 (2006), 16–20.

Lynch, Michael C., "Forecasting Oil Supply: Theory and Practice," *Quarterly Review of Economics and Finance*, 42 (2002), 373–389.

MacNeil, Robert, "Between Innovation and Industrial Policy: How Washington Succeeds and Fails at Renewable Energy," *Prometheus*, 34 (2016), 173–189.

Mani, Sunil, "Is India Becoming More Innovative since 1991? Some Disquieting Features," *Economic and Political Weekly*, 44, no. 46 (November 14, 2009), 41–51.

Manion, Melanie, "The Cadre Management System, Post-Mao: The Appointment, Promotion, Transfer and Removal of Party and State Leaders," *The China Quarterly*, 102 (1985), 203–233.

Maroufmashat, Azadeh, and Michael Fowler, "Transition of Future Energy System Infrastructure; through Power-to-Gas Pathways, *Energies*, 10 (2017), 1089.

Marx, Karl, *Capital*, Volume 1 (translated by Samuel Moore and Edward Aveling, edited by Friedrich Engels, Modern Library, New York, 1906), republished Dover Publications, New York, 2011.

Mathews, John A., and Hao Tan, "The Transformation of the Electric Power Sector in China," *Energy Policy*, 52 (2013), 170–180.

Maurer, John H, "Fuel and the Battle Fleet: Coal, Oil, and American Naval Strategy, 1898–1925," *Naval War College Review*, 34 (1981), 60–77.

Mayer, Jane, *Dark Money: The Hidden History of the Rise of the Billionaires behind the Radical Right*, Doubleday, New York, 2016.

McCarthy, Kieren, "Can't Do It the US Way? Then We'll Do It Huawei—And Roll Our Own Mobile Operating System," *The Register*, March 14, 2019.

McGlade, Christophe, and Paul Ekins, "The Geographical Distribution of Fossil Fuels Unused When Limiting Global Warming to 2°C," *Nature*, 517 (2015), 187–190.

McGrath, Matt, "Oil Change? Fossil Fuel Advocate to Run State Department," *BBC News*, December 13, 2016.

Meadows, Donella H., Dennis L. Meadows, Jorgen Renders, and William W. Behrens, *The Limits to Growth: A Report for the Club of Rome's Project on the Predicament of Mankind*, Universe Books, New York, 1972.

Mearsheimer, John, *The Tragedy of Great Power Politics*, W. W. Norton & Company, New York, 2001.

Merton, Robert K., "The Self-Fulfilling Prophecy," *The Antioch Review*, 8 (1948), 193–210.

Millennium Ecosystem Assessment, *Ecosystems and Human Well-Being: Synthesis*, Island Press, Washington, DC, 2005.

Ministry of New and Renewable Energy, *Annual Report 2016–2017*, New Delhi, 2017.

Minxin Pei, *China's Crony Capitalism: The Dynamics of Regime Decay*, Harvard University Press, Cambridge, MA, 2016.

Minxin Pei, "China's Governance Crisis," *Foreign Affairs*, 81 (2002), 96–109.

Montague, Brendan, "How Margaret Thatcher Came to Sound the Climate Alarm," *Ecologist*, August 21, 2018.

Montgomery, Carl T., and Michael B. Smith, "Hydraulic Fracturing: History of an Enduring Technology," *Journal of Petroleum Technology*, 62 (2010), 26–32.

Mowery, David C., and Nathan Rosenberg, *Paths of Innovation: Technological Change in 20th-Century America*, Cambridge University Press, Cambridge, 1999.

Musson, A. E., "Industrial Motive Power in the United Kingdom, 1800–70," *Economic History Review*, new series, 29 (1976), 415–439.

Nan Zhou, Gang He, and Christopher Williams, *China's Development of Low-Carbon Eco-Cities and Associated Indicator Systems*, Ernest Orlando Lawrence Berkeley National Laboratory, 2012.

National Climate Center, China Meteorological Administration, *Non-Party Stakeholder Submission to the Talanoa Dialogue of the UNFCCC*, Beijing, March 2018.

National Institution for Transforming India (NITI Aayog), *Draft National Energy Policy*, New Delhi, 2017.

Nehru, Jawaharlal, *The Discovery of India*, Oxford University Press, Delhi, 1985.

Nelson, Richard R., and Sidney G. Winter, *An Evolutionary Theory of Economic Change*, The Belknap Press of Harvard University Press, Cambridge, MA, 1982.

Neslen, Arthur, "India Unveils Global Solar Alliance of 120 Countries at Paris Climate Summit," *The Guardian*, November 30, 2015.

Ng, Wei-Shiuen, Lee Schipper, and Yang Chen, "China Motorization Trends New Directions for Crowded Cities," *Journal of Transport and Land Use*, 3 (2010), 5–25.

Nylander, Johan, "Chinese 'Ghost Mall' Back from the Dead?," *CNN*, June 24, 2015.

Odell, John S., and Susan K. Sell, "Reframing the Issue: The WTO Coalition on Intellectual Property and Public Health, 2001," in John S. Odell (ed.), *Negotiating Trade: Developing Countries in the WTO and NAFTA*, Cambridge University Press, Cambridge, 2006.

Office of the Leading Group for Promoting the Belt and Road Initiative, *The Belt and Road Ecological and Environmental Cooperation Plan*, May 2017. https://www.followingthemoney.org/wp-content/uploads/2017/06/2017_MEP_Belt-and-Road-Ecological-and-Environmental-Cooperation-Plan_E.pdf.

Office of the Leading Group for Promoting the Belt and Road Initiative, *The Belt and Road Initiative Progress, Contributions and Prospects*, April 22, 2019. http://www.xinhuanet.com/english/2019-04/22/c_137998357.htm.

Organisation of Economic Co-operation and Development, *China in a Changing Global Environment*, OECD, Paris, 2015.

Organisation of Economic Co-operation and Development, *Education Indicators in Focus*, 31, OECD, April 2015.

Organisation of Economic Co-operation and Development, *OECD Urban Policy Reviews: China 2015*, OECD Publishing, Paris, 2015.

Owyang, Michael T., and Hannah G. Shell, "China's Economic Data: An Accurate Reflection or Just Smoke and Mirrors?" *The Regional Economist*, Second Quarter, 2017.

Pearce, Fred, "Greenwash: The Dream of the First Eco-City Was Built on Fiction," *The Guardian*, April 23, 2009.

Peters, Glen P., Robbie M. Andrew, Tom Boden, Josep G. Canadell, Philippe Ciais, Corinne Le Quere, Gregg Marland, Michael R. Raupach, and Charlie Wilson, "The Challenge to Keep Global Warming below 2°C," *Nature Climate Change*, 3 (2013), 4–6.

Peters, Glen P., Gregg Marland, Corinne Le Quere, Thomas Boden, Josep G. Canadell, and Michael R Raupach, "Rapid Growth in CO_2 Emissions after the 2008–2009 Global Financial Crisis," *Nature Climate Change*, 2 (2012), 2–4.

Planning Commission, Government of India, *Twelfth Five-Year Plan (2012–2017)*, Volume I, *Faster, More Inclusive and Sustainable Growth*, Sage Publications India, New Delhi, 2013.

Planning Commission, Government of India, *Twelfth Five-Year Plan (2012–2017)*, Volume II, *Economic Sectors*, Sage Publications India, New Delhi, 2013.

Plekhanov, Dmitriy, "Quality of China's Official Statistics: A Brief Review of Academic Perspectives," *Copenhagen Journal of Asian Studies*, 35 (2017), 76–101.

Pool, Robert, "Solar Cells Turn 30," *Science*, new series, 241, no. 4868 (August 19, 1988), 900–901.

Postiglione, Gerard A., "Research Universities for National Rejuvenation and Global Influence: China's Search for a Balanced Model," *Higher Education*, 70 (2015), 235–250.

Radjou, Navi, and Jaideep Prahbu, "What Frugal Innovators Do," *Harvard Business Review*, December 10, 2014.

Railway Commission of Texas, *Eagle Ford Shale Task Force Report*, March 2013.

Rainforest Action Network, BankTrack, Indigenous Environmental Network, Oil Change International, Reclaim Finance, and the Sierra Club, *Banking on Climate Change: Fossil Fuel Finance Report 2020*, https://www.banktrack.org/article/banking_on_climate_change_fossil_fuel_finance_report_card_2020.

Rious, Vincent, and Nicolo Rossetto, "Continental Incentive Regulation," in Leonardo Meeus and Jean-Michel Glachant (eds.), *Electricity Network Regulation in the EU: The Challenges Ahead for Transmission and Distribution*, Edward Elgar, Cheltenham, UK, 2018.

Rosse, Robert M., "The Working of Communist China's Five-Year Plan," *Pacific Affairs*, 27 (1954), 16.

Rumpf, Julius, and Henrik Bjørnebye, "Just How Much Is Enough? EU Regulation of Capacity and Reliability Margins on Electricity Interconnectors," *Journal of Energy & Natural Resources Law*, 37 (2019), 67–91.

Rusong Wang and Yaping Ye, "Eco-City Development in China," *Ambio*, 33 (2004), 341–342.

Ryder, Brett, "First Break All the Rules: The Charms of Frugal Innovation," *The Economist*, April 15, 2010.

Ryggvik, Helge, "A Short History of the Norwegian Oil Industry: From Protected National Champions to Internationally Competitive Multinationals," *Business History Review*, 89 (2015), 3–41.

Saha, Biswatosh, "State Support for Industrial R and D in Developing Economies: Telecom Equipment Industry in India and China," *Economic and Political Weekly*, 39, no. 35 (August 28–September 3, 2004), 3915–3925.

Saraswati, Jyoti, "The Indian IT Industry and Neo-Liberalism: The Irony of a Mythology," *Third World Quarterly*, 29 (2008), 1139–1152.

Schleicher, Andreas, "China Opens a New University Every Week," *BBC* News, March 16, 2016.

Schneider, M., and A. Froggatt, *The World Nuclear Industry Status Report*, Mycle Schneider Consulting Project, Paris, Budapest, 2019.

Schneyer, Joshua, and Nicolas Medina Mora Perez, "How China Took Control of an OPEC Country's Oil," *Reuters*, November 26, 2013.

236 BIBLIOGRAPHY

Schumpeter, Joseph A., *Capitalism, Socialism and Democracy*, Routledge, 5th ed., London, 1976.

Schwartz, John, "Exxon Mobil Lends Its Support to a Carbon Tax Proposal," *New York Times*, June 20, 2017.

Schwartz, Moshe, Katherine Blakeley, and Ronald O'Rourke, *Department of Defense Energy Initiatives: Background and Issues for Congress*, Congressional Research Service Report for Congress, Washington, DC, 2012.

Scott, Joanne, "From Brussels with Love: The Transatlantic Travels of European Law and the Chemistry of Regulatory Attraction," *American Journal of Comparative Law*, 57 (2009), 897-942.

Scott, Richard, *The History of the International Energy Agency: The First Twenty Years*, Vol. 1, OECD/IEA, Paris, 1994.

Scoville, Warren C., "Technology and the French Glass Industry, 1640-1740," *Journal of Economic History*, 1 (1941), 153-167.

Sen, Gautam, *The Military Origins of Industrialisation and International Trade Rivalry*, Frances Pinters Publishers Limited, London, 1984.

Shabad, Theodore, "Communist China's Five-Year Plan," *Far Eastern Survey*, 24 (1955), 189-191.

Shabecoff, Philip, "Global Warming Has Begun, Expert Tells Senate," *New York Times*, June 24, 1988, Section A, 1.

Shao, Ken, "Taobao, WeChat and Xiaomi: How Innovation Flourishes in China's 'Fertile Land of Intellectual Property Piracy,'" in Gustavo Ghidini, Hanns Ullrich, and Peter Drahos (eds.), *Kritika: Essays on Intellectual Property*, Vol. 2, Edward Elgar, Cheltenham, UK, 2017, 22-43.

Shepard, Wade, *Ghost Cities of China*, Zed Books, London, 2015.

Sinn, Hans-Werner, "Public Policies against Global Warming: A Supply-Side Approach," *International Tax and Public Finance*, 15 (2008), 360-394.

Singh, Rhythm, "Energy Sufficiency Aspirations of India and the Role of Renewable Resources: Scenarios for the Future," *Renewable and Sustainable Energy Reviews*, 81 (2018), 2783-2795.

Skancke, Martin, Elroy Dimson, Michael Hoel, Magdalena Kettis, Gro Nystuen, and Laura Starks, *Fossil-Fuel Investments in the Norwegian Government Pension Fund Global: Addressing Climate Issues through Exclusion and Active Ownership*, Report by the Expert Group Appointed by the Norwegian Ministry of Finance, Oslo, 2014.

Sloop, John L., *Liquid Hydrogen as a Propulsion Fuel, 1945-1959*, NASA, Washington, DC, 1978.

Spencer, Dwain F., Michael J. Gluckman, and Seymour B. Alpert, "Coal Gasification for Electric Power Generation," *Science*, new series, 215 (1982), 1571-1576.

Srivastava, Sarvesh Kumar, Przemyslaw Piwek, Sonal R. Ayakar, Arman Bonakdarpour, David P. Wilkinson, and Vikramaditya G. Yadav, "A Biogenic Photovoltaic Material," *Small*, 14, no. 26 (May 31, 2018).

State Grid Corporation of China, *State Grid Corporate Social Responsibility Report*, Beijing, 2016.

Steffen, Will, Johan Rockstrom, and Robert Costanza, "How Defining Planetary Boundaries Can Transform Our Approach to Growth," *Solutions*, 2 (2011), 59-65.

Strum, Harvey, "The Association for Applied Solar Energy / Solar Energy Society, 1954-1970," *Technology and Culture*, 26 (1985), 571-578.

Strum, Harvey, "Eisenhower's Solar Energy Policy," *Public Historian*, 6 (1984), 37-50.

Sun Yan and Michael Johnston, "Does Democracy Check Corruption? Insights from China and India," *Comparative Politics*, 42 (2009), 1–19.

Szoldra, Paul, "14 Cutting-Edge Firms Funded by the CIA," *Business Insider*, September 21, 2016.

Tang, Rachel, *China's Steel Industry and Its Impact on the United States: Issues for Congress*, Congressional Research Service, Washington, DC, 2010.

Taylor, Peter, *Extraordinary Cities*, Edward Elgar, Cheltenham, UK, 2014.

Technology Executive Committee (UNFCCC), *Enhancing Financing for the Research Development and Demonstration of Climate Technologies*, UNFCCC Working Paper, November 2017.

Tollefson, Jeff, "US Government Abandons Carbon-Capture Demonstration," *Nature News*, February 5, 2015.

Tomory, Leslie, "Building the First Gas Network, 1812–1820," *Technology and Culture*, 52 (2011), 85–102.

Travis, Anthony S., "Perkin's Mauve: Ancestor of the Organic Chemical Industry," *Technology and Culture*, 31 (1990), 51–82.

Tripathy, Devidutta, "Global Pension Funds Warm to India's Solar Power Ambitions," *Reuters*, April 30, 2017.

Turner, Graham M., "A Comparison of The Limits to Growth with 30 Years of Reality," *Global Environmental Change*, 18 (2008), 397–411.

Ullrich, Hanns, "The Political Foundations of TRIPS Revisited," in Hanns Ullrich, Reto M. Hilty, Matthias Lamping, and Josef Drexl (eds.), *TRIPS plus 20: From Trade Rules to Market Principles*, Springer, Heidelberg, 2016, 85–129.

United Nations Centre on Transnational Corporations, *World Investment Report 1991: The Triad in Foreign Direct Investment*, UN, New York, 1991.

United Nations Conference on Trade and Development, *World Investment Report: Overview—Investing in a Low-Carbon Economy*, UNCTAD, New York, 2010.

United Nations Conference on Trade and Development, *World Investment Report 2018*, UNCTAD, New York, 2018.

United Nations Department of Economic and Social Affairs, Population Division, *World Urbanization Prospects: The 2014 Revision, Highlights*, New York, 2014.

United Nations Development Programme, "Accelerating the Commercialization of Fuel Cell Vehicles in China," UNDP, Beijing, September 5, 2016.

United Nations Development Programme (UNDP), *China Human Development Report. 2013: Sustainable and Liveable Cities: Toward Ecological Urbanisation*, Beijing, China Translation and Publishing Corporation, 2013.

United Nations Economic and Social Commission for Asia and the Pacific (UNESCAP), *Case Study: China's Low-Carbon City Project*, Bangkok, n.d.

United Nations Environment Programme, *The Emissions Gap Report 2013*, UNEP, Nairobi, 2013.

United States Bureau of Industry and Security, Department of Commerce, "Review of Controls for Certain Technologies," *Federal Register*, vol. 83, no. 223 (November 19, 2018), 58201.

United States Department of Energy, *Saving Energy and Money with Appliance and Equipment Standards in the United States*, Washington, DC, 2016.

United States Department of State, *U.S.-China Memorandum of Understanding to Enhance Cooperation on Climate Change, Energy and the Environment*, Washington, DC, July 28, 2009.

United States Energy Information Administration, *Country Analysis Brief: Sudan and South Sudan*, Washington, DC, 2014.

United States Energy Information Administration, *Quarterly Coal Report*, Washington, DC, April–June 2017.

United States Energy Information Administration, *Technically Recoverable Shale Oil and Shale Gas Resources: China*, Washington, DC, 2015.

United States Government Accountability Office, *Clean Coal: DOE's Decision to Restructure FutureGen Should Be Based on a Comprehensive Analysis of Costs, Benefits, and Risks*, Washington, DC, February 2009.

United States International Trade Administration, *2016 Top Markets Report: Semiconductors and Related Equipment*, Department of Commerce, Washington, DC, 2016.

van der Heijden, Jeroen, *Governance for Urban Sustainability: Responding to Climate Change and the Relevance of the Built Environment*, Edward Elgar, Cheltenham, UK, 2014.

Victor, David G., and Kassia Yanosek, "The Next Energy Revolution: The Promise and Peril of High-Tech Innovation," *Foreign Affairs*, 96, no. 4 (July/August 2017), 124–131.

Vogel, Ezra F., "Foreword," in Mary Ann O'Donnell, Winnie Wong, and Jonathan Bach (eds.), *Learning from Shenzhen: China's Post-Mao Experiment from Special Zone to Model City*, University of Chicago Press, London, 2017, vii–xiv.

Voslensky, Michael, *Nomenklatura: The Soviet Ruling Class, an Insider's Report*, translated by Eric Mosbacher, Doubleday, Garden City, NY, 1984.

Wald, Matthew L., "How to Build the Supergrid," *Scientific American*, 303 (2010), 56–61.

Wallerstein, Immanuel, *Historical Capitalism with Capitalist Civilization*, Verso, London, 2011.

Wallerstein, Immanuel, *World-Systems Analysis: An Introduction*, Duke University Press, Durham, NC, 2004.

Wang Ning, Lee Jason, Zhang Jian, Chen Haitao, and Li Heng, "Evaluation of Urban Circular Economy Development: An Empirical Research of 40 Cities in China," *Journal of Cleaner Production*, 180 (2018), 876–887.

Webb, Dominic, *UK Progress in Rolling Over EU Trade Agreements*, Briefing Paper 7792, House of Commons Library, London, April 26, 2019.

Wedeman, Andrew, "Xi Jinping's Tiger Hunt: Anti-Corruption Campaign or Factional Purge?," *Modern China Studies*, 24, no. 2 (2017), 35–94.

Weiss, Linda, *America Inc.?: Innovation and Enterprise in the National Security State*, Cornell University Press, Ithaca, NY, 2014.

Wester, Philippus, Arabinda Mishra, Aditi Mukherji, and Arun Bhakta Shrestha (eds.), *The Hindu Kush Himalaya Assessment: Mountains, Climate Change, Sustainability and People*, Springer, Switzerland, Cham, 2019.

White, Hugh, "Without America: Australia in the New Asia," *Quarterly Essay*, 68, November 2017, 1-81.

Wiens, Kyle, "iFixit: A Case Study in Repair," in Martin Charter (ed.), *Designing for the Circular Economy*, Routledge, London, 2019, 307–315.

Wood, Geoffrey, "Business and Politics in a Criminal State: The Case of Equatorial Guinea," *African Affairs*, 103 (2004), 547–567.

World Bank, *High and Dry: Climate Change, Water, and the Economy*, Washington, DC, 2016.

World Bank, *Russia Economic Report*, No. 351, Washington, DC, 2016.

World Bank, *State and Trends of Carbon Pricing 2019*, Washington, DC, 2019.

World Bank and Ministry of Planning and Investment of Vietnam, *Vietnam 2035: Toward Prosperity, Creativity, Equity, and Democracy*, World Bank, Washington, DC, 2016.

World Bank and PRTM Management Consultants, *The China New Energy Vehicles Program: Challenges and Opportunities*, World Bank, Washington DC, 2011.

World Bank and the State Environmental Protection Administration (P R China), *Cost of Pollution in China—Economic Estimates of Physical Damages*, World Bank, Washington, DC, 2007.

World Intellectual Property Organization, *Patent Cooperation Treaty Review 2017*, WIPO, Geneva, 2017.

Wright, Tim, "Growth of the Modern Chinese Coal Industry: An Analysis of Supply and Demand, 1896–1936," *Modern China*, 7 (1981), 317–350.

Wright, Tim, "The Political Economy of Coal Mine Disasters in China: 'Your Rice Bowl or Your Life,'" *China Quarterly*, 179 (2004), 629–646.

Wrigley, E. A., "Energy and the English Industrial Revolution," *Philosophical Transactions of the Royal Society* (2013), 1–10.

Xiaoliu Yang and Jinwu Pang, "Implementing China's 'Water Agenda 21,'" *Frontiers in Ecology and the Environment*, 4 (2006), 362–368.

Xi Jinping, *The Governance of China*, Vol. 1, Foreign Language Press, Beijing, 2014.

Xi Jinping, *The Governance of China*, Vol. 2, Foreign Language Press, Beijing, 2014.

Xinru Liu, *The Silk Road in World History*, Oxford University Press, New York, 2010.

Xuguang Song and Wenhao Cheng, "Perception of Corruption in 36 Major Chinese Cities: Based on Survey of 1,642 Experts," *Social Indicators Research*, 109 (2012), 211–221.

Yan Sun, *Corruption and Market in Contemporary China*, Cornell University Press, Ithaca, NY, 2004.

Yergin, Daniel, *Shattered Peace: The Origins of the Cold War and the National Security State*, Andre Deutsch, London, 1978.

Yokell, Michael D., "The Role of the Government in Subsidizing Solar Energy," *American Economic Review*, 69 (1979), 357–361.

Yong Guo, "Corruption in Transitional China: An Empirical Analysis" *The China Quarterly*, 194 (2008), 349–364.

Yongling Li, Yanliu Lin, and Stan Geertman, "The Development of Smart Cities in China," paper for the 14th International Conference on Computers in Urban Planning and Urban Management, July 7–10, 2015, Cambridge, MA.

Yuan Hu, Xuan He, and Mark Poustie, "Can Legislation Promote a Circular Economy? A Material Flow-Based Evaluation of the Circular Degree of the Chinese Economy," *Sustainability*, 10 (2018), 990–1012.

Yuhua Wang, "Court Funding and Judicial Corruption in China," *The China Journal*, 69 (2013), 43–63.

Yuxuan Li, Weifeng Zhang, Lin Ma, Gaoqiang Huang, Oene Oenema, Fusuo Zhang, and Zhengxia Dou, "An Analysis of China's Fertilizer Policies: Impacts on the Industry, Food Security and the Environment," *Journal of Environmental Quality*, 42 (2013), 972–81.

Zevenbergen, Chris, Dafang Fu, and Assela Pathirana, "Transitioning to Sponge Cities: Challenges and Opportunities to Address Urban Water Problems in China," *Water*, 10 (2018) 1230.

Zhong Xiang Zhang, "Carbon Emissions Trading in China: The Evolution from Pilots to Nationwide Schemes," CCEP Working Paper 1503, April 2015.

Zhu Boliang, "MNCs, Rents, and Corruption: Evidence from China," *American Journal of Political Science*, 61 (2017), 84–99.
Zuboff, Shoshana, *The Age of Surveillance Capitalism: The Fight for a Human Future at the New Frontier of Power*, Hachette Book Group, New York, 2019.
Zuoyue Wang, "The Chinese Developmental State during the Cold War: The Making of the 1956 Twelve-Year Science and Technology Plan," *History and Technology*, 31 (2015), 180–205.

Index